RECOLLECTIONS OF A
WESTMINSTER ANTIQUARY

OTHER BOOKS BY THE SAME AUTHOR

Westminster School: A History (1934, 2nd ed. 1951)
Unknown Westminster Abbey (King Penguin, 1948)
The History of the Coronation (1952)
History and Treasures of Westminster Abbey (1953)

1   The Keeper of the Muniments.

Recollections of a
WESTMINSTER
ANTIQUARY

Lawrence E. Tanner

C.V.O., M.A., Hon. D.Litt., F.S.A.

Keeper of the Muniments (1926-66)
Librarian, Westminster Abbey

5 ROYAL OPERA ARCADE
PALL MALL LONDON SW1

© 1969 LAWRENCE E. TANNER
All rights reserved
First published in 1969 by
JOHN BAKER (PUBLISHERS) LTD
5 Royal Opera Arcade
Pall Mall, London S.W.1

S.B.N. 212 98358 X

Printed and bound in Great Britain by
Thomas Nelson (Printers) Ltd
London and Edinburgh

Contents

5

Plates

PLATES

Foreword

DAVID WILKINS, writing during the lifetime of that learned antiquary, Thomas Tanner, Bishop of St Asaph (d. 1735),[1] described him as 'one whom all regard as the living treasure-house of our antiquities'. For one, like myself, who has lived for nearly eighty years more or less under the shadow of Westminster Abbey and made it the study of a life-time, it would be difficult not to have acquired something of the reputation of my distant kinsman.

Many, including myself, have written on the past history of the Abbey, and have been able to draw for their material on the inexhaustible 'treasure-house' of the Abbey Muniments, or, for printed sources, on that remarkable book Dean Stanley's *Memorials of Westminster Abbey* which still remains the chief 'treasure-house' of what may be called the anecdotal side of Abbey history.

Stanley was, perhaps, the first Dean of Westminster[2] to realize fully the part which the Abbey might play in the life of the nation. It was one of the main objects of his life to make the treasures which it contains better known to the ordinary person, 'to reanimate the inheritance of the past, to make the Abbey an eloquent memorial of all that was greatest and most famous in national history, to keep alive its power as the incentive to heroic action', and to make it in a way which it had never been before 'the centre and the representative of the highest aspects of religious and national life'.

It is part of the measure of the success which has attended the pursuit of these ideals not only by Stanley but by his successors in the

[1] Author of *Notitia Monastica* and *Bibliotheca Britannico-Hibernica*, etc.
[2] Dean of Westminster 1864–81.

9

Deanery that 'the Abbey' today has acquired a meaning to people all over the world, even though they might find it difficult to put into words, and that it excites in them a curiously personal, almost a proprietary, interest in all that concerns either its present history or the historic memories which have gathered round its past.

Each generation adds something to the treasure-house of Abbey history; but memories are short and the details of events which loomed large at the time all too quickly fade or become distorted as the years go on. Often in my work at the Abbey some question of detail has arisen which has proved unexpectedly difficult to answer, either because no one could clearly remember what really happened or because when, perhaps, an antiquarian discovery was made no one at the time made a careful record of what exactly was seen or done. How often, too, have I wished for a description by a contemporary of the appearance and characteristics of someone who was well known within the Precincts of the Abbey in his day, but of whom now little more is known than the bare outline of his life.

It is with some such thoughts as these in my mind that it has seemed to me to be worth while to try to record, however inadequately, some of the events at Westminster which have come under my personal observation, of which no one now, except perhaps myself, can give a first-hand account, and to weave such records and memories into the context of a long and happy life.

LAWRENCE E. TANNER

CHAPTER I

Early Days

'Grant's' – Westminster in the '90s – The 'streets out at the back' – Street Cries – School Shops – Tuttle Fields – St James's Park

In a notebook kept by my mother I find recorded that at the age of four I startled my nurse one day by remarking that 'I was born in Westminster Abbey', that I meant to be buried there, 'and have on my tomb Mr Lord General Baba Tanner'. As a general statement of my lifelong connection with the Abbey the remark was not without foresight, but as regards the place of my birth it would appear that my memory was at fault for, in fact, my first introduction to the Abbey was on 15th March 1890, on which day I was christened by Dean Bradley in Henry VII's Chapel. I have always understood that I behaved extremely badly and that the Dean found it somewhat difficult to restrain my loudly expressed disapproval of the whole proceedings. I was not born within the Precincts, but within sight of the Abbey at 53 Vincent Square on 12th February 1890. A few months before my birth my father, Ralph Tanner,[1] who was then an assistant classical master at Westminster School, was offered a House Mastership, and by the date of my baptism we had moved into No. 2 Little Dean's Yard, which was to be my home for the next twenty-nine years of my life.

In many ways the house was an interesting one. The centre house of the three on the south side of the Yard, it was built in 1789 by Robert Furze Brettingham, an architect of some note at the time. It cannot be said that it is a work of great imagination, but it still presents its satisfying and solid – some might say stolid – pedimented Georgian

[1] Both my Father's and my Mother's families came originally from Wiltshire. My Mother was a daughter of George Lewis Phipps Eyre, a member of a family well-known in Wiltshire for many centuries.

front to Westminster boys as it has presented it to generations of their forebears (Plate 2).

Both at Eton and Westminster the curious system prevailed in the past whereby the boarding-houses were kept by 'Dames' with a resident or non-resident usher to keep some kind of order. One such at Westminster, for instance, was Mrs Porten who numbered her nephew, Edward Gibbon, among her boarders, and of whom the historian wrote (in a phrase I sometimes used to quote to my father) that, scorning a life of dependence, 'she preferred the humble but genteel industry of keeping a boarding-house for Westminster School, where she laboriously earned a competence for her old age'! But the unique feature about my old home was that both it and the house which had preceded it on the same site had been kept by successive generations of a family called Grant. The last 'Mother Grant', or her deputy, disappeared in 1847 when a House Master was installed in her place, but the name remained and the house is still known as 'Grant's' (Plate 3). There is, I believe, no other instance at a public school of a boarding-house having kept a family name for almost two hundred years. The Grant family is now extinct, but a few years ago I was able to trace their representatives and it became possible to buy back from them a very charming pastel portrait of the 'Mother Grant' of about 1800. Now, once again, it hangs in the house with which the Grant family was so long connected.

An earlier 'conversation' piece of the Grant Family (Plate 4), painted c. 1737–47 by Francis Hayman, R.A., had been sold to a dealer many years before. In 1909, while I was still at the School, I saw this picture and wrote a description of it. It could then have been purchased for £50. It passed, however, into a private collection, and all trace was lost of it until 1963 when it came up for sale at Sotheby's and fetched £6,500! It was simply catalogued as 'The Grant Family' and no one knew of its connection with the School, but I was able to identify it from the description which I had written over fifty years before. The owners very kindly allowed a coloured reproduction of it to be made and this also now hangs 'up' Grant's.

In our time the House Master and his family lived on the ground and first floors with the dormitories of the boys on the floors above. Where and how the Grants slept in their day I cannot imagine, for most of the rooms on the first floor seemed to have been used at one time or another by the boys. There were names of former Grantites hammered out in nails on the floor boards, and my nursery had a long fixed marble washing-stand below the wide window which made a perfect parade ground for my very considerable army of toy soldiers.

The house was not merely full of young life but of memories of the past. Some families had come for generations, and the Grants had had among their boarders a future Prime Minister (Lord John Russell), and a future Archbishop of Canterbury (Charles T. Longley), while the oldest living Old Grantite when my Father first took over the house was the 6th Earl of Albemarle (1799-1891), who was the last officer survivor of the Battle of Waterloo.

At the back of the house was a long narrow yard which ran back to Great College Street to which access was gained by a door cut through the fourteenth-century stone boundary wall of the Monastery. Along the side of the yard was a range of buildings consisting of the boys' dining-hall and three rooms opening into each other, which were originally built as sick-rooms but which were used in our time, and long before that, as studies for the senior boys. They were known as 'Chiswicks' and derived their name from the old College house at Chiswick to which the School used to migrate in times of plague in the sixteenth and seventeenth centuries and which later became a kind of summer resort for the Head Master and Prebendaries until well into the eighteenth century. The name still survives although all this back part of the house has been rebuilt within the last few years.

It must be confessed that when my Father took over the house it had much of its primitive eighteenth-century character. There were no bathrooms and each boarder had to be content with a little tin hip-bath placed by his bed in the dormitories. They were filled with cold water from a tap on the landing outside. There was gas in the passages and in some of the rooms, but the boys still went to bed with the eighteenth-century round brass candlesticks (dating back to the Grant's time) each containing a queer little candle (a 'tolly') which lasted exactly half an hour – after that they went to bed in the dark! Gradually my Father managed to introduce such amenities as electric light, bathrooms, etc., but the complete modernization of the house came after his time.

Not the least of the charms of Grant's was the noble view from its windows of the south front of the Abbey Church. There are those who decry the exterior of the Abbey and who point out, what is indeed obvious, the incongruity of the eighteenth-century western towers, and no doubt such critics are technically correct. I can only say that I lived opposite that view for all but thirty years and saw it almost daily from my bedroom window under every condition of light and shade, and I never failed to be impressed by its noble outline or to marvel at the grandeur of its massive simplicity. Unlike the familiar view of the north front from Parliament Street, it is difficult to get an uninterrupted view of the south front of the Abbey, but from our windows it revealed its entire length, rising above the mellow red brick of Ashburnham House and at exactly the right distance to get its full effect. Seen in the light of a full moon or touched with snow against a blue sky or yet again on a day just sufficiently misty for the sun to give a pinkish tone to the stonework and flash on the great Rose and clerestory windows it could be entrancingly beautiful. It became part of one's life, a living presence by day and a vast mysterious silhouette against the sky at night, seeming to watch over us and to shield us from the outer world. And, indeed, it did shut out all sound at night. Except for the chiming of the quarters from Big Ben, the top of whose friendly face could just be seen from my bedroom window, we might have been in the depths of the country (Plate 5).

There was in fact much of the atmosphere of a quiet cathedral town in the Westminster of the '90s, and we, within the Precincts, were in every sense of the word a close community. Even in those pre-motor days, to turn into Dean's Yard in the day-time was to enter into a haven of peace, and when one was admitted, as a resident, through the postern gate after the great gates had been closed for the night one seemed to leave London behind. Actually some forty or fifty years before it must have been even more secluded. It was not until 1851 that Victoria Street ploughed its way through the little streets which then came close up to the Abbey. There are prints and water-colours which show Dean's Yard filled with charming seventeenth- and eighteenth-century houses. On the east side these still survive with much of the monastic buildings incorporated in them, but in the 1850s and 1860s Sir Gilbert Scott had reigned supreme as the Abbey Architect and Surveyor. It was he who built the Sanctuary houses and the Gatehouse to Dean's Yard which face Victoria Street, and he and his predecessor, Edward Blore, had also, with a heavy hand, dealt with the west and north sides of the Yard. But no one dared then to question that 'ecclesiastical gothic' was the proper thing for houses in a cathedral close, even if it did involve fitting sash windows into 'gothic' mouldings. Perhaps, however, even then there may have been some who ventured to wonder why the older houses and the quiet Georgian houses on the terrace on the south side of Dean's Yard (now pulled down and replaced by the Church House) seemed somehow to fit more easily into their surroundings. Many of these terrace houses, when I first knew them in the '90s, were still private residences.

It is curious to remember that in my childhood there was a sedan chair which was still in occasional use in the Precincts. It had belonged originally, I believe, to Lord John Thynne who was installed a Canon during the preparations for the coronation of King William IV in 1831 and who died in 1881. Lord John was a man of great character and business ability and for many years he was the dominating figure at Westminster. Rumour said, and I have been assured that it was true, that only to the Dean did Lord John give his whole hand, all others had to be content with a gradually decreasing number of fingers according to their position in the Collegiate Body. Lord John died before my time but his son, John Thynne, was established in a house in the Little Cloister and held the ancient but no longer arduous office of Receiver General to the Dean and Chapter. As there was no room for the sedan in this house the Dean and Chapter had solved the problem of its accommodation by the simple and to them obvious expedient of taking a chunk out of the hall of a Minor Canon's house next door, thereby ruining the proportions of what had been the medieval Infirmarer's Hall!

I have a very vivid recollection of meeting in the Cloisters Agatha Thynne (afterwards Lady Hindlip) returning in the sedan to her father's house after her presentation at one of Queen Victoria's after-noon Drawing Rooms in 1897. The sedan was then mounted on wheels. It lasted on over the turn of the century until one day the bottom fell out when some of the young men who then lived with Dean Armitage Robinson were taking the Dean's sister in it rather too vigorously to a service in the Abbey! That was the end of the Westminster sedan, and it is amusing to remember that it must have been just about this time or a little earlier that the Head Master of Westminster remarked at my Father's dinner table, amid somewhat incredulous laughter, that he quite expected that the day would come when Westminster boys would arrive and depart in motor-cars instead of hansoms and four-wheelers at the beginning and end of term. My Father took me to see the first motor-car rally in Northumberland Avenue in 1896 before they set out for Brighton; but I fancy that many of them failed to reach their destination. A few years before that date I remember seeing people enjoying the latest amusement at Bexhill-on-Sea, which consisted in solemnly riding their bicycles up and down a perfectly flat asphalt bicycle track of about a quarter of a mile or less, which had been specially constructed for this purpose along the sea front.

To revert for a moment to sedans. They survived longer, I think, in cathedral closes and university towns than elsewhere. My distant cousin, Miss Barbara Townsend of Salisbury, who died in 1939 aged over ninety, told me that she could just remember sedans depositing ladies at the lovely Mompesson House in the Close there which was her home for most of her life, and there is at Trinity College, Cambridge, a miniature four-wheel carriage in which the Master used to be pushed about the courts by the college servants. Such vehicles did in fact solve a very real problem for ladies living in cathedral closes when dining out in the precincts on a wet night. There were always anxious glances at the sky by my parents when they were giving a dinner party, for no carriage could approach our house, and Little Dean's Yard could be extremely wet to cross on foot. Our predecessor at Grant's, much to our regret, had done away with the old up-and-down front door steps. All three houses formerly had them, and they still survive in the house next door (No. 3). I have little doubt that that type of approach to a front door, so common in eighteenth-century houses, was designed to facilitate the use of sedans, which with their poles must have been awkward things to take up a straight flight of steps unless the occupant could be carried right into the hall.

How delightful entertaining was, and is, in the Precincts. It used to be a common custom to take one's guests into the Abbey after dinner – an unforgettable experience especially in the days before the Abbey was lit by electricity and one had to depend on the moon or the night watchman's lantern. My Mother used to tell a pleasant 'ghost' story of one such occasion; when going up into the Confessor's Chapel with her guests in the dark she put out her hand to steady herself on something round and white, which, to her horror, slowly and silently rose beneath her hand . . . and turned out to be the bald head of the night watchman who had been dozing by the side of the steps! Sometimes, too, in those days a message would come round from Sir Frederick Bridge, the Abbey Organist, to say that he was having a great singer or musician dining with him on such or such a night, and that they were going into the Abbey afterwards if anyone cared to join them. And then, with the Abbey in darkness save for a single light in the Organ loft, the whole building would be flooded with glorious sound from organ, voice, or violin.

I have known those who regularly saw in the New Year in the Confessor's Chapel, and I have myself more than once visited the tomb of 'our Foundress Queen Elizabeth' on 17th November (the date of her accession) and seen 'by the pale moonlight' that noble profile – the one contemporary representation which gives one some idea of the power and strength of that great Queen. Many and many a time, too, as the chimes of midnight approached, have I paused by the monument of old Daniel Pulteney at the east end of the south cloister in the hope that he would 'play up' and according to tradition turn over a page of the grimy book which he holds in his hand. But Westminster ghosts are disappointing and neither Bradshaw, who presided at the trial of Charles I and is said to pace along the South Triforium, nor the King's Scholar who plays a ghostly game of rackets in Little Dean's Yard, have ever 'obliged' as far as I am concerned.

When I first knew the little streets which lie between the Abbey and St John's Church they still retained much of the peacefulness and 'the appearance of streets in a very quiet country town' which Disraeli had noted in *Sybil* some fifty years before. These streets, with their pine-panelled houses – for oak was required for the Navy or reserved for more important houses – had altered little since they were built in the first decades of the eighteenth century. They had neither risen nor fallen in the social scale. They were still largely inhabited by old ladies of the Cranford type; though a few of them were no longer private residences, but provided 'apartments for a single gentleman' of a superior kind. In the eighteenth century many of them had been small houses kept by 'dames' for the boys of Westminster School – such as 'Mother Gibson' in College Street who numbered Warren Hastings among her boarders, or 'Mother Morel' in Cowley Street, where Philip Stanhope as a schoolboy was the recipient of the earlier letters of the great Lord Chesterfield. In the '90s one could walk the length of College, Barton, Cowley and North Streets and round Smith Square, and see an almost unbroken façade of eighteenth-century houses, nor was there anything to break the calm in which they were enveloped except the occasional clip-clop of a hansom cab, the rumble of a van or coal-cart over the cobblestones with which College Street was then paved, or the weekly visit of a hurdy-gurdy grinding out the popular songs of the time. This last could be heard from my nursery and as a small child I used to wonder what exactly was required of Daisy when she was asked to 'give me your hearts-a-do', which was all I could make of our housemaid's rendering of *Daisy Bell*.

Although referred to rather patronizingly by the inhabitants of the Close as 'the streets out at the back', with just sufficient stress to suggest that the fourteenth-century monastic wall, which bounds the north side of College Street, was still serving its original exclusive purpose, these little streets had a quiet dignity – as indeed they still have – which was altogether charming, and they had not yet been 'discovered'. It was only when the contents of both Houses of Parliament had been emptied into them that strange and unexpected things began to happen. Who could have supposed – least of all old Tom

Gayfere, the Abbey stonemason – that a hundred years or so after he had passed into oblivion, St John's Street would be renamed Gayfere Street, or that great folk would print the imposing name 'Gayfere House' on their notepaper. Still more curious is the history of poor little North Street which, after leading a blameless (or almost blameless) life for two hundred years, with a name correctly and adequately describing its geographical position in relation to St John's Church, was suddenly raised to the peerage as Lord North Street. One is left to wonder whether the L.C.C. realized that although the connection of the street with the eighteenth-century Prime Minister, Lord North, was in fact a genuine one, it was not, perhaps, the kind of connection which is usually considered suitable for commemoration.

In my childhood days some of the old street cries still survived. There was a distressing looking old man who used to walk about in a stove-pipe hat covered with fly-papers chanting the refrain 'Catch'em all alive, bluebottles and flies', and one who offered 'Alittlebitof-groundselforyourlittle —burrd'. The lavender cry was, I think, a rather self-conscious revival, but a genuine and rather charming cry on alternate high and low notes was 'Umbrellas and scissors and knives to grind'. 'Milk-o' and the cats-meat man call up memories, but the only two, perhaps, which survived to recent times were 'Chairs to mend' and the muffin-man (whose bell is always associated in my mind with sleepy Sunday afternoons in my childhood and old bound volumes of *The Sunday at Home* and *Leisure Hours*).

Some of the old shops connected with the School were also in existence. Ginger's, the school bookshop for over a hundred and fifty years, in College Street had only recently gone, and so had the circulating library kept by Mother Vickers in Barton Street (although her eighteenth-century plate-glass window on the west side of the street still survives), but Martin's, the hereditary school bootmaker, was still going strong, and hanging on his walls were amusing and awe-inspiring photographic groups of the bewhiskered and moustached 'swells' who had rowed in the School Eights of the '50s and '60s. At the corner of College and Tufton Streets was the best known of all, Sutcliffe's ('Suts'), the school tuckshop. It was hinted that as a girl the beautiful Miss Sutcliffe had turned the heads of susceptible youth, but as a I remember her she was an austere little old lady, who presided rather grimly (with the aid of a life-preserver) over a shop which, with its double bowed windows, had altered little if at all from the eighteenth century. The life-preserver might not have been entirely for show for a few doors further up the street, almost opposite to our backdoor, was a notoriously black spot known, appropriately enough, as Black Dog Alley, with one entrance in College Street and the other in Tufton Street. It was said that some of the worst characters in Westminster lived there, and no policeman would venture into it alone after dark. Even in the '90s there were terrible slums within a stone's-throw of the Precincts, where drunken brawls were common and children all too often went barefoot and in rags. Historically Black Dog Alley was interesting, for it marked the east and south sides of what had been the Abbot of Westminster's kitchen garden, the area of which roughly corresponded to the modern house of the Cowley Fathers.

All these little houses on the south side of College Street – in one of them the poet Keats had lodged – between Barton and Tufton Streets were demolished in 1903 and replaced by the School Science Buildings and St Edward's House. In the excavations on the spot a large number of spoons, pots and other objects were found, including a portion of a writhed Purbeck marble shaft which was originally part of the Shrine of Edward the Confessor. But the oddest find was a 'Greybeard' jug, probably dating from the early seventeenth century, which contained a piece of red cloth carefully cut into the shape of a heart and stuck all over with bent pins. This curious object was unquestionably a malevolent charm intended by the maker to work all kinds of evil on an unpopular neighbour.

At the same time, just below the surface of Tufton Street, a seventeenth-century brick bridge with much older stone abutments or flanking walls was disclosed. I saw the other end of this bridge on the other side of the street some years ago when the new Church House was being built. It must have replaced a much older bridge, probably of timber, which spanned the millstream on the site of College Street and formed the boundary of the original Isle of Thorney on which the Abbey was built. The bridge led to the Abbey vineyards (the old name of Romney Street was Vine Street) and to the Tuttle Fields beyond. I have seen a painting – indeed I reproduced it in my history of Westminster School[1] – of the view from the upper window of one of the last houses on the east side of Marsham Street about 1794, and it showed that even then the open fields came right up to Horseferry Road. In the distance, on the site of what is now Vincent Square, the artist had sketched in a tent, which he noted was used by the Westminster boys 'when they play at Cricket'. In fact Vincent Square is the last remaining portion of the Tuttle Fields, and it is still 'Fields' to those whose predecessors at the School had played

[1] *Westminster School: A History.* Country Life Ltd, 1934; 2nd ed. 1951.

there for centuries. The story was that, when at the beginning of the nineteenth century houses began to invade the Fields, Dean Vincent, himself an old Westminster King's Scholar and former Head Master, persuaded the Chapter to set aside ten acres for the use of the boys and that the land so reserved was marked out with a plough. It was pleasant, therefore, to be able to confirm this story by finding a few years ago among the Abbey Muniments an order to pay (13th November 1810) one Jonathan Green's account 'for marking out ten acres of ground in Tothill Fields as a play ground for the Westminster Scholars, and for the use of his team of horses and plough two days . . . to mark the said piece of ground with a deep furrough'. In the days when we used to go backwards and forwards between the School and Fields – going 'up Fields' or coming 'down Fields' as we used to call it – we were sometimes asked for 'a penny for the grotter', that curious little arrangement of grass, stones and shells which the children made on the pavements. It would be interesting to know the origin of the custom, which probably went back to remote times, but it is many years since I saw a 'grotto', and I am afraid that the custom is now extinct.

Outside Dean's Yard was the pitch of a well known Westminster character, 'Daddy' Chapman, the hot potato man, who for over forty years sold hot potatoes and chestnuts from his barrow with its little steaming oven near the Crimean Memorial. On the opposite side of the Sanctuary, at the corner of Tothill Street and Princes Street (recently rather misleadingly renamed Storey's Gate) was the old Aquarium with its twin towers. It may originally have contained fish, but, if so, it had fallen from its high estate and had acquired a rather dubious reputation, providing for its patrons such side-shows as performing fleas, strong men, the 'human' monkey, and (as I remember) a certain 'Dr Tanner' who fasted in a tank for an incredible number of days! Respectability returned when it was all swept away and the Central Hall erected on the site.

At the other end of Princes Street (the real Storey's Gate to the Park) was a fine stone-fronted late seventeenth-century house facing the Park. It was pulled down when the Ministry of Defence was built, but its façade was re-erected in the corner of the Horse Guards Parade where it fits so well into its surroundings that few people, perhaps, know its earlier history. St James's Park itself has altered but little except for the recent destruction of the old suspension bridge and for the fact that all through my childhood the greater part of the lake was filled with rowing boats which could be hired from a boat house at the south corner by Buckingham Palace. Only the east end, with the island, was reserved for waterfowl and ducks. Farther along, on the other side of the Horse Guards Parade, near the site of the fortress excrescence of the Admiralty, were tethered, as I well remember, the two cows kept by an old lady to whose forebears, I believe, the privilege of selling glasses of fresh milk had been granted by King Charles II.

The Mall is now a fine processional way, but at the time it was made it was thought to be a sad desecration to destroy the old Mall with its broad tree-lined walks and narrow carriageway running through the middle of it. These once fashionable promenades were normally used only by pedestrians, but I can remember them sometimes filled with carriages, many with a be-wigged coachman on the box and with two footmen at the back in cocked hats and holding long gold topped staves on the occasion of one of Queen Victoria's afternoon Drawing Rooms. The old state coach, of which the royal ones used at the Opening of Parliament, etc., are almost the only survivals, was a very imposing affair. Once in the 1920s, on the night of a Court at Buckingham Palace, I was walking home after a dinner and happened to turn into Queen Anne's Gate. There, to my astonishment and pleasure, in front of Lord Bute's house was drawn up his state coach with the two footmen in yellow liveries, silk stockings, cocked hats and holding their staves standing on each side of the open front door. The street was otherwise completely empty, and, seen in such a perfect setting, the centuries seemed to have rolled away. It must have been one of the last occasions on which it was used, although Lord Spencer told me that he used his coach at the 1937 Coronation.

Queen Victoria came so seldom to London in the last ten years of her reign that when she did so it was quite an event. She invariably drove about with an escort of household cavalry even if it was only from Paddington Station to Buckingham Palace. I can see quite clearly in my mind the tiny black cloaked figure of the aged Queen with a little white feather in her bonnet bowing to the left and right as she passed. Oddly enough she always had a Highlander in full dress and a footman seated in the rumble behind her. The last time I saw her was in March 1900, when she drove past the Abbey. On this occasion the Abbey Clergy and the Choir in their surplices took their places on a stand outside the West Door and sang the National Anthem as she passed. For the first time, too, within living memory a flag was flown on the North West Tower of the Abbey in honour of the occasion. It was the Union Jack which had covered the coffin of Lord Tennyson at his funeral in 1892.

A few years later, in 1906, the Dean and Chapter got into sad trouble for flying the Royal Standard without authority when King Edward VII opened Parliament. The matter was reported to King Edward, who was not likely to overlook an irregularity of this kind, and a severe letter was sent pointing out that the Royal Standard could only be flown over a building when the sovereign was actually under its roof. Dean Robinson, however, wrote so charming a letter of apology, pointing out the peculiarly royal associations of the Abbey, that the King was not only mollified but granted special permission for the flag to be flown whenever the sovereign opened Parliament in person. This privilege, therefore, is always exercised on these occasions.

CHAPTER II

Deans and Others

THE Dean throughout my childhood was Dr George Granville Bradley (Plate 7). He had been at Rugby under Arnold, to whose memory he was devoted although he always described him as 'terribly strict'. He had himself been a successful Head Master at Marlborough, and was distinguished both as a scholar and as a teacher–what schoolboy of my generation does not remember struggling with that doubtless admirable but somewhat dreary publication Bradley's *Additional Exercises*, a supplement to (what seemed to us) the already more than sufficient number of exercises in Arnold's *Latin Prose*? From Marlborough Bradley went to University College Oxford, where he made Oxford history, in his early days as Master, by sending down the whole of his college for an ebullient demonstration against an unpopular don.

But there was little that was ruthless about Bradley as Dean of Westminster. As I remember him he was a little, frail, courteous old man, who peered at one from behind steel-rimmed spectacles and was liked and respected by everyone at Westminster. He always wore a purple velvet skull-cap in the Abbey, and he was, I think, the last Dean of Westminster to observe the ancient custom of sometimes wearing round his neck his badge as Dean of the Order of the Bath when walking about the streets.

When he succeeded his lifelong friend, Stanley, as Dean of Westminster in 1881 he was faced with a difficult task. Stanley, brilliant and fascinating, was notoriously unbusinesslike, and he had left both the fabric and the finances of the Abbey in a deplorable state. With both these problems Bradley grappled successfully, but it was a constant burden and care throughout his tenure of the Deanery and it filled much of his time and thought. It was unfortunate, too, that the most spectacular of the restorations of the fabric carried out in his time, namely the restoration of the north front between 1884 and 1892, was, perhaps, the least successful. Sir Gilbert Scott, R.A., and after him Mr John L. Pearson, R.A., produced, indeed, a scholarly reproduction of what they thought had been its original form, but what the late Professor Lethaby called 'the smile of the old work', which up to that time had remained, largely disappeared under their rather heavy hands. In other ways, too, Bradley was hampered. Stanley had stamped his vivid personality on the Abbey, and Bradley felt bound, not only from admiration of his predecessor but by the expressed wish of the Queen, to continue 'to carry out and on' (as the Queen put it) the aspirations and views of 'the beloved Dean'. He made, therefore, few alterations at Westminster beyond greatly shortening the services – they seemed long enough, even so, to myself as a child! – and he always said that his successor would have to do a great deal more and would be freer to do it.

The Bradleys, with their lively and brilliant daughters, continued the Stanley tradition of making the Deanery a social and literary centre. I was, of course, too young, but my parents used to go to the Deanery parties where they were sure to meet interesting people. Tennyson was a lifelong friend of the Dean, although his admiration for the poet was not entirely shared by his daughters, who disliked what they called his 'pawing' ways. I remember one of them telling me that as a girl she was somewhat unwillingly detailed to take the great man to the Royal Academy, and was embarrassed rather than pleased to find the poet and herself the centre of interest. Tennyson, however, was unperturbed and affected indifference, merely growling 'Take me to all the pictures *with my lines under them*' – a curious and interesting sidelight on the Academy of the Victorian age.

In striking physical contrast to the Dean was the portly figure of the Sub Dean, Dr Robinson Duckworth (Plate 9). For nearly forty years (1875–1911) he was a familiar figure in the Westminster Cloisters. As a young Oxford tutor he had been a friend of the Revd C. L. Dodgson (Lewis Carroll). It was on a river excursion to Godstow with the three young daughters of Dean Liddell that Lewis Carroll composed and told over Duckworth's shoulder, who was rowing stroke, the adventures of 'Alice in Wonderland' for the benefit of Alice Liddell who was acting as their cox. As the story unfolded Duckworth remembered turning round and saying, 'Dodgson, is this an extempore romance of yours?' and he replied,

'Yes, I'm inventing as we go along'. Subsequently Alice Liddell begged that it might all be written down, and it was Duckworth who suggested that Tenniel should be asked to illustrate it.

Later Duckworth became Tutor and Governor to Prince Leopold, in which post he found favour with the Queen and, if rumour was to be believed, aroused something more than admiration in the most accomplished of the Queen's daughters. Be that as it may, the Queen vigorously urged his claims to the Westminster Canonry vacant by the death of Charles Kingsley. But both Disraeli and Dean Stanley hesitated, for they not unnaturally thought that someone more distinguished should be appointed, especially as Duckworth was a young man of under forty who was little known outside Court circles. However, as usual the Queen had her way, and although the appointment roused criticism at the time it was ultimately justified. He was, in fact, an admirable representative of the older type of Westminster Canon, and on state occasions when he wore his medals and decorations his handsome and dignified presence added a touch of distinction to the Westminster Chapter. I can see him now in his full-sleeved black geneva gown and medals, standing up School over sixty years ago admitting the new King's Scholars in the absence of the Dean, and can hear the fine and impressive sonority which he gave to the traditional form as each in turn knelt before him: 'Ego, Robinson Duckworth, hujus collegiatae ecclesiae prodecanus, admitto te . . . in discipulum scholarem hujus collegii juxta statuta ejusdem. In nomine Patris, et Filii, et Spiritus Sancti, Amen.'

He was the last Canon of Westminster to hold a living unconnected with the Abbey in addition to his Canonry. As the Vicar of St Mark's, Hamilton Terrace, for thirty-six years he was a greatly liked parish priest. If, as a preacher, he was unable to compete with his colleagues Farrar, Gore, and Hensley Henson in the Abbey pulpit, he could at least be relied upon to produce a sermon as mellifluous as it was sound.

Of Farrar I have no recollection. My father, who knew him well, thought little of *Eric* as a picture of public school life and was unimpressed by his sermons. He would have agreed with Henson's remark that in the pulpit Farrar's very real ability was obscured by 'the purple rhetoric of his preaching'. It offended fastidious hearers, and caused another of his colleagues on the Chapter to describe him rather caustically as 'the apostle of the immature'. Gore, although he added greatly to the prestige of the Chapter and drew vast crowds to the Abbey by his preaching and lecturing, belonged to the Church as a whole rather than to Westminster where, in some ways, he lived a somewhat austere bachelor life at his house in the Little Cloister together with two or three brothers of the Community of the Resurrection of which he was the Superior. In those far-off days entertaining in the Precencts was still in the dignified and slightly exclusive Barchester tradition. My Father, for instance, delighted to recall that as a very young man and soon after he joined the Staff in the early eighties he had overhead the Head Master's wife apologizing for his presence to her principal guest as they went down to dinner on the ground that 'we *have* to ask the junior masters sometimes'. Gore's weekly 'At Homes' for men, in order to discuss Church reform or social problems, when many of the guests were content to sit on the floor and the host sometimes lay happily stretched out on the hearth-rug, appealed perhaps to a younger generation rather than to those accustomed to the more conventional and dignified hospitality of the Precincts.

None the less Gore's appointment to the Bishopric of Worcester was received at Westminster with very real regret, and by no one more than by Armitage Robinson, who had recently been appointed a Canon, and found himself more in sympathy, perhaps, with Gore than with his other colleagues on the Chapter.

A more prominent if less distinguished figure in Westminster life both in Victorian and later times was Canon Basil Orme Wilberforce. A grandson of the philanthropist, he had something of an hereditary connection with Westminster, for his father, the celebrated Bishop of Oxford and later of Winchester, had been Dean of Westminster for a few months before his appointment as a bishop in 1845. Canon Wilberforce was the Bishop's youngest son and came to Westminster from a Southampton parish where he had been so appalled by the drunkenness which was then prevalent there that he had himself become an extreme advocate of total abstinence, even going so far, it was said, as to pour much of the contents of his father's fine cellar down the drain. On his appointment to the Canonry in 1894 Queen Victoria had written characteristically to Mr Gladstone to say that she gave her approval on condition that he informed the new Canon that however necessary total abstinence might be in individual cases it would not 'do' for him to press his extreme views in the Abbey pulpit. Mr Gladstone in his reply thought that the matter was 'of some delicacy', but promised to confer with the Dean of Westminster on the subject.

Wilberforce was an exceptionally handsome and distinguished-looking man with a fine clear cut profile. Throughout his life he was a convinced and fervant Liberal in politics, and a large and (as good

Conservatives in the Precincts thought) rather aggressive photograph of Mr Gladstone hung immediately inside the front door of his canonical residence. It was in this beautiful house (No. 20 Dean's Yard), which had formerly been part of the monastic Cellarer's quarters, that Dr Johnson had been entertained, as Boswell records, by his friend Dr Taylor, then a Prebendary of Westminster. Wilberforce's immediate predecessor in the house, Canon Rowsell, had rescued the fourteenth-century vaulted undercroft from its use as a cellar and had turned it into a dining-room. In this unusual setting Wilberforce, both as Archdeacon and as Chaplain to the Speaker, entertained a wide circle of political and other friends.

In the pulpit he had his own form of fluent eloquence which was eagerly listened to by a devoted, and largely female, following who approved of his somewhat original views and theology. Some of the more scholarly members of the Westminster community were inclined to be critical and used to quote with some relish such phrases as 'the seen embodiment of the Unthinkable Absolute', 'the Unconditioned Intellect' or 'the non-atomic swathing of the ego' as typical of those which the Archdeacon seemed able to produce in his sermons with endless and effortless facility.

Among all these dignified clerics, Sir Frederick Bridge (Plate 10), who held the office of Abbey Organist from 1875 to 1918, was a colourful and unforgettable figure. He succeeded Turle who had been appointed Organist as long ago as 1831. By all accounts Turle was a dear old man whom everyone liked. In his day he had been a competent musician whose chants are still remembered. In his later years, however, and with growing infirmities, he was not always in perfect accord with his choir, which led someone to remark that when he played the Abbey services 'the singers go before, the minstrels follow after'. It was due to Turle and to Dean Stanley that Bach's 'Passion' music was performed in the Abbey in 1871. It was the first time that it had been performed in any English cathedral or abbey church, and, although it set a precedent which has been widely followed, it was thought at the time to be a somewhat daring innovation.

There had, however, been previous 'Musical Festivals', as they were called, in the Abbey. The most notable was the celebrated festival on the centenary of Handel's birth in 1784. It was on this occasion that King George III, moved to tears by the Hallelujah Chorus, suddenly stood up. His example was followed by the whole assembly, and thus was initiated what is now a universal custom. Further festivals followed but they were then dropped for over forty years. In 1834 they were revived, and King William IV and Queen

Adelaide attended a performance in the Abbey of Handel's 'Israel in Egypt'. It was marked by an amusing incident. The King went to sleep and the Queen, wishing to rouse him, touched him on the arm and said 'What a beautiful duet, "The Lord is a Man of War" '. Thereupon the sailor King, catching only the last words and still only half-awake, started up and in a loud voice, which could be clearly heard, exclaimed 'Man of War, Man of War – how many guns, how many guns!'

Bridge found the music at the Abbey at a low ebb, and the great work that he did there is not now always remembered. The forty years or so that he presided at the organ saw the real emergence of the Abbey as a great national church under the fostering care of Dean Stanley and his successors. Bridge, with his boundless enthusiasm, was able to ensure that the music not only for the daily services but for the great special services which came to be held with ever increasing frequency, was raised to a high state of efficiency. To him, too, was due the rebuilding and enlarging of the organ which before his time was very old-fashioned and unworthy of the Abbey. It is difficult to realize now that when he first came nothing was ever sung in procession, and that hymns, except occasionally at the 'popular' Sunday evening service in the nave, were thought to be beneath the dignity of an Abbey service.

Bridge was in charge of the music at the 1887 Jubilee Service, and at the Coronations of King Edward VII and King George V, at both of which he made a point of selecting music representative of five centuries of English church music. He was himself keenly interested, and did much to interest others, in the compositions of early English composers. His delight was great when he discovered in the Abbey Library, and subsequently edited, some forty motets of Richard Dering which had lain there unnoticed and had never been reprinted since they were first issued in 1617 and 1618. Nor should it be forgotten that it was he who induced Sir Hubert Parry to compose the splendid opening coronation anthem ('I was glad' etc.) which was first sung at the coronation of King Edward VII, and has now taken its permanent place in the music of coronations.

Bridge, of course, had his foibles. He was in every sense a 'character', and with his unfailing good humour no one ever got the better of him. 'Why didn't you take up that tenor lead in the anthem', he once demanded of an Abbey choirman. 'I did, Sir Frederick.' 'Then why did you!' was the unanswerable retort! He enjoyed playing the Dead March in *Saul* with special drum-like effects peculiar to himself, which rattled the windows, but gained, as he said himself, little approval from his brother organists. In 1895 an electric or 'echo' organ was installed in the triforium above the south transept which could be played from the organ loft – and played it was on every occasion so that Bridge could enjoy the astonishment of the congregation who wondered where the sound came from. He was himself a prolific, if not always an inspired, composer. It must be confessed that our hearts rather sank when we saw that there was to be a Bridge anthem on Sunday mornings. But nothing ever shook his delightfully naïve enthusiasm for his own compositions. One would meet him in St James's Park taking the regular walk which most Abbey people took between the end of service and luncheon, and he would immediately say, 'Did you like the anthem? Lovely thing, wasn't it? I composed it.'

'Westminster Bridge', as Goss called him – and the sobriquet stuck – was quite irrepressible ('ebullient' as Dean Ryle once described him to me). 'Shocking and disgraceful service we had in the Abbey this morning,' he would remark, 'Bridge in the Organ Loft, Dam(n)s[1] in the Pulpit, and a Gamble[2] in the Sacrarium', and go off chuckling. I was once standing talking to him before going up into the organ loft for the service when an old lady came up to him and solemnly said, 'It's Leviathan day today, Sir Frederick'. 'No, is it? You'll see, I'll give a twist to his tail', and when we got to the verse in the psalm 'There go the ships, and there is that Leviathan whom thou hast made to take his pastime there', we were left in no doubt that Leviathan was enjoying himself, Bridge saying to me over his shoulder 'That fetched 'em, didn't it?'

It was a great delight to him to come and dine with us when one of my great-aunts was staying with us, for as a girl she had lived at Rochester where her father, General Bingham, had had a house in the Precincts just at the time when Bridge had been a choirboy at that cathedral, and together they were full of stories of the cathedral dignitaries of those days.

The phrase 'cathedral dignitaries' sounds curiously old-fashioned in these days, but in no other way could the 'Archdeacon Grantleys' of Victorian times have been adequately described. They were a fine race in their way. Well born, well bred, immensely dignified, and very sure of themselves and of their own importance, they dominated their respective cathedral closes. It amused me to find in *The Letters of Queen Victoria*[3] that one of my Mother's uncles might well have

[1] The Revd W. B. Dams, Minor Canon.
[2] The Revd H. R. Gamble, Canon.
[3] Vol. I, p. 236.

become a Westminster 'dignitary'. The Revd Charles Phipps Eyre, my grandfather's elder brother, was Rector of Marylebone and a very well-known London clergyman in his day. In 1864 Lord Palmerston submitted his name together with one other to the Queen for appointment to a vacant Canonry at Westminster with the Rectorship of St Margaret's. Her Majesty, however, chose the other candidate. Had she chosen my great uncle, whom I can just remember as an handsome scholarly old gentleman, he might well have been a senior member of the Westminster Chapter when my Father and Mother came to live in the Precincts.

It is worth remembering that the Canons of Westminster were always formerly known as Prebendaries. The old designation died out, I think, partly as a result of the institution of large numbers of Honorary Canons in other Cathedrals in early Victorian times, but the Canons of Westminster are still designated 'the Prebendaries of Westminster' in certain official documents such as the Procedure for Coronations. In ordinary parlance, however, they were always referred to as 'Doctor So-and-So' and never as Prebendary or, in later times, as Canon. Dean Robinson was always very particular about this, and refused to use the rather new-fangled term 'Canon So-and-So' for a Canon of Westminster. The older usage (i.e. Dr So-and-So) is now, perhaps, only preserved on the front-door plates of the canonical residences. I well remember the consternation which was caused in the Cloisters when in 1906 the newly appointed Canon Barnett (who did not hold a doctor's degree) placed on his front-door a plate inscribed 'The Revd Canon and Mrs S. A. Barnett'. But when the redoubtable Mrs Barnett tackled Dean Robinson on this and other cherished Westminster traditions, such as the sanctity of the College Garden, which she described as 'mere prejudice', she was met by the bland and characteristic reply, 'You must know, Mrs Barnett, that I am a person who is *entirely* ruled by prejudice.' The offending doorplate, however, with its double indiscretion disappeared, and in due course one with the simple inscription 'The Revd S. A. Barnett' took its place in the Little Cloister among those of his 'doctored' colleagues.

The older usage had the advantage – or disadvantage – that no one could confuse a Prebendary with a Minor Canon. Nowadays the ordinary layman, unversed in the subtleties of the ecclesiastical hierarchy, assumes that all alike are Canons, and the mistake is a not unnatural one. But there was, and is, a very real distinction. The Canons Residentiary are members of the Chapter and are appointed by the Crown. The Minor Canons, on the other hand, grew out of the Singingmen or Vicars Choral and were, and are, appointed by the Dean with the consent of the Chapter, primarily to act as deputies for the Canons for choral purposes. Originally, like the Gentlemen of the Choir, they were usually non-resident with the exception of the Precentor, who always had a house in the Precincts. Their sole duty was to sing the services and preach when they were required to do so. Until 1822 they eked out their very insufficient incomes by certain statutory fees for burials, etc., and by the right, with the Lay Vicars, to take the fees for showing the tombs within the Abbey.

Dean Stanley has recorded that in his time as Dean (1864–81) 'the memory of old inhabitants of the Cloisters still retained the figure of an aged Minor Canon, who on Sundays preached two-thirds of the sermons in the course of the year, and on week-days sat by the tomb of the Princess Catherine, collecting from the visitors the fee of two shillings a head, with his tankards of ale beside him.' Further amusing evidence of the way the Minor Canons were regarded at the beginning of the nineteenth century is to be found in the customary for the Latin play at the School where it is noted that 'invitations are also sent to the Minor Canons, Bellringers, and Cleaners'. I have seen a letter from a former Minor Canon of mid-Victorian days which stated that even then the Minor Canons never dared to go into the College Garden until after dark. The fact is the more remarkable, and discreditable, when it is remembered that the Minor Canons at any rate from Victorian times were usually university men.

The great change came in 1840 when the number of Prebendaries was reduced from twelve to six. This meant that several of the prebendal houses became vacant and henceforth were offered to the Minor Canons in rotation. Residence within the Close, together with additional duties and offices such as those of Sacrist, Librarian, or Custodian attracted men of better calibre and with other than purely musical qualifications. The Minor Canons of Dean Bradley's time were fully representative of those Minor Canons who in the last hundred years or so have made their own contribution to the distinction of the Collegiate Body.

The Precentor, Dr John Troutbeck, and his predecessor the Revd Samuel Flood-Jones, were both very well known in the musical world of their day. Troutbeck, who had married a sister of Canon Duckworth, was largely responsible for bringing Bridge as Organist to Westminster and together they did much to raise the standard of music at the Abbey. Troutbeck was an early Wagner enthusiast and his English translations from the operas are still in occasional use at concerts. His house in Dean's Yard was a centre of hospitality.

Another of the Minor Canons of those days, the Revd J. H. Cheadle, whose venerable appearance was enhanced by an unusually long beard and skull-cap, was a highly dramatic reader whose annual rendering of certain Old Testament Lessons we looked forward to with eager anticipation. It was a great moment when Balaam in a voice of thunder which rang through the Abbey exclaimed, 'I would there were a sword in my hand, for now I would KILL thee'. And then the ass would reply in a quavering falsetto of infinite poignancy, 'Am I not thine ass, upon which thou hast ridden ever since I was thine unto this day?' Such dramatic reading is now very rare, but it was not uncommon at one time and, at least, it was unforgettable.

In 1902 Dr Bradley, who was then over eighty, resigned the Deanery of Westminster, which he had held for over twenty years. He was succeeded by Dr Joseph Armitage Robinson (Plate 8) who continued as Dean throughout what are now known as 'Edwardian' times. At Cambridge Dr Robinson had been the foremost theologian of his day, and it had been with some reluctance that he had given up his work there in 1899 in order to accept a Canonry at Westminster to which was attached the Rectorship of St Margaret's. His further appointment three years later to the Deanery of Westminster a few months after the Coronation of King Edward VII, was not entirely unexpected by those who knew how large a part he had played in all that related to the history and preparations for that ceremony.

But it was not easy for him, as a junior member of the Chapter, to succeed the venerable, urbane and courtly Dean whom all had regarded with affection. Robinson was a bachelor, something of a recluse, rather formidable, perhaps, to the ordinary person and with little but academic experience. On the other hand, even on his appointment at the age of forty-four, he was a man of most striking and arresting appearance whose commanding personality made an instant impression on everyone with whom he came in contact. A scholar of European reputation both as a teacher and as a preacher, his sermons, with their deep sincerity and intellectual distinction, were remarkable and outstanding even at a time when the Chapter numbered Gore and Hensley Henson among its preachers.

Gore's appointment to the Bishopric of Worcester a few months before Robinson's appointment to the Deanery was a blow to Robinson for with Gore he had been on terms of closer friendship than with any other of his colleagues on the Chapter. Henson had succeeded Robinson as Rector of St Margaret's, but, as he himself wrote in later life, the Dean and he 'were too dissimilar to be intimate', and the gulf between them widened year by year. Rightly or wrongly Henson

2 Little Dean's Yard, Westminster School. The centre house is 'Grant's'.
From a lithograph, c. 1845.

3   H.M. Queen Elizabeth II standing on the steps of 'Grant's' with the Head Master (J. D. Carleton, Esq.), Nov. 1960.

4   The Grant Family. Painted by Francis Hayman, R.A., c. 1740–7.

felt that as a Canon of Westminster he ought not to keep silent on public questions about which he felt strongly. In consequence he took a leading part in the controversies of the time in which, with his natural pugnacity, he too often seemed to be the storm centre and to go out of his way to say and do things which pained his friends and angered his foes. It is difficult for those who remember Dr Henson in after life as a wise and sympathetic Bishop who had won the respect and affection of many in his diocese, to recall the almost shuddering dislike and distrust in which both he and his views were held by many earnest churchpeople in the first decade of the century – and it must be admitted that he did little to conciliate those who differed from him.

The Dean, on the other hand, disliked controversy and saw no reason why one of his Canons should appear on the platform at public meetings or write provocative letters to the newspapers. His own interests lay in quiet research, and more and more of his spare time was devoted to studying the history of the Benedictine monastery at Westminster as revealed in the hitherto almost unknown but un-rivalled collection of original account rolls and documents to be found in the Abbey Muniment Room. For this kind of work both the Dean and his devoted friend and secretary, the Revd R. B. Rackham, were peculiarly fitted and the results of their researches have been of first class importance for the medieval history of the Abbey.

Unfortunately much of this work had to be done against a back-ground of distracting domestic controversy which dragged on for nearly six years. In July 1905 Canon Henson, who for some time had been discontented with the way things were managed at the Abbey, gave formal notice to the Dean that he was about to raise not only 'the whole question of the authority of the Chapter as distinct from that of the Dean', but also to obtain a decision whether the Dean was or was not the Ordinary of the Church and College. The questions about to be raised were admittedly difficult and delicate because so much depended on usage and custom but, as the documentary evidence in the Muniment Room shows, in spite of mis-understandings they should have been capable of amicable settlement with a little good will on both sides. Unfortunately, as might have been expected by those who remember them, no compromise was likely or even possible with Canon Henson and the Dean as the protagonists.

The Dean, with his knowledge of the history and customs of the Abbey, was genuinely convinced that except in certain agreed cases the function of the Canons was, as he put it, that 'of counsel not determination', and that he had in fact rather gone out of his way to consult them on such matters as he felt necessary. From that position he refused to move for he felt that to give way on this point would be to surrender the historical and statutory position of the Dean of Westminster. The Canons, on the other hand, had evidently found their autocratic Dean very difficult. They maintained, with some justice, that decisions had been taken and instructions given by him alone which they felt should clearly have been submitted to the Chapter. The Dean was never very ready in debate. He was far more in his element in the quiet of his study, composing pamphlets setting out the historical background and furnished with a wealth of detail derived from the Muniments. These he had privately printed and circulated to the Chapter. For the later historian these pamphlets have a far greater value than the details of the controversy which provoked them. But at the time the Canons were not much interested in such things as Dean Atterbury's disputes with his Chapter at the beginning of the eighteenth century. It was the Dean's position at the present day which they wished to have clarified and on this point the Dean was impervious to argument.

Eventually three of the Canons, against the wish of the Dean and with the rather unwilling consent of the rest of the Chapter, pushed matters to extremes and submitted certain specific questions to the Sovereign as the Visitor, by whom they were referred to the Lord Chancellor for decision. The result, although with qualifications, was substantially a victory for the Dean who, it was declared, 'ought to be treated as the Ordinary'.

There is no doubt that the Dean was deeply distressed by the whole matter and that it was one of the reasons, although not the chief one, which led him a few months later to exchange the Deanery of Westminster for the less onerous Deanery of Wells when that Deanery became unexpectedly vacant. But it would be a mistake to allow these dissensions to obscure, as has too often been done, what was in fact in many ways a memorable tenure of the Deanery. If there were some members of the Collegiate Body who found him difficult to work with, there were others who realized how much this erudite, if autocratic, Dean was able to do for the Abbey, through his profound knowledge of its history and architecture, and his wholehearted devotion to what he considered to be its best interests. As perhaps was to be expected, he found his chief friends among those who shared his antiquarian interests, such as Professor W. R. Lethaby, the Abbey Architect and Surveyor, and Dr E. J. L. Scott, the Keeper of the Muniments (Plate 6). Equally happy was his close

relationship with the Organist (Sir Frederick Bridge) and with successive Precentors (the Revd H. G. Daniell-Bainbridge (1899–1909)
and the Revd T. R. Hine-Haycock (1909–12), who were responsible
for the various services. As the last named was to write to the Dean
when he heard of his impending retirement: 'The Abbey is an
absolutely different place from what it was, owing entirely to you –
and it is impossible to put into words what the effect of your presence
and administration have been to us. In all details as well as in big
things, we have got accustomed to lean on you for guidance and
judgement.'

It might have been supposed that the Dean, as something of a
scholarly recluse, would have had little in common with the young.
Nothing could be further from the truth. He was at his best with them,
and he seemed to have an instinctive sympathy with and understanding of their difficulties. He liked to have young men to live
with him who had just come down from the University, and the
'Young Gentlemen' or Y.G's, as they were usually called, became a
feature of his life both as a Canon and subsequently as Dean and did
much to brighten the somewhat austere atmosphere of his home. They
were made, too, to help him with whatever he happened to be
interested in at the time. One 'budding' architect, I remember, was
able to draw for him, to his great delight, measured plans of the
Deanery, etc. Another, better known in later life as the Revd P. B.
Clayton, made a study, under the Dean's guidance, of the medieval
encaustic tiles in the Abbey and wrote a learned paper on them
which is still the standard authority on the subject.

The Dean's relations with the School were equally happy. In my
last year at Westminster he expressed a desire to get to know a few
of us at the top of the School, and we were able to persuade him to
talk to us on the early history of the Abbey. These informal lectures
round his dining-room table were entirely delightful. Here to the full
he gave of his best, and the charm with which the story was unfolded, the profound knowledge lightened with flashes of humour, the
vivid insight into the past and the revelation of the patient care with
which each small fact had first to be established and then fitted into
the fabric of the whole, gave us an invaluable insight into the mind
and method of a great scholar and antiquarian, and was an unforgettable experience for those of us who were privileged to be present.

The friendship, if I may so call it, which he had extended to me at
Westminster was continued when he exchanged Westminster for Wells,
and was cemented when, as Lord High Almoner, he nominated me
Secretary of the Royal Almonry. I often stayed with him at Wells or

went over to see him if I happened to be anywhere in the neighbour-hood. Rather to the surprise of his friends, who had always thought of him as a confirmed bachelor, he had married in 1914 Miss Amy Faithful, the close friend and companion at Lambeth of Mrs Randall Davidson. The marriage was a very happy one. She brought order into his life, and insisted that his work, which had previously been prolonged into the small hours, assisted by pots of stewed tea and an endless chain of cigarettes, should be done at more reasonable hours. The result was that both his health and his eyesight improved.

At Wells his beautiful medieval Deanery gave him endless pleasure, and indeed it was the perfect setting for one who himself became increasingly 'medieval' and striking in appearance as he grew older. I remember asking him soon after he got to Wells if he had had to do much to the Deanery. He replied: 'My predecessor had eight daughters. All of them had taste. I am engaged in removing the traces of their taste!' On another occasion he took me over to the Cathedral to show me what he had been doing there. When we got there there was a large crowd of tourists gazing open-mouthed at the famous medieval clock which was just about to strike. The Dean gave one look at them, murmured 'horologiolatry', and passed on.

Just as at Westminster, he now became absorbed in the early history of the great cathedral in his care, and especially in the lives of its Saxon bishops. He also made himself an authority on its medieval glass, of which he made a close study and found that many of the details in the windows had been wrongly re-set at different times. He had them all taken down, and then with intense eagerness and detective work he was able to re-sort and re-arrange the glass with his own hands, and eventually to bring ordered beauty where previously there had been much confusion.

CHAPTER III

Westminster School, 1900-9

In September 1900, without having been previously at a preparatory school, I had been admitted to Westminster School. The circumstances were somewhat exceptional. I was a delicate child, my Mother had recently died, and my Father, no doubt, thought that I should be happier if I continued to live at home as a half-boarder in his house (Grant's).[1] I think now that it was probably a mistake. I was too young to be suddenly plunged into a public school even under these favourable conditions. After all, I was only in my eleventh year, the youngest boy in the school, and although everyone, both masters and boys, were very kind, it took me some time to settle down and begin slowly to climb the long ladder of promotion from the lowest form to the History VI.

When I first went to Westminster the Head Master was the Revd William Gunion Rutherford (1881–1901). When he retired in 1901 he was succeeded by the Revd James Gow, who was Head Master for the next eighteen years.

They were something of a contrast. Rutherford was a son of the Manse, a classical scholar of wide reputation and an authority on New Testament Greek. With his abundant white hair and striking appearance he was an imposing and revered figure, exactly portrayed by 'Spy' in a cartoon in *Vanity Fair* (Plate 11). He was rarely to be seen about the school except in a gown, cassock, and bands. Without much previous experience of an ancient public school, which was jealous of its traditions and customs, the reforms which he had felt it

---

[1] The boarding houses had a certain number of day boys attached to them who were known as half-boarders.

necessary to make in his early years as Head Master were in some instances unfortunate and had aroused intense hostility among both the boys and Old Westminsters. By 1900, however, he had largely lived down this unpopularity and, although he was always rather awe-inspiring, there were many boys who had found in him a wise and sympathetic counsellor.

His successor, Dr Gow (Plate 12), was also a classical scholar, and had been a Fellow of Trinity College, Cambridge. He had originally intended to be a barrister, and had been called to the bar at Lincoln's Inn, but after a few years he abandoned the law to become Head Master of Nottingham High School. There he had been very success-ful, but after six years he was appointed in 1901 to succeed his old friend, Dr Rutherford, as Head Master of Westminster. It gave him the opportunity to take Orders, which he had wished to do for some time but which for various reasons he had felt unable to do as long as he was at Nottingham. He had not the imposing presence of his im-mediate predecessor at Westminster, and it was perhaps unfortunate that an autocratic manner and an uncompromising directness of speech without wasting words too often tended to obscure the essential kindness of his character.

He was at his best in the form room, especially when taking upper boys, as I found one summer term when he created a special form for about half a dozen of us which he took most of the time himself. It was all pleasantly informal. We sat round a table in the Library, and there was always a slight uncertainty whether the Head Master would be able, or would remember, to turn up. When he did he gave us his best, and I owe much to the experience. Sometimes, bored with our efforts, he would say 'I'll do a bit', and then, a sheer delight, he would translate a couple of hundred lines or so straight off in a way which fascinated us. Never before had most of us managed to get through more than thirty or forty lines in a school 'hour', and those cluttered up with notes, references, etc. I remember one incident: we were doing Horace in an edition edited by himself. We came across a difficult passage which he translated, saying 'Well, that's what it seems to mean; let's see what the note says about it.' He then pro-ceeded to read aloud to us his own note on the passage. It was very long, very learned, and not very informative. At the end he paused, squinted at us in his characteristic way over the top of his gold-rimmed spectacles, smiled, and said quietly 'Thank you for nothing!' Dr Gow was very much alive to the advantages which a London school could offer to senior boys with special aptitudes. Musical him-self, he would encourage them to go to concerts, or to art exhibitions or to productions of Shakespeare's plays, often letting them off school hours in order that they might do so.

I have come to think that in many ways Dr Gow did much for Westminster, but at the time, as is shown in the very full journal which I kept in my last year at the school, I failed to understand him and found his abrupt manner disconcerting and tongue-tying. It was probably my own fault, but even when I was at the top of the school some of my contemporaries seemed to find it less difficult to get into an easy relationship with him than I did.

It was far otherwise with John Sargeaunt (Plate 13), the Master of the VI Form, for whom, like everyone who came under his influence, I had the most profound admiration. He was in every way a most remarkable man; classical scholar, man of letters, botanist, an historian with a unique knowledge of the eighteenth century and its personalities whom he almost seemed to have known personally, and himself a well-known figure in many spheres both literary and social. I know of no other instance of an assistant master at a public school who not only had a 'leader' in *The Times* on his death, but thirty-five years later another 'leader' on the centenary of his birth, as well as a place in the *Dictionary of National Biography*.

An hour with J.S. (as he was always called) was an unforgettable experience. As it has been truly said, he taught almost entirely by digression, and 'what you got from J.S. was a minimum of particular teaching and a maximum of general education', conveyed in a way which was as delightfully informal as it was stimulating. It didn't matter what the particular subject was, some word or reference would start him talking and it was fascinating to follow his train of thought as apt quotations, anecdotes, or personal reminiscences followed one another in apparently effortless and inexhaustible supply. Perhaps two extracts from my journal will give some faint and imperfect idea of his scope and variety and the impression which he made on one at least of his pupils.

Friday, March 12th 1909
Influenza and bronchitis don't seem to have affected the spirits of J.S., who was more entirely delightful this morning than he has been this term. We are doing the last 200 lines or so of the 'Midsummer Night's Dream', not one would think a very productive subject, but J.S. was full of stories and quotations. He quoted Coleridge's lines,

> *When the ivy-tod is heavy with snow*
> *And the owlet whoops to the wolf below,*
> *That eats the she-wolf's young.*

39

As J.S. remarked you would almost freeze to death if you said them often enough. He was pointing out at the time the wonderful effect of the lines:

> The iron tongue of midnight hath hold twelve:
> Lovers to bed; 'tis almost fairy time.

... J.S. explained, which interested me, that everybody 70 years ago, for instance when Pickwick was published, said 'wuz' for 'was', and it was only cockneys who said 'wos', hence Mr Weller senior always says 'wos'. J.S. remarked Lord Lansdowne always says 'wuz'. 'Yes, he wuz'[1]. This reminds me of another remark of J.S's that 'no English poet took more trouble to get the sound 'sss' out of his lines than Tennyson, consequently you very rarely find the sound in his poems. He called it 'kicking the geese out of the boat.' When Thisbe speaks of Pyramus's 'eyes as green as leeks', J.S. made the characteristic observation 'They *are* rather impressive if they are the right green!'

Here are two of J.S's stories. 'Theodore Hook used to come through a churchyard late at night and always said he saw a ghost in the porch. One night a friend dressed up in a sheet and went and sat in the porch. Theodore Hook looked in as usual and simply remarked cheerfully 'Oh! There are two of you tonight are there?' and passed on leaving the friend horribly scared!

J.S's comment on the line: 'That had in it a crannied hole or chink' (the Wall in Act V, Sc. i): 'I knew a Squire's wife who never had much brain and lost all she had in making a new rockery, who said, "It will be so nice when all the little holes are filled up with *crevices*!"'

Friday, May 14th 1909
3rd hour went to J.S. He spoke of surnames and I learnt, which amused and interested me, that Ming-ees = Menzies, Bred-doll-ban = Breadalbane, and the other ones I knew before. This was *a propos* of the pronunciation of Cromwell which J.S. said was of course 'Crummell', and that when the statue was unveiled outside Westminster Hall only Lord Rosebery and one other distinguished man called him by his right pronunciation. He quoted the pompous Mayor of Oxford who referring to his year of office remarked 'I feel that I have fulfilled my duties with partiality on the one side and impartiality on the other!'

He also told us ... that once when Swift, Harley, and Bolingbroke (Bullingbrook as J.S. called him) were driving down to see the Queen, Harley and Swift began to play road-whist.[2] In the midst of Bolingbroke's learned disquisition on politics, Harley bursts in 'I'm up; there's a Cat!'

---

[1] After listening to Lord Lansdowne in the House of Lords (24th June 1909) I noted: 'Incidentally I satisfied myself that Ld. Lansdowne does say "wuz" for was'!

[2] The game in which each person scores so much on seeing certain animals on his side of the road.

He also quoted Dr Johnson's remark to one who asked him if he was a botanist: 'No, Sir, I am not, and before I could be one I should have to turn myself into a reptile', alluding to his shortsightedness. 'Johnson had many defects' adds J.S., 'but in many respects he is one of the most admirable men in literature.'

Sooner or later in all his digressions J.S. was sure to quote Boswell whom he seemed to know by heart. Indeed it was said of him at the time that he and Mr Asquith, the then Prime Minister, who were both members of the Literary Club (The Club), were the only two members who could be relied upon to quote Boswell on any subject with perfect accuracy.

I have often thought that what Johnson once said of Burke might well have been said of J.S. When Boswell remarked that Burke had 'a constant stream of conversation', Johnson replied 'Yes, Sir; if a man were to go by chance at the same time with Burke under a shed, to shun a shower, he would say—"this is an extraordinary man".'

I suppose that after J.S. my Father (known to many generations of Westminsters as 'The Buck') was the best known and most liked of the other assistant masters of my time (Plate 14). He, himself, was the most modest of men, but as a very distinguished Old Westminster wrote to me after his death—and it was true—'Your father was loved and admired by every generation of Old Westminsters who knew him ever since he became a master at Westminster. He has influenced for good hundreds of Westminsters, and the School owes him a deep debt of gratitude for all he did in raising the tone and standard of life amongst the boys. . . . I always thought that your father was an ideal House Master, and that the boy was fortunate who went up Grant's and there came under the influence of your father's remarkable personality.'

My last years up Grant's were very happy ones, for by then I had made many friends who shared my own interests. Chief among these was R. E. Clifton Gordon,[1] who was afterwards at Pembroke College, Cambridge, with me, Adrian Boult,[2] and Guy Chapman,[3] and we four formed what we called (with memories of Walpole and Gray) the 'Quadruple Alliance'. Other close friends, especially in my last year at the School, after the others had left, were D. Morrice Low[4]

[1] d. 1920.
[2] Sir Adrian Boult, C.H., D.MUS., etc.
[3] Professor G. P. Chapman, C.B.E., M.C., author of *Beckford, a Biography* and other books.
[4] D. M. Low, author of various books on Edward Gibbon, the historian, etc.

and Robin Barrington-Ward.[1] In that year (1908–9) Barrington-Ward was Captain of the School, Low was Head Townboy (Princeps Oppidanorum) and I was Head of my House, so that all three of us were in a position of considerable authority.

I have seen it seriously argued somewhere that the decade 1900–10 was the high-water mark of public schools in England. It is a satisfactory hypothesis for those whose schooldays, like my own, fell within the period, but there is, in fact, something to be said for it. Certainly the older public schools had by then recovered their poise which had been rudely shaken by the evidence given about them before the Public Schools Commission in the 1860s, and had adapted their traditions and customs to more modern conditions, while the younger public schools (e.g. Marlborough, Wellington, Radley, etc.), founded in the 1840s and 1850s, were by then firmly established.

Conditions at Westminster, as revealed by the Commission, were no worse than at Eton or Winchester. Indeed in some ways they were better, but none the less it had been harder hit than either of the others. Apart from the general trend at that time in favour of country schools, it cannot be denied that Westminster in the mid nineteenth century was an unattractive place. Those responsible for the welfare and finance of the School had done little for it. The open fields which had once stretched from Westminster to Chelsea had been largely built over, and had contracted into the ten acres which the foresight of Dean Vincent had reserved for the School's Playing Fields. The clear water of the Thames had become foul with much of the drainage of London, and in summer emitted a stench which at times – as I was assured by one who was a master at the School in the 1850s – could be smelt in Dean's Yard.

By 1900, however, so much had been done to improve the amenities of the neighbourhood by slum clearance, re-building, and better drainage systems, etc., that the alleged unhealthiness of Westminster, although the legend died hard, was seen to have been largely due to local conditions which were no longer operative. Partly as a result of this, partly by the recommendations for the future welfare of the School made by the Commission and embodied in the Public Schools Act of 1868 and partly by successive Head Masters and the able staffs which they gathered round them, the School had recovered much of its reputation and prestige. There was no longer any question of its removal to the country. The value and advantages of its unique position at the very centre of affairs had been recognized, and both it

[1] R. McG, Barrington-Ward, D.S.O., M.C., Editor of *The Times*, 1941–8 (d. 1948).

and the other public schools were accepted, rightly or wrongly, as making a definite and unchallenged contribution to the educational system of the country. Furthermore, within their walls, there was a general sense of security in that it was believed that nothing would upset the general pattern of things.

We, who were at Westminster during this decade, as is clear from my journal from which I have already quoted, shared in that sense of security, which was to be finally shattered by the 1914–18 War. We were neither thoughtless nor were we over thoughtful. We did not question the value of our traditions and customs. We were quietly proud of being Westminsters, and jealous of the School's prestige. We were not unduly games-ridden like some other schools at that time. Games had their part, and a large part, in our lives, but, as again my journal shows, the leaders at that time had also wider and other interests. Those who did not conform to normal public school standards were treated tolerantly on the whole and, as they got higher in the school, if they were good fellows their 'eccentricities', if we may so call them, became their assets. The youthful 'crank', if that is not too strong a word, is none the worse for being temporarily suppressed and made to conform outwardly – if he is any good he will come into his own in time and be valued for the particular contribution which his single talent makes to the whole.

Mercifully the word 'teenager' had not then been invented, and we were able to develop naturally as schoolboys according to our ages without articles in the Press, nor was it possible for us in those days to be asked to give our views either on wireless or in television interviews. If we moved on traditional lines we were not, I think, hide-bound, and the tone of the school taken as a whole was admirable. We carried out our duties (those of us who were in authority) to the best of our ability, and with a real sense of responsibility. We never thought it wrong to exercise the authority which had been delegated to us.

We were content, perhaps too content, with our little world as we found it, but we were not entirely uncritical of it and some at least of the things which we discussed among ourselves as desirable for the welfare of the school, but of which there then seemed but little prospect, have in the course of time come to pass.[1] But none of us ever supposed that there might come a time when criticism would be levelled at the whole public school system as a privileged anachronism in a changing world.

[1] e.g. an increase in the number of boarding-houses, the revival of 'Water', etc.

Such, at any rate, are some of the impressions which I get from re-reading my journal which with all its inevitable immaturity does give, I think, from the very triviality of the events which it records a not uninteresting day to day picture of the Westminster of sixty years ago as seen through the eyes of a senior boy who was also Head of his House.

Perhaps a few extracts from my journal will illustrate these impressions.

Sept 23rd 1908
(the evening before Term began)
The first arrival was a new boy called Smurthwaite.[1] I went and talked to him, and showed him round the House, etc.

I told him he would be my fag, and he seemed relieved at the mildness of my aspect and appeared surprised as he had pictured himself arising at 5.30 to make me cocoa (I can see myself at *that* hour drinking cocoa!). I mentioned that he would be 'lag of Hall' [i.e. the lowest boy in the House] and to my astonishment he said he was so glad that he would begin right at the bottom . . . The next arrival was S., a curious contrast, poor child, he is utterly lost and miserable, not knowing whether he is on his head or his heels.

Oct 8th
Today the new boys commence fagging, so I got hold of Smurthwaite and told him that he needn't fetch my Father for lunch. To which he replied in a disappointed manner 'Oh! needn't I. I should so love to!' I had to say no I was afraid he couldn't. I then found S. and gave him first choice whether he would take my boots down at 9 and tidy my table, bringing my boots up again at 9 in the morning, or whether he would make my toast when fires begin. I advised him to do the former as I didn't see him in my mind in the midst of a scrum round the fire. He chose as I suggested, and turning to Smurthwaite I said 'Then you will make my toast', to which this remarkable child replied 'Is that all, can't I do something more. I should so love to'! Much taken a-back I said 'Well, if you are so anxious you can bring my boots in the morning at 9 if you like', on which he thanked me profusely. I asked S. how he was getting on, and he seemed to think better, again impressing on me the fact he got on well with his Dormitory. I think as a matter of fact he is settling down, the clouds on his face seem clearing.

I had a tremendous long talk with Barrington-Ward this afternoon which extended from 1-45 to 3. I find that we have much in common and I think that we shall get very friendly. I hope so, as it is a very good thing when the head Town Boys are friendly with the head Kings Scholars,

[1] On leaving Westminster he went to Sandhurst, became a 2nd Lieut. in the Black Watch, and was killed in action at Ypres in October 1914.

apart from the fact of personal friendship. He took me into College, and showed me various things. . . . B-Ward and myself then walked round and round Dean's Yard and discussed School matters. We found our likes and dislikes were very similar. It seems to me a very good thing that Low is a friend of mine and B-Ward, and we are all frightfully keen on the School. I do not think the Town Boy and King's Scholar friction will be *en evidence* this year, not at any rate if we can prevent it, for B-Ward and myself think the same about it.

. . . In Deb Soc this evening . . . the debate ['That this House approves of the system of fagging'] was fair, not very good. B-Ward got up and made an impassioned speech on the evils of the fagging system and the deceitfulness, etc, it led to. The House drank it in open-mouthed to hear the Captain saying such things. I was intensely amused. When he sat down he passed across to me the laconic note 'Exactly as I expected, the House is *far* too honest'! In a pause I found myself upon my legs unknowing whether to speak for or against, eventually I followed B-Ward's lead, but was hampered by continually thinking of arguments the other way . . . The motion was carried by acclamation. . . .

Going round Dormitories tonight I found one of the new boys out of bed and the others all but likewise, and the light on. Really they are a nuisance. I am afraid if this happens again I shall have to sit on them which I hate doing to new boys.

Oct 21st

That disgusting little 'Professor' was out of bed again tonight. What am I to do?

[He was another new boy, who was known as 'the Professor' from his large round glasses and from his amusingly precise and somewhat solemn way of talking.]

Oct 22nd

It is no good, I tried hard to be 'a very great seigneur indeed' tonight, but like Rowland Edwards and his philosophy 'my cheerfulness kept breaking in'! In other words I had up the 'Professor' for being out of bed last night. He said he hadn't heard the half strike [i.e. Big Ben]. 'Have you a watch' said I. 'Yes' says he, 'only it is always slow'. My fatal mouth, it would twitch do what I would, and I fear he saw. However I sent him out, and after a decent interval had him back and delivered this not over brilliant harangue, horribly conscious of the fact that Hobson [my admirable second monitor and eventual successor] inwardly gurgling, was standing next to me. 'We have decided to'—brutal me! I paused here—to let you off this time . . . It seems impossible to impress on you new boys that you must be in bed by the half' etc. etc. . . . However we have decided to let you go this time, so you may go, but don't ever be late again or you won't receive such lenient treatment.' Hobson dashed my pride by saying that he didn't believe he was a bit impressed.

However, later in the evening when I went round Dormitories I noted 'the children were so much in bed tonight that only, or so it seemed to me, the tops of their heads were visible . . . truly it seemeth efficacious for the moment!'

From time to time a grimmer entry appears in the journal. Here, for instance, is one which begins cheerfully:

'Oh! Thou bloudie man! I am fairly "steeped in gore" today, owing to the ruthless slaughter of three children' for the breach of some house rule. I see that I noted that 'it was a fair "kop",' and that as they stood completely silent when I asked if they had any excuse to make, and as Hobson and I could think of no reasonable excuse to be lenient, the law had to take its course.

Here are my reflections at the end of half my term of office as Head of Grant's.

Feb 24th

Thus ends half of my term of office and I think, on carefully considering it, I may say truthfully that things are going all right. Certainly I am proud to say we have won the only two possible things we could win, Juniors and the Pancake [won by a Grantite]. For the rest—what shall I say? Without hesitation I can say that for me my first half has been entirely happy. Nothing, no one could have been nicer to me than my House has been. I cannot speak too strongly of how deeply I feel this. My slightest efforts have been greeted with an instant response, and this cannot but be gratifying to one in the position of Head of the House. I have tried, and tried very hard, it was the least I could do, to do and give of my very best, and to do my utmost for my House.

I could say the same at the end of my last term, with an added tribute to Hobson and my other monitors for the way that they had backed me throughout, and had helped me to make decisions in such problems as arose from time to time.

During this year my friendship with Robin Barrington-Ward and Morrice Low became close and intimate. Robin had great charm, and my journal has many references to my good fortune in having such a wise and sensible person as Captain of the School. Morrice was my constant companion. We went up Fields together and watched matches and our senior and junior teams playing cricket or football, for although neither of us was any good at games we were both anxious to show that we were keenly interested in the various activities of our respective Houses. Together we walked miles, exploring London and seeking for Westminster prints and portraits in the print shops. We attended debates in both Houses of Parliament and, perhaps rather unexpectedly, those of the Lower House of Convocation and the Church Assembly in the Church House in Dean's Yard. I see, too, that together we went to organ recitals in the Abbey, that we visited the Royal Academy, and that we often turned into Christie's where I picked up quite a lot of knowledge of silver and furniture.

It was something of a blow to me when Robin won a scholarship at Balliol, and Morrice one at Oriel, so that, as I was going to Cambridge, our close companionship could not be continued at the University.

When I look back I am conscious of how much I owe to the School, not only for the lifelong friends which I made there, but for the opportunities which it gave me to see things and to develop on a wider stage than would have been possible, perhaps, in the necessarily restricted setting of a country school.

It was impossible to be at Westminster without realizing that one was at the very centre of affairs. One had only to look at night from one's dormitory window to see just beyond the east end of the Abbey the light in the Clock Tower when the House was in session with the cheerful face of Big Ben beneath, whose chimes regulated much of our social life. Then there were the great state and other services within the Abbey, although these were not so numerous when I was at the School as they have since become. But, as related elsewhere, I was present as a small boy at the Coronation of King Edward VII in 1902, and I well remember the funeral of the old Duke of Cambridge in 1904. His father, Adolphus, Duke of Cambridge (1774–1850), was the youngest and most respectable of the sons of King George III. He was also the most popular, although his habit of talking aloud in church was sometimes a source of embarrassment ('No, no, it was my brother William did that' etc.). He used sometimes to come to the Abbey for service, and a Westminster boy remembered his turning to Dean Buckland during the service and saying in a loud voice, 'I say, Dean, what's a shawm?' His son was something of a link with the past, for after the death of Queen Victoria he was the last surviving grandson of King George III, and for a few months before her birth he had been the heir presumptive to the throne. Although he was actually buried at Kensal Green, it was the first royal funeral service at the Abbey for a great number of years. It was held with full military honours. King Edward was the chief mourner and five Field Marshals and thirteen Generals were pall-bearers. But what has remained in my mind even more than the actual service was the scene when the body was brought to the Abbey the night before to rest in St Faith's Chapel. On this occasion the south cloister was lined on each side by Grenadiers, and the long lines of guardsmen in their bearskins with bowed heads and reversed arms in the gloom of the very dimly lit cloister as the flag-wreathed coffin was borne between them was extraordinarily impressive.

Another feature of Westminster, which was at least as old as the eighteenth century, was, and is, the custom for many of the boarders either to go home for the weekends, if their parents lived in or near London, or to visit relations and friends on Sundays. This might, perhaps, be unsettling for a small boy, but I am quite sure that it was immensely valuable for an older boy not merely to keep in touch with his family in term time as well as in the holidays, but to have the opportunity to meet people unconnected with the daily routine of his school life.[1] It was certainly so in my own experience, and I am more than grateful to those who invited me to their houses.

I remember one such occasion when Canon H. C. Beeching invited Barrington-Ward and myself to a dinner at his house in the Little Cloister at which the other guests were all men of letters, including Sir Sidney Lee, E. V. Lucas, A. C. Bradley, John Sargeaunt, and F. Anstey Guthrie. Canon Beeching was himself a writer, essayist and poet of great charm and distinction, who published while a Canon of Westminster a valuable life of Dean Atterbury based upon the Atterbury MSS which he had persuaded the Dean and Chapter to buy for the Library. He had, too, a very pretty wit, which is shown in a little poem which he circulated privately among his friends entitled, 'Instructions for the Morning Preacher in Westminster Abbey' (see Appendix, page 195).

Another house at which I was a constant guest both as a boy and in later years, was that of the Alexander Murray Smiths. He was the younger son of George Smith, the publisher and friend of Ruskin, Charlotte Brontë, Thackeray and many others and the originator of the *Dictionary of National Biography* and of the *Cornhill Magazine*. For some years he was himself an active partner in the family firm of Smith, Elder & Co. In 1893 he had married Emily, the fourth daughter of Dean Bradley. She had spent her early life at Marlborough and at University College, Oxford, of both of which places her father had been Master. Later as one of the lively and

---

[1] The great Lord Chesterfield writing (*c.*1743) to his son, Philip Stanhope, who had been invited by the father of one of his Westminster schoolfellows to dine on a Sunday, reminds him to adopt 'an easy, civil, and respectful behaviour . . . to take care to answer with complaisance when you are spoken to', to avoid 'an impertinent forwardness', and to remember that 'an outward modesty is extremely becoming'. He was afraid that 'your various occupations of Greek and cricket, Latin and pitch-farthing may possibly divert your attention' from such matters.

5 View from the upper windows of 'Grant's'.

6   On the leads above the South Cloister. (*Left to right*) Professor W. R.
Lethaby, Dean Armitage Robinson, Dr E. J. L. Scott.

talented 'grown-up' daughters of the house she, herself a god-daughter of Tennyson, had met and known most of the eminent later Victorians who came to the Deanery in Bradley's time. She had been the devoted friend of my Mother and, after her death, she had done her best to fill the terrible gap in my young life by adding me, so to say, to her own nephews and nieces. All her life she had a great love for the Abbey, and had written several books illustrating what may be called the anecdotal side of its history. In some ways 'Aunt Nem' (as she became to me) and her husband were an amusing contrast. He very tall and silent, and she very small and vivacious. At their beautiful house in Queen Anne's Gate (once the home of Jeremy Bentham, and left by them to the National Trust), there were always interesting people, whom I met at Sunday luncheons and suppers.

Thus on 17th March 1933 I noted in my Diary:

Lunching today with the Murray Smiths I was interested in meeting old Miss Trench [daughter of Archbishop Trench who was Dean of Westminster from 1856 to 1864] and to hear that she remembered an old Verger at the Abbey called Burroughs who told her that he was one of those who helped to shut the Cloister Door against Queen Caroline when she tried to enter at the Coronation of George IV.[1]

Miss Haldane [sister of Viscount Haldane, sometime Secretary of State for War and afterwards Lord Chancellor] who was also at lunch told us that when the Kaiser lunched with them at Queen Anne's Gate before the [1914–18] War, they had some framed photographs of the German Army Manoeuvres hanging on the wall. Some of the Kaiser's entourage drew his attention to these, 'You see, Sir, here are pictures of your Army.' 'Yes', said the Kaiser cocking his eye at the Haldanes, 'and *how long* have they hung there?'

Lord Haldane had attended the German Army Manoeuvres as the guest of the Kaiser in 1906.

Belonging to an earlier generation was that most loyal of Old Westminsters the late Sir Clements Markham (1830–1916), sometime Secretary and afterwards President of the Royal Geographical Society and as such mainly responsible for choosing Captain Robert Falcon Scott to lead the Antarctic Expeditions of 1901 and 1910. Sir Clements had heard that I was interested in Westminster history, and I see that it was in 1906 that he wrote to me inviting me to spend a

[1] On 25th June 1934 I see that 'I took round College Garden today a Miss Harding, whose Grandfather was at Westminster at the time of George IV's Coronation. He often told her that he remembered standing by the Cloister Door and seeing the Queen arrive. "She wore a black wig, rather crooked, and was crying and much distressed".'

weekend with him as he thought that he might be able to give me some help in my 'antiquarian researches'. He was then getting on for eighty and I was sixteen but, as the D.N.B. remarks, he had 'a genius for friendship especially with the young', and any shyness I might have felt was soon dispersed for I remember that almost his first remark was 'all my life I have regretted that I didn't ask questions when I was young for I might have preserved so much'. He himself had been at Westminster, in the early 1840s, as had been his father, his grandfather, and his great-grandfather (Archbishop Markham) before him, and he had all the 'gentle kindness of manner and engaging winning softness of voice and look' of the Archbishop as described by one of his contemporaries.

For the next ten years I used frequently to go and see him, always to be greeted by 'Well, how's Westminster?' He had no son to carry on the Westminster tradition, but when he died I was touched and surprised to find that he had left me all his Westminster books and papers.

He told me once, sitting in his study in Eccleston Square, that as a Westminster boy he had been out with a gun over all that part of Pimlico, then swampy fields, in search of snipe, but added characteristically, 'I don't think there really were any snipe'. Shooting snipe in the Tuttle Fields, which then stretched from Westminster to Chelsea, was something of a legend, but it was very curious to hear about it at first hand from someone who had actually tried to do it. It was only a very few years after Sir Clements had left the School that Cubitt started to develop Pimlico by laying out streets and squares – Eccleston Square among them – and in consequence the Tuttle Fields ceased to exist except for the ten acres of Vincent Square, still known as 'Fields' to every Westminster boy.

Sir Clements had a vivid recollection of his school days and of the Westminster of his time. He could remember old Bishop Monk (1784–1856) who found no difficulty in combining his episcopal duties at Gloucester and Bristol with a lucrative Canonry at Westminster, and was the last of the Westminster Prebendaries to wear a white wig. Two of his daughters, old ladies of portentous age, always came on Sundays to the Abbey in my childhood and sat opposite to our pew in the Choir. Dressed in the fashion of a byegone age, with large feathered hats, they had a disconcerting and, to a child, slightly alarming habit of suddenly nodding their heads, opening their mouths and gnashing their teeth with a clatter which could be heard across the aisle. Sir Clements could also remember dining with his step great-uncle, Archdeacon Bentinck, and seeing an ancient peer, a 'hang-over' from Regency days, enter the room with a flat cocked hat (*chapeau bras*) under his arm which he retained throughout the evening.

Like many Westminsters before and since Sir Clements used to go over to listen to the debates in the House of Commons, then being rebuilt after the 1834 fire. It was on one of these occasions that Disraeli remarked as he passed, with an amused glance at a Minister who was struggling to express himself with but poor success, 'Why do you come here, my boy – to take a lesson in *eloquence?*'

This privilege of going over to the House was one of which I myself made full use on wet half holidays and at other times. In those days six seats were usually kept for King's Scholars, but the rest of us had to take our chance and send in our names to the Serjeant-at-Arms, who usually managed to find a place for us. People, then as now, interested me more than politics as such, and I was endlessly fascinated by the procedure of the House and by the contrasting personalities of those who then held the stage. Those were the days of Asquith, Balfour, Joseph Chamberlain, Lloyd George, just coming to the front as President of the Board of Trade, and a youthful and aggressive Winston Churchill. Mr Asquith, always weighty and impressive, seemed to belong to an older and more dignified Parliamentary tradition, and was capable of rising on special occasions to a measured eloquence and perfection of phrase to which no one else could attain.

More exciting, at any rate to one of my age, was Chamberlain, then passionately advocating tariff reform. With his keen, alert face, so curiously and, indeed, startlingly like the face of the younger Pitt as depicted on his statue in St Stephen's Hall, he would sit poised like a hawk on one of the back benches impatiently awaiting the moment when he could swoop and in a magnificent flood of words, which seemed to carry all before it, demolish the arguments of the previous speaker. There was no one, I think, in the House at that time who had quite that type of overwhelming eloquence. There could hardly be a greater contrast between the passionate earnestness of Chamberlain and the seemingly careless indifference of Mr Balfour with his hesitations and fastidious choice of words. How often have I watched him lazily uncurl his long legs from a sprawling position on the front bench and advance to the box with his hands grasping the lapels of his frock coat. He would then begin to speak with infinite charm and detachment. Before long some one on the opposite side of the House, misled and annoyed by what seemed to him merely verbal play and frivolous handling of a serious subject, would interrupt with what he thought was a telling interjection, only to find himself instantly annihilated by some completely unanswerable and smiling retort showing that the speaker knew very well what he was talking about. I saw it happen again and again, and no back bencher ever seemed to learn how dangerous it was to interrupt that master of verbal swordsmanship.

Over all presided, with great dignity, first Mr Speaker Gully and then Mr Speaker Lowther. I never look at the painting of Mr Speaker Gully in my Club, which depicts him standing in his robes and about to put the question, without instantly recalling, after over sixty years, the exact tone of his voice as he said: 'As many as are of that opinion say "Aye" . . . and contrary "No" . . I *think* the "Ayes" have it . . Ayes to the right, Noes to the left, etc.

I suppose that everyone who has been at Westminster has been influenced to a greater or less degree, consciously or unconsciously, by its surroundings and by the way the School nestles under the Abbey Church. To go into 'Abbey' daily as the school chapel, to be present at its services on great and small occasions, 'to make a two' (as the phrase was) round Cloisters, and, if one was adventurous, to explore the Triforium and the roofs hoping no one would spot one, and to be ever conscious of its majestic and dominating presence, these things make an ineffaceable impression on a Westminster even if, at the time, they were all rather taken for granted as part of one's ordinary school life.

My own case was, of course, exceptional. After all, Westminster was my home long before I entered the School, and I cannot remember a time when the Abbey and its services and its monuments ('the gentlemen in stone' as I am told that I called them at an early age) were not a part – and a large part – of my life.

But I think that my first real interest in the Abbey was aroused when my Mother took me as a small boy to hear a lecture on it by Mrs Murray Smith. The lecture was illustrated by lantern slides taken from the somewhat imaginative illustrations in her own large book on the Abbey. Somehow or other these illustrations caught my imagination both then and subsequently when I was old enough to read the book, and, although they may not come up to the highest standards of antiquarian accuracy, to this day I never think of certain episodes in the history of the Abbey without instantly visualizing them as they are represented in the pages of her book.

As the years went on and I came to know more about the history of the Abbey and the spell of its beauty grew upon me, I came to have a feeling for it which it is hard to put into words. Perhaps the poet and authoress, the late Victoria Sackville-West, came nearest to it when, in one of her books, she wrote of the love which she and her family had for their own beautiful home, and said that 'to all of us Knole meant as much as any human being. It was different from one's love for any human being. It transcended it'. That feeling, call it what you will, is something, perhaps, known only to those who have experienced it, and have either lived in or have been brought up in the shadow of great and historic buildings.

And it wasn't only the Abbey; there was in addition the School with its own historic buildings and great traditions which exercised a like spell upon me. Pre-eminent among these buildings is the Great Hall or 'School' as it is called, once the Dormitory of the monks. No school in the kingdom has so noble and majestic a Hall of Assembly, roughly comparable in size – it measures I believe 96 feet long by 34 feet broad – and shape to such Halls as those of the Middle Temple or of Christ Church, Oxford. In this room for centuries practically the entire school was taught, and the Shell Form, familiar in many more modern public schools, derives its name from the form at Westminster which was taught in front of the shell-like apse at the end of School. When my Father first came to Westminster in 1881 School was still used for teaching and he often told me how distracting it was for a young man to try to teach with other forms all round him. But very shortly afterwards it was found possible to build many new class-rooms and School became, as it is today, a Hall of Assembly for the whole school. But with a difference. In 1941 an incendiary bomb gutted the interior, leaving only the four walls standing. Among the ashes, lying several inches thick upon the floor after the fire, I picked out the iron bar which formerly crossed School at a height of about twenty feet from the ground. From this bar in earlier days hung a curtain which divided the upper from the lower school. But in later days it was, and still is (for it has been re-erected), the bar over which the pancake is tossed on Shrove Tuesday. No one knows the origin of this curious Westminster custom, but Jeremy Bentham mentions it as taking place when he was at the School in the middle of the eighteenth century, and it is probably very much older. Formerly the whole school scrambled for it, but now one boy is elected to represent each Form (Plate 15).

A curious incident connected with the 'Greaze', as it is called, which happened on one occasion while I was at the School, comes to mind. The College Cook duly tossed the pancake, which sailed over the bar, and as it fell the combatants rushed forward to try to catch it and then fell in a heap on the floor. One boy, perhaps because he was at the far end of the line, was a fraction of a second late and as he prepared to hurl himself on the top of the struggling mass of boys, by an extraordinary chance the pancake, undamaged, rolled out from beneath the Greaze. Whereupon he picked it up, stood with an amused smile watching the Greaze struggling for nothing. When time was called, and the Greaze disentangled itself, he claimed and was awarded the traditional prize of a guinea by the Dean. The boy was my friend and contemporary—the present Chancellor of Cambridge University, Lord Adrian, O.M., F.R.S.

The new 'School' which has arisen on the ruins of the old is in every way worthy of its predecessor, and cannot fail to impress present and future Westminsters. But for those who remember School as it was before 1941 (Plate 16) there must always be sadness. Nothing can quite replace the loss of the great sixteenth-century hammer-beam roof, the hundreds of names painted on the walls with the long family lists, Randolphs, Markhams, Phillimores and the rest who had come for generations, and the impressive display of coats of arms painted on the panelling (nearly two hundred of them) of the more distinguished peers and commoners who had been bred at Westminster. Even as a small boy one could not fail to be conscious of a sense of continuity and of being a part of 'something greater than we knew', and this was to grow as one progressed up the school and to develop, as regards myself, into a lifelong devotion and loyalty to its interests.

CHAPTER IV

Cambridge

Cambridge Characters – Sydney Cockerell – Dr Tanner –
Professor Gwatkin – Undergraduate Life – Pembroke Dons –
The Winchester Reading Prize

I WENT up to Pembroke from Westminster in October 1909. My
grandfather had been at Trinity under the redoubtable Dr Whewell,
but in 1872 my eldest uncle won a scholarship at Pembroke from
Sherborne, and in 1876 my father followed exactly in his footsteps.
At that date Waterhouse had just rebuilt the Hall, and the College
was trying to reconcile itself to the glaring ugliness of both its new
Hall and its new Library with its clock tower. Fortunately the original
fourteenth century front to Trumpington Street with the addition of
Christopher Wren's Chapel beyond, together with the north side of
Old Court and the charming inner or Ivy Court with the Fellows'
Garden beyond had been left untouched and preserved the dignity
and beauty of an earlier age.

Cambridge itself had changed outwardly but little in the thirty
years or so which had elapsed between my father's time and my own.
It retained, as, indeed, compared with Oxford, it still retains, much
of the character and peacefulness of a university town. The ancient
one-horse tram, with its morning and evening complement of Bed-
makers and their 'helps' (that unique race of 'Bedders' and "elps")
still ambled up and down K.P.[1] and Trumpington Street; hansom
cabs still plied between the station and the colleges; the University
Library, where I spent many happy hours, was still in its ancient
home near the Senate House; and from my first-year rooms in
Trumpington Street one could see just across the road the fallow deer
in the so-called Peterhouse deer park although it was little more than
a small enclosure which has since then been swallowed up by an

[1] King's Parade.

55

extension to the Fitzwilliam Museum. If bicycles were many, motors, as far as the University was concerned, were few. When evening fell it was possible to go the length of Trumpington Street, K.P., and Trinity Street, and meet no one unconnected with the University.

There were, too, still to be seen about the streets, as there always are in a university town, some well known characters and a few survivals from an earlier age. One such survival was the Revd Peter Mason, the Senior Fellow of St John's, a frail old man whom I used to see wheeled about the streets in an invalid chair. His claims to fame were popularly said to be that in his youth he had walked from Cambridge to Oxford in less time than it took to accomplish that notoriously wearisome journey by train, and that he had once written a Hebrew Grammar in a series of letters to a Duchess. The first was a product of fertile undergraduate imagination, although it is an undoubted fact that he did indeed, among other pedestrian feats in his youth, walk the eighty miles from Cambridge to Oxford in two days. It is no less true, incredible as it may seem, that in 1853 Messrs J. Hall & Son of Cambridge published a slim little volume from his pen entitled *Gently Flowing Waters . . . an easy practical Hebrew Grammar . . . arranged in a series of letters from a teacher of languages to an English Duchess.* Therein the curious may find that each chapter begins 'My Lady Duchess', and contains such enchanting sentences as 'Your Grace has condescended to approve of my plan of comparing the irregular verbs' to so- and- so, and 'I call Your Grace's particular attention' to this or that, etc!

Far otherwise than frail was the burly figure of Sir Robert Ball (irreverently known as 'Zerubbabal') Lowndean Professor of Astronomy, that most genial popularizer of science, whom one used to see about the streets. He used to tell how, returning to the Observatory one evening, he was so struck by the brilliance of Venus in the evening sky that he felt impelled to draw the attention of a passing policeman to her, only to be met by the stolid reply 'All right, Sir Robert, I'll keep my eye on her'! Another well-known figure, whom one regarded with awe as a metaphysician of immense reputation, was Professor McTaggart of Trinity, nervously edging his way sideways along the pavement as if in constant fear of attack from behind.

Less well-known then than he was to become in later years was (Sir) Sydney Cockerell who had recently been appointed Director of the Fitzwilliam Museum. He was already showing how much could be done to improve what hitherto had been a rather cheerless museum not merely by re-arranging the exhibits and re-hanging the pictures

7 Dr George Granville Bradley, Dean of Westminster 1881–1902.
8 Dr J. Armitage Robinson, Dean of Westminster 1902–11, High Almoner 1906–33.
9 Dr Robinson Duckworth, Canon and Sub Dean 1875–1911.

10   Sir Frederick Bridge, Organist 1882–1924. Author of
Samuel Pepys – Lover of Music.

11   Dr William Gunion Rutherford, Head Master of Westminster 1883–1901.

12 Dr James Gow, Head Master of Westminster 1901–19.

13 John Sargeaunt, Esq., ('J.S.'), Assistant Master 1890–1918.

14 Ralph Tanner, Esq., Assistant Master 1881–1919. My Father watching a House Match up Fields (Vincent Square).

but by placing large bowls of flowers and expensive rugs in the galleries.

Perhaps because my lodgings in my first year were almost opposite I often found my way into the Fitzwilliam, and I remember with gratitude his friendliness and how he would stop and talk to me and tell me of his latest acquisitions. I well remember, too, the thrill when one day he told me that he had just had given to the museum a large collection of unpublished letters, etc., written to the eighteenth century poet William Hayley, the friend of Cowper and Blake, and asked me if I would catalogue them for him. I don't suppose that the catalogue was very well done, but it was a task which I greatly enjoyed, for there was a fascination in handling original letters and in familiarising oneself with the literary circle in which Hayley moved.

My father had been 10th classic in the Classical Tripos of 1880, but I elected to read history. Taken as a whole, and with one or two notable exceptions, the history lecturers were an uninspiring lot. Curiously enough, in view of his brilliant books, the most disappointing was Professor G. M. Trevelyan (afterwards Master of Trinity) who used to read his lectures in the Hall of Trinity in a rapid and completely expressionless monotone. I can remember other arid hours spent with other lecturers in the same Hall, but they were redeemed by studying the heraldry in the windows and the great picture of Henry VIII over the High Table. Occasionally the old Master of Trinity, Dr Montagu Butler, used to appear at these lectures and sit under the picture; rather to our amusement, for there was a story that on one occasion two visitors who had been laughing at the unmistakable facial resemblance between the Master and Henry VIII were astonished to hear the soft voice of the Master, who unbeknown to them had come in behind them, saying 'Ah! you are looking at that picture. Terrible, terrible, vice in every line of his countenance'!

I was present on one occasion when Dr Butler attended a lecture by the Professor of Poetry. He sat in the front row and completely disconcerted the lecturer by keeping up a soft but audible commentary on how interesting he was finding it. This he varied by dropping off to sleep, and after a few minutes waking with a start. Then he still further disconcerted the lecturer by surveying him at the distance of a few feet through a pair of small field glasses which hung round his neck.

The two outstanding history lecturers of my time were my very distant cousin, Dr J. R. Tanner of St John's, and Professor H. M. Gwatkin of Emmanuel. Dr Tanner with his round face and twinkling eyes behind his gold-rimmed spectacles, was always good value. He lectured on what he once described to us as 'the primrose path of English Constitutional History'. His lectures were an admirable blend of wit and learning. What could be more grateful to a roomful of undergraduates, for instance, than the casual remark that some historic personage had 'exercised the strict economy of leaving bills unpaid'. It was not surprising that his lectures attracted large classes for he gave us in a skilful and attractive way the kind of valuable facts which could easily be embodied in our notes.

Equally outstanding, but in quite a different way, was Professor H. M. Gwatkin, who lectured to us on European history. He appeared to be much older than he really was, and one was always told that he had taken four 'Firsts' and lost a sense for each of them. Certain it is that he was practically blind, almost deaf, and had no roof to his mouth, or at any rate had so remarkable an intonation that until one got used to it, it was almost impossible to understand what he was saying – certain words would stand out with startling clearness but the rest was a jumble which sometimes came out in rushes, and required patience, skill, and long practice before it could be disentangled and become intelligible. Some gave the task up as hopeless after the first lecture, but those who persevered found him infinitely brilliant and stimulating.

His entry into the lecture room was unfailing comedy. He would arrive looking very frail, advance up the room slowly unwinding his many mufflers, deposit them and his coat on what he believed to be a desk, but was not improbably one of the ladies from Girton or Newnham, who always sat together in the front row. He would then hold out his hand saying hopefully 'any papers? any papers?' (but none were ever forthcoming), climb on to his dais, tilt his chair back to a quite impossibly dangerous angle until his head rested on the wall behind him, retrieve half a sheet of notepaper from some inner pocket which he would hold within less than an inch from his best eye for a minute or two, and then begin with some such sentence as: 'It-will-generally-be-found' that when the *Spanish* fleet sets-out-to-sea it is in a *moshst dishgraceshful* condition'! Then would follow what some one has called 'the incisive sentences, the brilliant pictures, the revealing aphorisms, and the lively asides' which were a constant delight to the listener. Here are two which I remember after nearly sixty years. One day he gave us the admirable advice 'You should read Stubb's Constitutional History and leave out all the constitutional parts and you will pick up a great deal of history'. On another occasion he dismissed some king with the words

'So he died and went-to-*Hell* – we *know* he went to hell because the Pope said he did'.

He was a recognized authority on early Church history and his *Studies in Arianism* was the standard work on the subject. When he became Dixie Professor of Ecclesiastical History in 1891, at the age of forty-seven, he decided to take Orders. According to his own account one of the questions in the Ordination Examination was 'Give a brief account of the Arian heresy' – 'So I wrote down what I thought the Examiners would like, and then I referred them to my book'. I once attended a course of lectures given by him on Biblical criticism, for the sheer pleasure of hearing him lecture, and can remember the placid satisfaction with which he ended one lecture by saying 'Next time we-shall-*eashily* finish the Woman taken in *Adultery*'!

The decade before the first World War, although, for those who lived through it, by no means as secure and untroubled as later writers would have us believe, was probably the last decade in which the ordinary life at Cambridge was very much as it had been in the time of our fathers and grandfathers. Much of what one took for granted seems unbelievable and prehistoric to a modern generation. To begin with, the number of undergraduates has more than doubled. When I first went up in 1909, the number of undergraduates was about 3,700 and, perhaps, 200 women at Girton and Newnham. In 1968 there were 9,153 men in residence and 1,164 women.[1] There was, therefore, in those days no great scramble for places. No one shared rooms in College with anyone else. One had one's own set of rooms consisting of a sitting-room, bedroom, and small pantry where one's bedmaker washed up, etc. Bathrooms were few and might be some distance away across the Court.

Except for dinner in Hall one had all one's meals in one's own rooms. Breakfast was still a regular meal at which to entertain one's friends, although the pots of beer with which the meal began in my father's time no longer appeared. One was frequently asked out to breakfast with one of the married Dons at his home or, more rarely, with the Master, who had his invariable formula with which to dismiss us – 'I have my work and, doubtless, you have your lectures. Good morning!' Tea in one's rooms, with plates piled high with muffins and crumpets ordered from the Buttery, and coffee after Hall were other occasions for entertaining. Sherry was completely out of fashion, and widespread cocktail drinking was not yet. To entertain any of the ladies from Girton or Newnham was unheard of,

[1] Whitaker's Almanack 1968.

indeed, my recollection is that one seldom saw them about the streets. When they came to lectures they arrived in a waggonette, carefully chaperoned by a Don, and sat together in the front rows. If a Freshman was called upon by a senior man, either of his own or of any other College, he was still expected to return the call by continuing to go to the senior man's rooms until he found him at home. On Sunday afternoons it was usual to call on such Dons and their wives as one knew. I can recall one Sunday when masses of Freshmen chanced to call almost simultaneously on a certain Don's wife. After every chair had been requisitioned from bedrooms, etc., they sat in inarticulate rows, as at a meeting, too shy either to talk or to depart!

Chapels were compulsory, but no one, I am afraid, could say that they were very edifying in my day at Pembroke. Mozley, the Dean, had no note of music in him and, if he was not gasping for breath with chronic asthma, read the Service in a rapid sing-song, with old Heriz-Smith, a senior Fellow, repeating the Psalms, firmly, loudly and invariably at least half a verse behind the rest of the congregation. In those days undergraduates read the lessons on weekdays. My Pembroke uncle used to tell of one in his day who, after studying the key to the lessons for the day, confidently gave out 'Here beginneth 2. Tim. 4'. In my own day someone informed an astonished congregation that the woman of Samaria in her agitation left her *waterproof* instead of her water pot at the well. I was present, too, on another occasion when an unfortunate young man had neglected to find the place beforehand. On arrival at the lectern he was appalled to discover that he was faced with the problem of finding in a hurry one of the most minor of the Prophets. With scarlet face and trembling hands he turned the pages backwards and forwards. Hosea, Amos, Micah and the rest flitted before his agonized gaze as he sought the elusive Nahum. Then to our shameless amusement, the Master rose in his stall and in a pained and reproving voice read the lesson himself, while the miserable young man, hopelessly left at the post, knew not whether to remain at the lectern or return to his seat.

The Master throughout my time was Canon Arthur James Mason who had been elected to the Mastership in 1903. Looking back I think that to the ordinary undergraduate he seemed to be a little aloof – as, perhaps, a Master of a College ought to be – although we were conscious of the charm and dignity with which he presided both over the College and over the University of which, at that time, he was Vice-Chancellor. But his gentle manner, his beautifully modulated voice, and his fastidious tastes (he abhorred tobacco), seemed to have little in common with the rather robust and predominantly athletic traditions of the College.

The Master, therefore, was rather an unknown quantity to most of us including myself. And then something happened which completely altered my whole conception of him. About a fortnight before I took the first part of my Tripos in my second year, I had been overworking and had something in the nature of a breakdown. I recovered, however, sufficiently to go the day before the examination – it was a Sunday – and pay, as was then the custom, a 'duty' call on the Master and Mrs Mason. I have no recollection of that call, but that evening as I was sitting rather miserably in my rooms I heard a step outside, and the Master put his head round the door. He said that Mrs Mason and he had thought that I looked so ill that I was to pack up my things at once and come and stay at the Lodge over my Tripos, so that I could be properly fed and looked after and rest between the papers.

I thought then, and I think now, that it was one of the most charming things that a Master could do for an undergraduate whom he scarcely knew. At the Lodge I was at once made to feel that I was one of the family, and a very delightful family it was, with the Master adding to the gaiety of meals by the grave and amused courtesy with which he answered, and endeavoured to stem, the inexhaustible flow of questions from his three small children, all, then, under the age of ten. I stayed with the Master, I think, for nearly a fortnight—he wouldn't let me go until I had completely recovered—and during that time he went out of his way to invite my personal friends to meals.

Of the Pembroke Dons of my time those who most readily come to mind, besides my Tutor, W. S. Hadley, are Professor E. G. Browne, the Persian and Oriental scholar, the Revd J. Kenneth Mozley, and (Sir) Ellis Minns, and from all of these I received much kindness and hospitality both in their college rooms and in their homes. 'Johnny' Browne was a tremendous talker and his volubility in those years was not lessened by the fact that he was bitterly opposed to the then government's policy towards his beloved Persia. From my room beneath his I used to hear the distant rumble of that ceaseless flow. Mozley, too, was a great talker and delighted to argue, and argue brilliantly, on any subject. He was to become a Canon of St Paul's but, partly owing to ill-health, he never seemed quite to fulfil the promise of those earlier years. Ellis Minns, the Librarian, was rather different. Most undergraduates who strayed into the Library were rather oppressed by his vast learning and by his habit, at that time, of pouncing on any unguarded statement with a devastating rejoinder. But that was only Minns' way, and when one got to know him well – and he was really a very friendly person – he was excellent company. I had a very real affection for him, and often stayed with him after I had gone down. It was very amusing to see him 'twittering' – i.e. standing on the tips of his toes and rubbing the palms of his hands together in intense enjoyment – before he launched one of his verbal shafts at oneself or another. But some there were who took it all a little too seriously and were offended and hurt by his outspokenness.

Better known, perhaps, than any of these was H. G. Comber, whose friendships extended to all Pembroke men and to many beyond the College. It was often said that he lived in a world of his own entirely populated by 'Blues', and 'Comber and his Blues' was rather a byword in the College. But 'labels are always libels' (as I once heard Dean Inge remark in a sermon in Pembroke Chapel), and while it was true that Comber's most intimate undergraduate friends were drawn from the athletic set, it was not the whole truth. He had many other friends, including myself, who had, alas, no shadow of a claim to any athletic blue blood, and when I had rooms in Ivy Court there were few mornings when he did not stop at my window for a friendly word on his way to and from the old Combination Room.

I loved those rooms in Ivy Court. In the eighteenth century they had been inhabited for a brief period by that wayward genius and poet Kit Smart, and they were immediately beneath the rooms later to be those of the poet Gray and, after him, of the younger Pitt. It was pleasant to think that they had once passed and repassed my door, and there was a tradition that the Pembroke undergraduates of Pitt's time used to lay bets which side of the entrance he would lurch against as he emerged into Ivy Court, for even in those early days he was fortifying his feeble constitution and aggravating his tendency to gout by what his biographer calls 'floods of port wine'. Before I moved into these rooms, in my third year, the seventeenth-century panelling was painted a dingy and muddy brown, but I persuaded the College to have it repainted white. When I went down in 1912 these rooms were taken over by Arthur Bliss,[1] and in 1925, when the Hall was lengthened by the inclusion of the old Combination Room, they were turned into the present Senior Parlour by throwing my bedroom and sitting-room into one and by making a door through from the Hall.

In 1910, while I was still a Freshman, King Edward VII died, and

[1] Now Sir Arthur Bliss, Master of the Queen's Musick.

I listened in the Senate House to the Master of Pembroke, as Vice Chancellor, reading the letter from the Privy Council commanding him to proclaim the new Sovereign. This letter followed the traditional Tudor form and ended 'Your loving friends', followed by the signatures of some members of the Privy Council. At this time, owing to the Parliament Act, political feeling was running very high. I remember the Master telling me, with some amusement, that when he saw that the first signature was 'Winston S. Churchill', he could not bring himself to read 'Your *loving* friends, Winston S. Churchill' etc., but thought it better to prevent any possible groans or other demonstrations from the undergraduates in the gallery by changing it to 'Your loving friends (signed) Three of the Privy Council'! It is forgotten now how unpopular Winston Churchill was at that time, and that his unpopularity was not entirely confined to the Conservative party.

The Senate House is associated in my mind with another scene, when my friend, Clifton Gordon, and I competed for the Winchester Reading Prize in 1912. We had entered our names rather light-heartedly, and we were, I remember, a little disconcerted to find that there were fifty or sixty other undergraduate competitors seated round the Senate House. The judges were A. C. Benson, then a Fellow and later Master of Magdalene and Professor E. F. Kenney. We were given passages of poetry and prose of gradually increasing difficulty to read, and to begin with elimination must have been fairly easy. But when Clifton, myself and four others were the sole survivors there seemed to be nothing to choose between us, and I began to wonder if it was going to be fought out between Clifton and myself. Then for no very obvious reason Clifton was eliminated, and eventually I divided the prize with a Christ's man, both of us being 'declared to be of equal merit'! Clifton was a beautiful reader. He was, in fact, a better and more versatile reader than myself, and both in Westminster and Pembroke Reading Societies it was an unfailing pleasure to read a scene with him and to see how instantly he responded to the slightest inflexion in one's voice, or how inimitably he would render a comic part such as, for instance, Sir Fretful Plagiary in Sheridan's *Critic*. It was no surprise, therefore, when he won the prize outright the following year.

CHAPTER V

Ceremonial at the Abbey

Dean Ryle – The Revd Francis Westlake – Burial of the Unknown Warrior – Queen Alexandra's Lying-in-State – Installation Service of the Order of the Bath – Bishop Boyd Carpenter – Dr R. H. Charles

---

In November 1910 while I was still up at Cambridge Dean Armitage Robinson resigned the Deanery of Westminster. For some time his eyesight had been giving him increasing trouble, and he dreaded the inevitable extra work and strain involved in the preparations for the approaching Coronation of King George V in which he would necessarily have had to take a prominent part. It was, therefore, a relief to him when a vacancy at Wells enabled him to retire to a Deanery where the duties would be less exacting than at Westminster and where he would be returning to the county of his birth.

The new Dean was Herbert Edward Ryle (Plate 17) who had just resigned the Bishopric of Winchester also owing to ill-health. He was in many ways a great contrast to his immediate predecessor at Westminster. No one could be more charming than Armitage Robinson when he chose, but he was always slightly alarming especially to those who did not know him well, and there were times when he was petrifyingly unapproachable. He was frequently disconcerting in his remarks, and sometimes seemed to enjoy being wilfully mischievous. On one occasion, for example, at Wells a poor young man who had incautiously made some youthful and passing criticism about the afternoon service was introduced by Armitage Robinson to the Archbishop of Canterbury (of all people), who happened to be staying at the Deanery, as 'my young friend Mr X who has views about the way the services should be run'!

Ryle was never either alarming or unapproachable. He would never deliberately make a disconcerting remark, nor could one imagine him enjoying being wilfully mischievous. He had extraordinary

15 H.M. King George V, H.M. Queen Mary, H.R.H. The Prince of Wales with the Dean (Bishop Ryle) at the Pancake Greaze 1919. The winner, D. Moonan, K.S. (holding the remains of the pancake), is presented to H.M. The Queen.

16　School before it was bombed. A photograph of Latin prayers up school taken in the 1930s.

17　Bishop H. E. Ryle, Dean of Westminster 1911–25.

personal charm. At the same time there was a certain aloofness about him which marked him out from more ordinary mortals. In this and in other ways he resembled his slightly older contemporary Arthur James Balfour, who was always 'Prince Arthur' to his friends and contemporaries. Certainly the gods had given Ryle every gift. His career had been almost an unbroken triumph – Eton, King's, the Presidency of Queens' College, Cambridge, and the Bishoprics first of Exeter and then of Winchester. Almost, but not quite; for, by an apparently cruel fate, ill-health had deprived him not only of an almost certain 'First' in the Classical Tripos and also of his 'Blue' for athletics at Cambridge, but now, after being appointed Bishop of Winchester at the age of forty-six, he was forced to resign again for reasons of health, just when he appeared to be marked out for the Primacy.

And yet, in the end, perhaps his best work was to be done at Westminster where he ruled for fourteen years with conspicuous success. He came as a peace-maker after a difficult period at the Abbey, and for that task no man was better fitted. No one could resist the charm of his personal fascination. He had, too, something of that beautiful simplicity and humbleness of heart which character-ized Archbishop Davidson. And yet he was every inch our Abbot (as he liked to call himself), in every way head and shoulders above everyone else at Westminster, moving with calm dignity and dis-tinction as the central figure at all services and functions. It was entirely due to him that the Abbey once again, and after many cen-turies, became the setting for weddings of members of the royal family, and both for these and for the series of Memorial Services after the 1914–18 War a standard was set which, perhaps, had never previously been realized. In working out the details of these services he was greatly helped by members of the Collegiate Body – as he was the first to acknowledge in the charming letters of thanks which he invariably wrote to them after each service was over – and, perhaps pre-eminently by the Custodian, the Revd Francis Westlake, who had a remarkable 'flair' for ceremonial and for foreseeing and providing for every possible contingency. Nothing was too small to escape Westlake's notice. Often I have been with him in the Abbey the night before a big service when everything had been prepared and all the chairs had been set out, but even then he would not be satisfied until he had personally checked every detail, made sure that the cards were on the right seats, verified the numbering, and even taken the trouble to sit on a chair in a back row or near a pillar to see whether it was possible by moving it slightly to ensure that the occupant would get a better view. How he did it all I don't know, for he refused to have a telephone or typewriter at hand, and the many applications for seats were disposed in heaps on the floor of his study in accordance with their merits. The last heap, I remember, he used to refer to pleasantly and generically as 'the Clapham Spinsters', being applications from those whose claim for a seat ('in the choir, please') were non-existent. But although he was often desperately overworked he never allowed himself to be flurried, and had his reward in the smoothness with which everything invariably worked out on the day.

Probably, after the Coronation, the most impressive service in Dean Ryle's time was the burial on 11th November 1920, of the Unknown Warrior. Whether it was he or another who first conceived the idea it seems impossible to say, but it was Ryle who realized its potentialities and it was he who carried it successfully through its initial stages when even in the highest quarters there were doubts and hesitations. No one who was present at that service could ever forget it. The solemn music, the vast congregation which included four Queens and mainly consisted of those who had lost sons or near relations in the War, the nave lined by a hundred V.C's through which was slowly borne the coffin draped with the Ypres Union Jack, and followed by King George V, as chief mourner, with the Prince of Wales and the Duke of York, the Prime Minister (Mr Lloyd George) and his Cabinet, and Members of both Houses of Parliament.

But in some ways even more moving than the service was the final scene of all. All that afternoon and evening there had poured through the Abbey a ceaseless stream of those who came to pay their tribute. Then, at last, at 11 p.m. it became necessary finally to close the doors, but Francis Westlake and I stayed on until nearly midnight in the silent and empty Abbey in order to superintend the filling in of the grave, and thus to be the last to see the Warrior laid to his rest. Into that grave was poured soil brought from every country where our troops had fought during the War, even as, by tradition, soil was brought from the Holy Land in order that the Shrine of Edward the Confessor might be placed upon it. As we stood watching the slowly filling grave the gravediggers, I remember, began to talk, not irreverently but unemotionally, asking each other as they emptied the bags of earth 'where this lot came from' etc., and the contrast to the scenes of emotion which had been witnessed round the grave earlier in the day almost inevitably brought to mind the gravedigger scene in Hamlet.

The Abbey is always impressive at night, and one other scene, also on a November night, remains imperishably in my memory. Just five years after the burial of the Unknown Warrior, Queen Alexandra lay in state in the Abbey before her interment at Windsor on the following day. No Sovereign or Queen Consort had either lain in state or been buried in the Abbey since George II had been buried in Henry VII's Chapel in 1760, and none has done so since. It had been a day of sadness for the passing of a much-loved Queen, and for met personally, a day of great sorrow, for my friend, Francis Westlake, had died very suddenly a few minutes after he had returned to his house in the Cloister from taking part in the Queen's funeral service. Late that evening, after the Abbey was closed, I went and sat quietly in a seat in the choir, alone except for the Queen's flower-covered coffin resting on its catafalque at the foot of the altar steps surrounded by lighted candles and guarded by Gentlemen-at-Arms and Yeomen of the Guard who stood motionless and with bowed heads. Except for the distant murmur of traffic nothing disturbed the complete and absolute silence, save, only, that from time to time there was heard from the far end of the nave the measured tread and clank of sword on stone pavement as a fresh guard passed up the Abbey to replace in silence those whose period of duty was over, and to become in their turn frozen into immobility. For a long time I sat there fascinated and soothed by the scene. When at last towards midnight I left the Abbey I turned and looked up the nave and through the choir gates to where, framed as in a picture, that splendid and motionless group kept their silent watch through the long hours of darkness to the pale grey winter's dawn. Always shall I remember that picture. It was incredibly impressive and moving (Plate 18).

Queen Alexandra's funeral service took place, actually, a year or two after Dean Ryle's death, but it has been estimated that between 1914 and 1925 nearly a hundred special services of all kinds were held in the Abbey, and this alone would have made his tenure of the Deanery remarkable. It was not, however, only in the greater services that he made his influence felt. He was himself both by temperament and upbringing an evangelical, but he felt strongly that the Abbey should hold a middle position and not be afraid of ceremonial magnificence in its right place. He, therefore, warmly encouraged the Revd Jocelyn Perkins, the Sacrist, who was doing so much to rebuild the English liturgical tradition and, more especially, the traditional 'use' and colour sequence at the Abbey. During his time processions round the church and ambulatories with banners, candles, and clergy in copes began to take place on high days and festivals. There were some perhaps who doubted whether the 'middle position' was not being exceeded. 'Rather the road to Rome wasn't it', as the Archbishop was said to have remarked after attending one of these services as an ordinary member of the congregation, adding quickly 'but I *like* your way of going to Rome!'

The note of pageantry was struck quite early in Dean Ryle's time when in 1913 the Abbey had its first state ceremony, apart from a coronation, since Queen Victoria's Jubilee in 1887. At the Dean's suggestion King George V decided to re-inaugurate Henry VII's Chapel as the Chapel of the Most Honourable Order of the Bath, and to revive the ceremony of Installation which had not been held there since 1812. The old tattered banners, which had hung in the Chapel for over a century, were taken down, and new banners of the then existing Knights Grand Cross were hung in their place, thus providing a splendid and much needed splash of colour in the Chapel.

The service itself was held on 22nd July 1913 and was a very magnificent and colourful affair. I was one of the Stewards who corresponded to the Gold Staffs at coronations. Like all the men in the congregation we wore levee dress or uniform, and for the first and only time we were provided with white batons tipped with red and ornamented with the three crowns badge of the Order. I borrowed a suit from a cousin which had belonged to Sir James Wigram, a former Vice Chancellor in the Court of Chancery and to my great satisfaction wore with it ruffles and a lace jabot instead of the more usual white tie. Ruffles with court dress were becoming old fashioned but were still allowed to be worn. I think that this was the only occasion when the Knights, together with the Great Master (H.R.H. The Duke of Connaught), the Sovereign and the Clergy came over in procession from the Prince's Chamber in the Palace of Westminster and entered and left the Abbey by the old Sovereign's entrance in Poets' Corner. At subsequent Installations (I have been present at all but one of them) they robed in the Chapter House and Norman Undercroft and came in procession through the Cloisters. In 1928 the King decided that, if it was a fine day, it would vary proceedings if the Knights went in procession outside the Abbey, at the conclusion of the service, by way of the churchyard from the north transept door to the great west door. As this intention had not been advertised and as passing traffic had not been stopped the sudden emergence of this colourful procession caused no little surprise. It recalled, though in the opposite direction, the scene depicted in Canaletto's painting of the Installation of 1747 which has always hung in the Deanery and shows the Knights coming out from the great west door and winding their way back to the Palace of Westminster.

It is a somewhat remarkable fact that within five years of Dean

Ryle's appointment his entire Chapter had changed. Either owing to death or to promotion none of the Canons remained who had welcomed him on his installation at Westminster. Their places were taken, both then and subsequently, by men of outstanding distinction. Some like Canon E. W. Barnes and Canon William Temple had still, so to say, their best known years before them. So, too, had Canon E. H. Pearce, although during the eight years he was at Westminster before he became Bishop of Worcester he, together with Francis Westlake, was to enrich Westminster literature by their invaluable researches among the documents preserved in the Abbey Muniment Room. For others Westminster was to see the close of their distinguished careers. Such were Bishop Boyd Carpenter, who was appointed to a canonry on his retirement from the See of Ripon in 1911, and Dr R. H. Charles who succeeded Canon S. A. Barnett in 1913.

Boyd Carpenter succeeded Duckworth in the beautiful house in the Little Cloister which had been built by Busby after the Restoration in 1660, but which was, alas, to be totally destroyed by an incendiary bomb in 1941. Both Duckworth and Boyd Carpenter had been much about the Court of Queen Victoria, and it was curious to go into the Bishop's drawing-room and to find apparently exactly the same signed royal photographs which had been there in profusion in the time of his immediate predecessor. The Bishop was one of the most eloquent preachers of his day, but although he might well have been embarrassed by his own extraordinary fluency every word was so perfectly enunciated that there was never any difficulty in hearing him in the pulpit. The Abbey is notoriously a difficult place in which to speak, but he would have scorned the use of microphones and loud-speakers even if they had been installed in his day.

There were those who rather unkindly said that the Bishop's sermons were only for 'consumption on the premises', and that while one was impressed by the eloquence at the time one carried away little that was remembered afterwards. I do not think that this was true. I remember a course of sermons which he preached in the Abbey on the Jewish Kings. There was one particularly eloquent sermon about a certain King ('As I see him he was a man of courage' and so on and so on). At the time it struck me that I did not seem to remember much about that particular King, and afterwards I found that all that was known about him was contained in exactly six verses in the Bible. But taken with its surrounding setting it was all perfectly fair deduction. Another sermon, this time on the good Samaritan, was, I think, the most vivid piece of word-painting that I have ever heard, with the whole congregation apparently watching the scene as he unfolded it with almost breathless interest.

The Bishop was a tiny little man with a somewhat whimsical expression and a charming and delicate sense of humour who endeared himself to everyone at Westminster by his friendliness and ready sympathy. In the 1914–18 Zeppelin and other raids – they seemed bad enough in those days, when at the warning sound of the Head Master's bell we used to sprint across Little Dean's Yard with the boys and take refuge in the Norman Undercroft – the Bishop used to appear in his dressing-gown and keep us all amused until 'the tyranny was overpast' and we could return to our beds.

Scholarly as he was, Boyd Carpenter would have been the last to claim for himself that he was a profound scholar or still less that he was one of European reputation. Those titles were pre-eminently reserved for his near neighbour in the Little Cloister, Dr R. H. Charles. Charles was in the direct line of succession to those incredibly learned sixteenth and seventeenth century scholars whose vast folio tomes fill the shelves of the Chapter Library. He had made himself the greatest living authority on Apocalyptic literature, and to this he devoted his days. When one went to see him on Abbey business one would usually find him sitting at his table wrapped up in a rug and completely surrounded with books propped up in every direction. He would push these aside and receive one courteously and eagerly, but there would be a swift glance at the clock at the beginning and end of one's visit, and one knew that the ten minutes or so would have to be added later to the allotted span of the day's work to compensate for the time lost by one's visit.

From the Apocalyptic world he would emerge at intervals to deal in his own way and to his own complete satisfaction with the more ordinary problems of everyday life. An Irishman to the core, he had all the characteristics of his race and, perhaps not least, an endearing perverseness which led him to do and say the most unexpected things. Who but he, for instance, would have booked, to everyone's astonishment, the tennis court in the College Garden for an afternoon, and then have sat on a deck chair in the middle of it because, as he explained, 'the X's have lately been using it too much and it should be for everyone's use'. There was also an occasion when as Treasurer he and the Chapter Clerk attended a legal consultation. But it was Charles who took charge of the interview and explained the law with complete confidence and to his own satisfaction to an amused and eminent King's Counsel who, when he managed to get in a word, found his objections waved aside as 'totally irrelevant'.

I remember meeting him one day in pouring rain and, as we stood with dripping umbrellas, he 'held me with his glittering eye' while he expounded to me at great length what he called 'an epoch making discovery' which he had made on some abstruse point in Apocalyptic literature. As, according to his wont, he seldom finished any sentence he began, I was not much wiser at the end, but I managed to convey my intense interest and he went off quite happily, cheerfully remarking that he liked the rain 'because you see it flushes the sewers'.

It was he, too, when a suitable memorial to a former Dean was under discussion, who threw out the suggestion that a new lavatory for the Canons might well be considered.

CHAPTER VI

Weavers and Westminster

The Weavers' Company – Silk-weavers of Spitalfields – Octo-
centenary – Westminster History VI – Ralph Tanner and Dr
Gow – From 'Grant's' to No 6 Dean's Yard – Pupils – Ash-
burnham House – The Royal Almonry – Abbey History – The
Society of Antiquaries – Abbot Islip's Obituary Roll – The
Keepership of the Muniments

DEAN RYLE's tenure of the Deanery, which spanned the years 1911–
25, saw the beginning of several new interests in my own Westminster
life, including within a few months of his death my appointment as
Keeper of the Muniments.

After the 1914–18 War in which, owing to low medical grading, I
was only able to work first at Lord Robert's Field Glass Fund and
then, later, to hold a commission as a Lieutenant on the General List
at the Headquarters of the Navy and Army Canteen Board, I had
been in some doubt as to my future career. I had eaten my dinners
at Lincoln's Inn and passed most of my law examinations, but I did
not feel much drawn to taking up the law as a profession, although I
could have joined an uncle who was a well known Chancery barrister.
But all my life things have turned up for me in unexpected ways.
In the spring of 1919 I was on a fishing holiday in Dorset when I
suddenly received a telegram from Geoffrey Radcliffe, a Westminster
friend who was on the Court of the Worshipful Company of Weavers,
asking me if I would care to come up on a certain date in order to be
interviewed with a view to my possible appointment as Clerk to the
Company. The interview was successful, and hardly was my appointment confirmed than I was equally unexpectedly offered a History
Mastership at Westminster. Neither of these was a whole-time post
and, after some consideration, I found that it would be possible to
combine the two.

I knew then very little about City Companies and their work, but
from the first I was fascinated by the traditions of the City and by
the customs of my Company. The Weavers' Company is the oldest

of all the City Livery Companies. An entry on the Pipe or Great Roll of the Exchequer for 1130 records a payment by the Company in that year, and this entry is the first known reference to a City Company. The Company, also, still possesses a charter granted to it by Henry II in 1156 conceding 'to the Weavers of London . . . all the liberties and customs which they had in the time of King Henry, my Grandfather', and this is the first royal charter granted to any London Guild. The senior officer of the Company is termed the Upper Bailiff, a title unique among City Companies and older, in this connection, than either Master or Prime Warden or even that of Lord Mayor.

Like most of the other City Companies the Weavers eventually lost the active control of their craft, but the connection with weaving has remained strong, and both on the Court and among the Livery there are the heads or representatives of many of the leading firms in the textile industry. When I first became Clerk, for instance, a prominent member of the Court was the late Sir Frank Warner who was probably, at that time, the best known and most respected Weaver in the industry. The constant and invaluable interest which he took in the work and affairs of the Company is carried on today by his son-in-law, Sir Ernest Goodale, the present head of his firm. The Company, too, played its part indirectly at the last Coronation, for the Queen's purple velvet robe, all the hangings in the Abbey, the Homage Throne, the Chair of Estate, and the Faldstools with their trimmings were all supplied by firms represented on the Court of the Company. It was partly to mark this that the Court held a special meeting at Messrs Warner's factory at Braintree when the two hand-loom weaveresses who wove the velvet for the Queen's robe were made Honorary Freewomen of the Company.

Another Honorary Freewoman is H.R.H. Princess Alice, Countess of Athlone, whose husband, the Earl of Athlone, twice served as Upper Bailiff. For over forty years, until his death in 1957, he was an active member of the Court and by his friendliness and charm endeared himself to all its members. By a happy inspiration, when the Princess was made a Freewoman in 1947 instead of the usual casket a genuine weaver's shuttle was procured. The scroll of the freedom was wound round the bobbin and enclosed in the shuttle, to which a silver lid had been added bearing the Arms of the Company and the date.

Much of the work of the Company is concerned with administering its charitable endowments and almshouses. It also can and does do much to foster research work and good design by financing senior research studentships in Textile Technology and Design tenable at Leeds, Bradford and Manchester Universities. Besides this the Company makes grants to enable post-graduate students to travel in order to study and be trained in the latest developments in the textile industry in America and elsewhere both at home and abroad.

The old handloom silk-weavers who formerly congregated in Spitalfields and district are now almost extinct, and the craft itself has tended to move to Essex and to the north of England. Thirty or forty years ago, however, the Company used to pay pensions to a few survivors, or their immediate descendants, and many of them bore names which showed their Flemish or Huguenot origin. Both the Flemings and later the Huguenots had been intimately connected with the history of the Company. Regarded at first as hated aliens, both in turn not only overcame opposition but eventually contributed greatly to the strength and prosperity of the Company. It was, therefore, not unfitting that as part of the celebrations of the Company's octocentenary the Court paid a state visit to Belgium. There we were entertained at Brussels by the celebrated Burgomaster Max, and visited Ghent, Courtrai, and other cities connected with the weaving industry.

My connection with the Weavers' Company has been an uniformly happy one, and I owe much to the many friendships which I have formed both with members of the Court and of the Livery. When I retired from the Clerkship in 1960, after forty years' service, the Court not only paid me the unusual honour of electing me as one of their members, but made it possible for me to serve as Upper Bailiff in 1963–4.

The offer of the Mastership of the History VI at Westminster, which I was able to combine, as related above, with the Clerkship of the Weaver's Company, had come as a complete surprise to me for I had never considered taking up scholastic work, but it led to thirteen years of great happiness.

The Form which I took over in the summer (Election) term of 1919 from my rather easy-going predecessor, was a lively and amusing one. They had done pretty well what they liked in the Library – very much as we did when I was myself a member of the form some ten years before. I do not think that their reading had been confined to history when, as had frequently happened, they had been left to their own devices in the Library. I was not unduly concerned about this for most of them were leaving at the end of the term, and I always had in mind how much I had myself owed to having been let loose to browse in a good library at that age. It had taught me the importance, as Dr Johnson insisted, of looking 'at the backs of books', for, as he once remarked, 'knowledge is of two kinds. We know a subject ourselves, or we know where we can find information upon it.' I remembered, too, how I had often spent a whole afternoon not in reading history but in filling out the notes which I had hastily taken down during an hour with John Sargeaunt and tracking down the quotations etc., with which he had illustrated his teaching.

The end of that summer term saw other changes at the School, for both Dr Gow and my Father retired. My Father would have liked to have retired before this, but the 1914–18 War had supervened and he had felt that he ought to remain in order to see the School through a period of difficulty and stress. It was a sad time for him personally for the mounting casualty lists which included the names of so many boys who had left the School but a short time before, and, above all, the death as the result of wounds of my only brother in September 1914 were crushing blows. He was concerned, too, at the gradual deterioration in the health of the Head Master. For some time Dr Gow had had trouble with his eyesight, and this got steadily worse after he, too, lost a dearly loved son who went down with his ship in the Battle of Jutland. As his senior Assistant Master my Father felt that the least he could do was to try to lighten the Head Master's responsibilities and to give him all the help which he could. Like everyone else at Westminster he was full of admiration for the iron self control and courage with which this proud and self-reliant man faced the increasing probability of total blindness. Outwardly calm and imperturbable, he remained 'cheerful and helpful and firm'. Once, and once only, did he privately reveal to my Father something of the misery which he concealed so successfully in his daily work as Head Master. After his retirement he became totally blind, and when he died four years later he was buried as he had wished in the church-yard at East Budleigh, a Devonshire village where he had often taken duty during the summer holidays. There his gravestone bears the strikingly simple inscription: J. G. Olim Archidid. Westmon. Obiit A.S. MCMXXIII.

Westminster seemed to me to be a strange place at the opening of the winter (Play) term in September 1919 without the familiar figures of Dr Gow and my Father, and more than once I found myself absent-mindedly turning towards 'Grant's' only to realize with a shock that it was no longer my home. I was lucky however. Partly to provide accommodation for the staff of his private practice for whom there was no room in the Chapter Office, and partly to give me a home, Sir Edward Knapp-Fisher the Chapter Clerk had taken No. 6 Dean's Yard, a house on the terrace at the south-west corner of Dean's Yard. It had previously been a private residence, and a large room on the first floor with a bathroom attached provided me with a bed-sitting-room where I lived very happily for the next nine years.

When the old Monastic Granary was pulled down in the middle of the eighteenth century some of the blocks of stone from it were used to construct a raised terrace. On this terrace it was planned to build a row of houses, partly to provide additional boarding houses for the School. For one reason or another, however, only a few of these houses were actually built, and the rest were left unfinished until they were finally completed in 1815. My house was one of the older ones. It had a small garden backing on to Great Smith Street, and boasted a mulberry tree and a vine which did their best, although not very successfully, to produce fruit in season. It was interesting that the curve of the garden wall, which was, perhaps, older than the house, followed almost exactly the curve of the stream which had formerly bounded the monastic precinct. The view from my windows of the Abbey and the western towers across Dean's Yard was entrancing, especially in spring when the trees were beginning to unfold their leaves (Plate 20).

Although the centre house on the terrace, once a well-known Westminster Boarding House ('Mother Pack's') had been taken over by the Church House, there were some houses still in private hands. Next door but one from me lived Sir Henry Craik, M.P., and I was sometimes awakened by a cavalcade consisting of Sir Henry, the Head Master (Dr Costley-White), one of the Masters (Mr J. S. Rudwick), and others setting out for their morning ride in Hyde Park. Further along the terrace, in the other direction, lived Sir Robert Hudson and, next to him, Mr Justice Sankey. The Sankeys were old friends of my Father's family. I remember on one occasion dining with them shortly before a General Election when Lord Justice Macmillan was the only other guest. After the ladies had left the dining-room, we fell to talking of the first Labour Government and both Judges expressed the opinion that Labour was not yet fit to govern. Less than a month afterwards our host was Lord Chancellor in a Labour Government!

In Dr Costley-White, who had succeeded Dr Gow, I found a very sympathetic Head Master who was content to let me run my Form of historians in accordance with my own ideas. I always tried to keep the Form as small as possible; to choose recruits for it with care in order that it might not become a refuge for the idle; and so to arrange the time-table that, apart from my actual teaching, there were several hours in every week in which the boys were free either to read history by themselves or make such other use of the Library as they liked without undue supervision by their Form Master. I aimed at establishing, and I never seemed to have any difficulty in doing so, an atmosphere of informality, friendliness and confidence in which, without seeming to do so, I could encourage them to develop and educate themselves. I wanted them to look upon me as a slightly older friend to whom they could talk naturally and spontaneously about anything which happened to interest them at the moment. It was the personal relationship between myself and my historians which I valued, and by which I felt that I could be of most use to them.

Someone once said to me that if a boy was obviously going eventually to get a 'First' at the University there was not really much that one could do about it. It was, perhaps, crudely put, but I saw what was meant and that it might be more rewarding to regard *all* my 'geese' as potential 'swans'. Certainly it was a source of continual pleasure and interest to me to see how much could be done by sympathy, encouragement, and, perhaps, a little gentle chaff, to help my 'not so clever' boys to gain in self-confidence and thereby enormously to improve their work. Some of my stricter colleagues may, perhaps, have been inclined to think that I allowed my boys too much freedom from the formality of the class room. But I knew that they would never abuse the trust which I put in them, and that they would always respond to my lightest word.

Turning out some old letters recently, I found amongst them two, which I had quite forgotten, written from Oxford by two of my former historians which seem to show that I had not been entirely unsuccessful in my methods. The first wrote. 'I may have been wrong ... but I always used to think of you more as a personal friend than as a form master, and hoped that you entertained a similar feeling towards me.' The other, evidently written in reply to my congratulations on his having become President of the Oxford Union, amusingly remarked, 'I am sure that the Presidency was won in the playroom of the History Form!' I was also amused to read in the *Spectator* a few years ago an article on his early days by the distinguished novelist, Angus Wilson, who was in the Form from January 1931 to January 1932. From this I learnt with interest that 'Mr Tanner was very civilized. He taught us to behave with decorum and good sense. He read to us from Max Beerbohm and from Lord Chesterfield's Letters ... we sat in the pleasant surroundings of the

Ashburnham Library and read and talked. There, in the intervals of acquiring a passion for mediaeval history that has survived, I talked my head off and read all the novels of Dostoevsky, Turgenev and Tolstoy. A very pleasant time indeed.'

I am not sure that I might not have mildly protested against quite such extensive Russian fare, and I could imagine myself gently removing one of these novels from his protesting hands and silently substituting in its place some such book as Tout's *Empire and Papacy* ('Tout comprendre est tout pardonner' as someone once remarked!).

We certainly sat and worked in pleasant surroundings (Plate 19). Ashburnham House, supposed to have been designed by Inigo Jones, but more probably built by his pupil John Webb about 1660, is one of the most delightful houses of its date in London. For many years the London home of the Earls of Ashburnham it subsequently became one of the Prebendal houses until it was purchased by the School in 1881. Fortunately it was undamaged during the last war. Its charming staircase, so well known to architects, and its beautifully proportioned and panelled state rooms have a grace and charm which are completely satisfying. Its garden, too, has historic associations, for it is on the site of the monastic Refectory. The Refectory was unroofed and dismantled at the Dissolution of the Monastery, but the whole of the north wall, backing on to the south cloister, remains, and also, as I have seen from time to time, much of its tiled floor although it is hidden beneath the grass. It must have been a noble Hall. I sometimes used to tell my historians that Parliament grew up in their back garden, for the Refectory, as well as the Chapter House, was often used in medieval times as the meeting place of the earliest Houses of Commons. No doubt the Commons felt more free to formulate their views within the neutral ground of the monastery rather than within the walls of the Palace of Westminster where silent acquiescence was expected for any demands which might be made upon them; even as today they stand at the door of the Upper House to listen in silence to the 'gracious speech' from the Throne at the Opening of Parliament.

Those twelve years with the History VI and VII were very happy ones. If at the end of the summer (Election) term one felt a natural sadness as those to whom one had become attached passed on to the University or elsewhere, their places were filled year by year by others to whom in due course one became equally attached. If among the many whose 'memory is fair and bright' one can only mention a few of those, who in their last year or years at Westminster, passed through the Form in my time, it is merely to illustrate the variety of ways in which some of them have since become eminent. They included two who became bishops, a dean, an ambassador, the head of an Oxford college, a very distinguished actor, the biographer of King Edward VII, a well-known novelist, a Chief Metropolitan Police Magistrate, the Recorder of a great provincial city, and the learned medievalist and historian of Oxford. One other I will mention by name, the late Dom Gregory Dix, the eminent liturgiologist, who remained a dear and devoted friend throughout his all too short life.

Although my work as Master of the History VI and VII necessarily filled most of my time I had many other activities. I was becoming increasingly interested in the work of my City Company which, apart from the meetings of the Court, involved a good deal of committee work connected with the almshouses and other charities, and the furtherance of such matters connected with the textile industry in which the Company could play a useful part. Then, as Easter approached, the work of the Royal Almonry, of which I had been appointed Secretary in 1921, greatly increased, and there were all the arrangements to be made in connection with the annual Maundy Service, although, as will be seen in a later chapter, it did not then arouse the public interest which has since attached to it.

Fortunately, from my point of view, the Weavers' Company, unlike other City Livery Companies, was not confined to act within the City of London, but by its original charters was given jurisdiction over the weavers of London, Westminster and Southwark. When, therefore, I was appointed Clerk the Court agreed, as the Company had no Hall, that its offices need not be in the City but could be situated in Westminster. The office of the Royal Almonry was already almost next door to my rooms on the terrace of Dean's Yard, and it was possible to provide accommodation for the Weavers in the same house, and some years later to move both offices to a house in Queen Anne's Gate. Even so I do not think that I could have combined these different activities satisfactorily if I had not been able confidently to delegate much of the routine work for both the Weavers and the Almonry to Mr E. E. Ratcliffe, who was to be my loyal and devoted assistant for over forty years.

Besides all this I was becoming more and more absorbed in the history of the Abbey and the School. Nor was I alone in this. The impetus given by Dean Robinson and Professor Lethaby to the study of the history and architecture of the Abbey continued unabated in the ten years or so after the close of the 1914–18 War. These years saw the publication of the Revd H. F. Westlake's monumental

History of Westminster Abbey (1923) based very largely on original research amongst the documents in the Muniment Room; the invaluable volume (*The Inventory*) on the structure and contents of the Abbey issued by the Royal Commission on Historical Monuments (1924); and Professor Lethaby's *Westminster Abbey Re-examined*, in which he summed up all that he had learnt from his minute study of the Abbey and its contents as its Architect and Surveyor. These three books were and are of first-class importance.

Westlake had been appointed a Minor Canon in 1909, and had married a daughter of the Master of the King's Scholars in 1913. In 1918, on the death of Dr E. J. L. Scott, he became Keeper of the Muniments. He and I became the closest of friends. Together we explored every nook and corner of the Abbey. When he was writing his great book we discussed every problem as it arose, sometimes adjourning to investigate matters on the spot. His enthusiasm was infectious and nothing deterred him. Once at least we were only able to solve a problem by a hazardous crawl on all fours from which we emerged dirty and dishevelled but triumphant. It was with Westlake's encouragement that I wrote a small book (my first-born) on *Westminster School; Its ' Buildings and their Associations* which necessitated much research among the muniments and elsewhere and embodied a good deal of information which had not previously been known.

Westlake's unexpectedly sudden death from a heart attack in November 1925 was a tragic loss not only to the Abbey but to myself. One of his last acts was to put me up for the Society of Antiquaries of which I was elected a Fellow in February 1926. I was no stranger to their Library and rooms at Burlington House. Many years before, as a small boy in the under school at Westminster, I had formed a friendship with Maurice Hope, the only son of Sir William St John Hope, the Assistant Secretary. At that time the Assistant Secretary had an official residence at Burlington House using what is now the Council Room as his dining-room. I often used to lunch with the Hopes on Sundays. Sir William was extremely kind to me, allowing me the run of the Library and encouraging me to pursue my antiquarian interests. One day, about 1904, Maurice Hope and I, wandering round the Cloisters, found that the Office of Works was clearing out the Pyx Chamber preparatory to opening it to the public. Among the rubbish waiting to be carted away we spotted several little medieval wooden tally sticks. We each took a few of them and Sir William read and translated for us the writing on them which showed that they dated from the end of the thirteenth century. I have

18   The lying in state of H.M. Queen Alexandra, Nov. 1925.

19   The History VII Form, Westminster School 1932.

20   View from the Terrace, Great Dean's Yard. From a lithograph, *c.* 1845.

them still, and wish now that I had taken more of them. Such tally sticks are not too common, for it was the carrying out of an unfortunate order to burn two or more cartloads of them which caused the pipes and flues under the floor of the House of Lords to become red hot and started the fire which destroyed the old Houses of Parliament in 1834.

This was not my only connection with the Antiquaries, for I was present, too, at a meeting of the Society in 1907 in College Hall when Sir William Hope read his paper 'On the earlier Funeral Effigies of the Kings and Queens of England'. The meeting was unusual in two respects. In the first place it was, I believe, the only occasion when the Society has met outside its own rooms. At that time the earlier effigies (usually known as 'the Ragged Regiment' as distinct from the later wax effigies) were kept in a locked cupboard in the Islip Chantry Chapel and were almost unknown to antiquaries and never seen by the general public. On this occasion they were all laid out on the tables in College Hall and caused much interest to a crowded audience.

In the second place, Lord Dillon the President, who presided, handed back to the Dean (Dr Armitage Robinson) Abbot Islip's Obituary Roll which the Society had borrowed as long ago as 1791. The story is a curious one. The Islip Roll is one of the major treasures of the Abbey. On the death of a medieval Abbot it was customary for the community to send a circular letter or brief to other monasteries notifying the Abbot's death and asking for prayers for the welfare of his soul. Each monastery to which it was sent then added its name to the Roll, as it was called, with a statement that prayers had been duly offered. Several of these Rolls exist in various collections but the Islip Roll is an unusually elaborate example. It commemorates the death of Abbot Islip in 1532. The Roll is on vellum. It is embellished with five pen and ink drawings, one of them showing the Abbot's Herse in front of the High Altar. It is most carefully drawn, and is the only known drawing showing the interior of the Abbey in monastic times. It used to be confidently said that the drawings were by Holbein, but experts are now agreed that it is Flemish work and probably from the hand of Gerard Horenbouts, a Flemish artist who is known to have been working in England at the time. For some reason the Roll was left unfinished. It was completely lost and unknown until 1747 when one of the Westminster Prebendaries, Dr R. Hay-Drummond, bought it from a dealer and gave it back to the Dean and Chapter. In 1791 Dean Thomas lent it to the Society of Antiquaries in order that drawings might be made from it which were subsequently engraved and published in *Vetusta Monumenta*. The Dean and Chapter, however, not uncharacteristically at that time, apparently forgot all about the loan and the Antiquaries failed to remind them of it. It was not until 1906, 115 years later, that Dr Montague James, then Provost of King's College, Cambridge, when examining manuscripts in the Library found a reference to the loan in one of the Catalogues. A request was made for its return, and Lord Dillon at this meeting gave it back to the Dean who, amid some amusement, expressed his satisfaction that the Antiquaries had at last finished with it.

My Fellowship of the Antiquaries and membership of other antiquarian societies brought me many new friends and interests. On Westlake's death in 1925 the Dean and Chapter had asked me to take over the Keepership of the Muniments, and although much of the work connected with it could be done by correspondence I became increasingly convinced that with a collection of this importance greater facilities ought to be offered to students than the very limited space in the Muniment Room could provide. As related elsewhere a munificent grant from the Pilgrim Trust made this possible and also provided for a more or less whole-time Keeper.

I, therefore, retired from the Mastership of the History VI and VII, although I did so with great regret. It was sad, too, to sever a connection with the School which in a way was something of a record. For one term before his retirement my Father and myself had been on the staff together, and this meant that between us there had been an unbroken span of fifty-one years at the School. However, as Keeper of the Muniments I was still able to keep in close touch. There was, therefore, a charming appropriateness in the epigram written by my old Westminster friend Morrice Low, and recited by the Captain of the School at the Election Dinner in College Hall on 25th July 1932:

In Laurentium E. Tanner magistratu abiturum

You, Sir, who with your father joined have seen
More than twice twenty-five elections flow—
Good-bye, alas! Our memories will keep green.
Do you forget not, how so far you go,
Transported into Time's remoter stages—
Write to us sometimes from the Middle Ages.

CHAPTER VII

Controversies and Discoveries, 1925-37

Dean Foxley Norris – the Sacristy Controversy – the Sacristy Committee – Archbishop Davidson – Improvements to the Abbey Fabric – W. R. Lethaby – The Censing Angels – Thirteenth-Century Murals – Foundations of the Confessor's Church – The Anchorite's Cell

ON Dean Ryle's death in 1925 it was widely expected that the appointment would be given to the Sub Dean, the Revd William Hartley Carnegie, who was Rector of St Margaret's and Chaplain to the Speaker of the House of Commons. He was a strikingly handsome man, whom no one could fail to like, and he would have filled the position with dignity and distinction. Moreover he had married, as his second wife, the widow of Joseph Chamberlain. She was a born hostess, and together they had made their house, 17 Dean's Yard, a centre for the social, political and ecclesiastical world. Many years before as the young American bride of the statesman, then in the plenitude of his power, Mrs Chamberlain had captivated Queen Victoria who had noted in her Diary: 'Mrs Chamberlain is very pretty and young-looking, and is very ladylike, with a nice, frank, open manner', and again a, few years later, 'Mrs Chamberlain looked lovely, and was as charming as ever'.[1] At that time, too, there was a story that the Prince of Wales (afterwards King Edward VII), no mean judge in such matters, had been heard to remark that Mrs Chamberlain was 'teaching all our Duchesses good manners'. At any rate there was no doubt that the social traditions of the Westminster Deanery would have been fully maintained by the Carnegies.

But Carnegie himself had, perhaps, no great desire to hold the prominent position which a Dean of Westminster must necessarily occupy. Although the most sociable of men he hated publicity and anything remotely savouring of self-advertisement. During Dean

[1] *Letters of Queen Victoria* (1886–1901), Vol. J, p. 498, and Vol. II, p. 378.

Ryle's last illness, when as Sub Dean he had been in charge, some question had arisen on which he had had to give a decision which had aroused controversy in the press, and he had not enjoyed the experience. It may well be, therefore, that he was not entirely sorry when the appointment was given to the Dean of York, the Very Revd William Foxley Norris.

If Dean Ryle in his quiet and dignified way had been a contrast to his austere and ascetic predecessor at the Deanery he was no less a contrast to his genial and pugnacious successor. One could not imagine anyone under any circumstances referring to Ryle by a nickname, or still less speaking of him as 'Bertie Ryle', but it was quite common to hear his successor called 'Bill Norris' by his friends, and it seemed not to be unsuitable to his expansive and kindly personality. A big burly man, he was the most accessible of people, at home with all sorts and conditions of men, a first-class after-dinner speaker, enjoying a good story and able to cap it with a better which he would tell with irresistible mock gravity and humour. He had very considerable artistic ability, especially as a painter in water-colours, and he would sometimes amuse himself at meetings by making brilliant, if surreptitious, pencil portraits of clerical dignitaries. As both he and I were fishermen he had an engaging habit of embellishing his letters to me with little pen and ink sketches. I see that I have two of these stuck into my fishing diary; one of himself fishing ('This is how I am occupied – or like to think I am – in the most lovely river on earth'), and the other of myself battling with an immense trout ('I hope that this is a true record').

A north countryman by birth, he had spent most of his ministerial career in Yorkshire, and for York and its Minster he had a deep and abiding affection. There were some, indeed, who were inclined to be restive at the frequency with which – perhaps unconsciously – he tended to bring York into his conversation and to praise the beauty of the Minster and all things connected with it, to the implied disadvantage of the Abbey.

At York as Dean he had had pretty much his own way, or at any rate he had been able to overcome opposition, and at Westminster no doubt he expected to find himself in a similar position. In theory the Dean at Westminster is supreme and is answerable to the Sovereign alone. Many years before, Lord Salisbury, the Prime Minister, in speaking of Dean Stanley had summed up the absolute power of the Dean over Westminster Abbey by remarking 'bless my soul, if the man wanted to put up a statue to the Pope nobody could stop him'. But actually, of course, things are not as simple as that.

Whatever may be the Dean's actual or theoretical powers, in the last resort there comes a point, as Foxley Norris found, when the public, the press, and the Collegiate Body can raise a formidable opposition before which he has to bow. With the public and the press the Dean was quite ready to deal. He enjoyed and was never afraid of a good straightforward controversy, and he was at his best at what would now be called a press conference. Faced by his critics he could give as good as he got, and his good temper, his keen sense of humour, and his readiness and resilience would carry the day for the time. But if in addition he found himself in conflict with the Collegiate Body things became more difficult.

Such a situation arose in 1928-9 when the Westminster world and a wide circle beyond it was considerably agitated by what came to be known as the Sacristy controversy. In itself the thing was simple enough. In the preceding thirty years the Sacrist, the Revd Dr Jocelyn Perkins, had done a great work. When he was first appointed Sacrist what may be called the ornaments or ecclesiastical furnishings of the Abbey were in a deplorable state and quite unworthy of a great church. Gradually he had built up a wonderful collection of plate, banners, altar frontals and suchlike, towards which various donors had been proud to contribute. Unfortunately there was no place where all these treasures could be adequately housed and preserved under proper conditions.

The Abbey is, in fact, curiously circumscribed in space when any question of expansion arises. To the south the Cloisters, the Canonical houses and the buildings of the School nestle under the shadow of the Abbey Church; to the west are Victoria Street and the entrance to Dean's Yard, and to the east are Old Palace Yard and the Houses of Parliament. Only on the north is there anything in the nature of a Cathedral Close, and even there the larger part of the green space belongs to St Margaret's Church, of which it was formerly the Churchyard.

In 1928 the Dean (Dr Foxley Norris) was offered a large sum of money by an anonymous donor for the purpose of providing a proper Sacristy. After carefully considering various alternative sites, none of which were entirely satisfactory, the Dean and Chapter decided to choose what appeared to them to be the site least open to objection, and to build a Sacristy on the north side of the Abbey immediately to the east of the north transept where it was thought that it would be largely hidden from the north by St Margaret's Church and from the west by the projecting front of the north transept. As soon as this project was known opposition became vocal. 'Hands off the Abbey' is always a popular slogan, and many who had given no thought to the practical difficulties with which the Dean and Chapter were faced in providing for the efficient running of a great national church, plunged into the fray with cries of vandalism and desecration. It was admittedly a difficult problem and to meet the more restrained of these criticisms the Dean and Chapter erected on the proposed site a full sized plaster model of the design which had been made by Mr Walter Tapper, R.A., the Architect and Surveyor to the Fabric.

Unfortunately, far from allaying fears this merely added fuel to the flames. A body was formed which called itself the 'Council for the Protection of Westminster Abbey'. This body considered that any addition or alteration to the exterior of the Abbey was an act of sacrilege, and was loud in its denunciation of what it held to be a disfiguring excrescence. Actually the model suggested an inoffensive but not very inspired little gothic building which, tucked away in a corner, would soon have weathered and ceased to attract attention. A more serious and, indeed, a real ground for criticism was that the proposed Sacristy was probably only large enough for immediate purposes and made little provision for the future, and, further, that it was likely to cost considerably more than the sum which had been offered by the anonymous donor.

The Dean, however, made no secret of the fact that he still considered the 'model' site not only as the best but as the only practical solution of the problem. Autocratic by nature, he was never afraid of a fight, and with the support of Mr Tapper – the *mot* at the time was 'the Dean and Tapper of Westminster' – he was prepared to brave opposition, even though his Chapter, who had originally voted for the scheme, were beginning to have doubts and to waver in the face of opposition. He made, however, one more effort at conciliation. With the approval of the Chapter he asked Archbishop Lord Davidson of Lambeth to be the Chairman of a Committee 'to advise the Dean and Chapter generally on the subject of the proposed new Sacristy'. The Committee consisted of the President of the Royal Institute of British Architects (Sir Banister Fletcher, R.A.), the President of the Royal Academy (Sir William Llewellyn), the President of the Society of Antiquaries (Sir Charles Peers), and the acting Chairman of the Society for the Protection of Ancient Buildings (Mr J. F. Green). To this Committee were subsequently added Lord Newton and Sir Kynaston Studd in order to represent the opinion of 'the ordinary man in the street', and I was asked by the Dean to act as its Honorary Secretary.

The Committee met several times in the Jerusalem Chamber during the autumn and winter of 1929 and reviewed the whole subject. It visited the fourteen possible sites in turn, and it had the advantage of hearing evidence from all those directly interested. It soon became apparent that most of the suggested sites were unsuitable for one reason or another, and that the whole question was much more difficult and complicated than the protagonists on either side were prepared to admit. Eventually the Committee rejected the 'model' site, although they felt that it had strong points in its favour, and suggested that the Dean and Chapter should reconsider a scheme whereby the crypt of the Chapter House should be linked by means of an underground passage and stairway with a low building to be erected in the considerable space between the buttresses of the outside walls of the side chapels by the Poets' Corner door. A Sacristy on this site would be conveniently close at hand and would have easy access to the High Altar. It was felt, too, that it would be almost entirely screened by the flying buttresses of the Chapter House, and that it would not interfere with the external architecture of the Abbey. It also had the advantage that if further space was needed at any time it would be perfectly possible to make an underground extension between the Chapter House crypt and Old Palace Yard. The Report of the Committee was unanimous, but it was recognized from the first that the Committee was appointed merely to advise and report and that the final decision must rest with the Dean and Chapter. In the event the Report, for various reasons, was never implemented and the problem of a Sacristy remained and remains unsolved.

The work in connection with this Committee had the great interest for me that for some weeks I was in close touch with the Archbishop. It was not the first time I had met him. Some years before, I had dined at Lambeth, and in August 1925 he and Mrs Davidson and the then Bishop of Dover (Dr Bilbrough) were staying at the Inveran Hotel, Invershin, Sutherland, at the same time that my friend, Bernard Tennant, and I were there during the course of a motor-tour in Scotland. I had heard originally of this delightful Hotel from the Ryles and had stayed there several times. It was very small and, as it never advertised, it was known only to those who went there on the recommendation of others. Its setting was perfect, with the River Shin flowing just below the house and the moors all round. Some years later, I believe, the hotel was burnt to the ground. It was a favourite haunt of the Archbishop, who was an enthusiastic fisherman and desperately anxious to catch a larger salmon than his brother bishop. On this occasion there were, I think only two other men staying in the Hotel. The Archbishop was very friendly and charming, and usually came out after breakfast to smoke a cigarette and talk to us all on fish and fishing before the day's 'work' began. Even on Sundays, when of course, there was no fishing, after we had had the unique experience of attending a little service in their sitting-room conducted by the Archbishop of Canterbury and the Bishop of Dover in the wilds of Scotland and to the sound of the Shin, the two bishops could not resist going down to the river to look at a stick they had put there after breakfast in order to find out if the river was rising or falling!

When I was appointed Secretary to the Sacristy Committee the Davidsons asked me to dine with them in Cheyne Walk. After dinner the Archbishop took me up to his room when we had a long talk, and I remember his fixing me with his kind but curiously penetrating eyes and asking me many searching questions. I suppose that I came through the ordeal satisfactorily and was 'approved', for from that moment he showed me unlimited kindness and never seemed to mind how often I came to see him. It was an immense pleasure and privilege to work with him. After the meetings of the Committee we used to go through the Minutes together at his home (at his suggestion they were rather more detailed than such things usually are). I felt rather like an undergraduate reading an essay to my tutor, but it was very rarely that I could get him to alter a word, and usually all he said was 'quite right, I am very glad that you put that in', or (with a chuckle) 'well, that's what he *did* say, wasn't it?' Just occasionally he would say, 'Wait, let me think for a moment', and then he would suggest some wording which was exactly right.

When we had finished he would say 'don't go', and would begin to talk of all manner of things and persons from the stores of his wisdom and experience. On these occasions I remember sometimes thinking of a sentence of Lytton Strachey's about the aged Queen Victoria; 'there she was, all of her – the Queen of England, complete and obvious; the world might take her or leave her; she had nothing more to show, or to explain, or to modify.' Davidson had been a great Archbishop and, like Queen Victoria, it was his sincerity and his essential humility which were so impressive. Of all the well-known people I have come across in my work I have always thought that Archbishop Davidson and Sir J. J. Thomson, o.m., the physicist and sometime Master of Trinity, were in a class by themselves, something altogether in a bigger mould. On this point there is an interesting passage in the Revd A. W. Hopkinson's *Pastor's Progress:* . . . 'in

21 Bishop P. F. D. de Labilliere, Dean of Westminster 1938–46.

22 The Chapter Library.

24 H.M. King George VI arranges an Almonry group after the Maundy Service 1946. (*Left to right*) H.H. Princess Marie Louise, the Author, the High Almoner (Dr Woods, Bishop of Lichfield), the Sub Almoner (Revd W. H. Elliott), H.M. Queen Elizabeth, and children of the Royal Almonry.

25 The Almonry group as finally arranged, 1946.

26 After the Maundy Service 1942. (*Left to right*) the Author, Archbishop Lang, H.H. Princess Marie Louise, the Dean (Bishop Labilliere).

those days, some of us, in our ignorance, were inclined to think and speak of Archbishop Davidson as a successful courtier and statesman, and I once asked his chaplain, Edward Hertslet, how he appeared in the company of really great men like (Bp) Talbot or Gore. His rebuke was prompt, "when Davidson comes into the room, everyone else sinks into insignificance." It was a wonderful testimony, though most people would call it exaggerated.'

It may have been so, but it was certainly true of the way he dominated the Sacristy Committee, and it was not merely because he was, as one might have expected, a consummate chairman. It was actually the last public or semi-public work that he did before his death, but his mind was as clear as it had ever been. He was dealing with experts and somewhat technical questions, but it was fascinating to see the way he immediately seized on the essential points, his refusal to be drawn into matters beyond the concern of the Committee, his open-mindedness ('Well of course *I'm* prejudiced. But I think it *is* a prejudice, and I always distrust myself on such matters'), his powers of conciliation and humour, and his quiet but remorseless exposure of any overstatement.

I think that he thoroughly enjoyed the correspondence and the work involved – he used to lament to me sometimes the smallness of his daily post compared with Lambeth days – and he was disappointed, although not entirely surprised, when our Report was shelved by the Dean and Chapter. It was characteristic of him, too, that although we wrote the Report together, he minimized his own part and insisted on calling it 'your Report' so as to give me the credit for drawing it up.

The Sacristy and other controversies, little less violent, which marked Dean Foxley Norris's rather stormy tenure of the Deanery have tended to obscure the fact, as such controversies will, that these years saw much that was of value and of archaeological interest at Westminster. So much has been done in recent years to clean the interior of the Abbey and its tombs, that it is well to remember that the initiation of a scheme of systematic cleaning was due to the Dean, and was carried out by Professor W. R. Lethaby and Sir Walter Tapper who successively held the office of Surveyor to the Fabric at this time. Some, indeed, of this work was tentative and has had to be re-done for, as so often happens, the methods employed by the experts of one generation do not always commend themselves to those of the next. To take but one example. Forty years ago the best advice available advocated the use of wax to provide a preservative film after cleaning murals and monuments, but it is now generally recognized that such treatment has unforseen results and can, indeed, be definitely harmful.

On the whole, and in spite of some anxious periods, Westminster has escaped the heavy hand of the restorer in the last sixty years. Professors Micklethwaite and Lethaby and Sir Charles Peers were essentially conservative by nature, and were far more anxious to preserve than to make any additions of their own. Lethaby, indeed, has left it on record that 'the systematic cleaning of the structure and monuments . . . has given me more pleasure during my little term than almost anything else – the one greater pleasure is new work I have *not* done in the ancient church'.[1]

In fact the 'new work' which Lethaby actually did at Westminster was something greater than anything which he could have designed to be built with hands. In his two books on the Abbey[2] he broke entirely new ground, and these books have been the foundation upon which almost all subsequent research on medieval craftsmen has been based. Here, almost for the first time, the veil of anonymity which it was assumed concealed those who designed and worked on Westminster and on our other great medieval cathedrals was lifted. Lethaby showed that it was possible from surviving account rolls at Westminster and elsewhere not only to give their names but in many cases to identify the same craftsmen at work at different times in different places.

With regard to Westminster itself during his twenty-one years as Surveyor (1906–27) he taught us all to look at the Abbey Church with new eyes. It was a delight to go round with him and to see the care with which he studied every stone and detail; to share his enthusiasm for some delicate piece of carving or colouring, and to discuss with him some of the many problems and secrets which are part of the inexhaustible fascination of the Abbey. He himself, with all his unrivalled technical knowledge and unique understanding of gothic architecture, was the most humble-minded of men who knew well that the key to those mysterious problems could only be found, if at all, by years of intensive study of the craftmanship which went to its building.

Dean Foxley Norris's enthusiastic interest in the remodelling of the Library and Muniment Room, in the cleaning of the wax effigies, and in the opening of the urn which was reputed to contain the bones of the Princes in the Tower will be mentioned later, but

[1] *Westminster Abbey Re-Examined*, p. 233.
[2] *Westminster Abbey and Kings' Craftsmen* (1906) and *Westminster Abbey Re-Examined* (1925).

there were other events of no less interest. When in the course of cleaning the south transept a staging was erected in 1930 under the Rose Window, it was a supreme delight to be able to examine at close quarters the thirteenth-century Censing Angels in the spandrels immediately below the window. Partly owing to their height from the ground these entrancing figures, as lovely as anything in Europe of their date, were very little known and most of the guide books scarcely mentioned them. It is true that Professor Lethaby had examined them from a scaffolding some years before and had noted their supreme quality and that there appeared to be traces of colour on them. But it was now possible to examine them at leisure under the best conditions and to have them photographed from every angle. We found, too, that originally they had been brightly coloured. Their wings had been picked out in gold, red, black and green, their vestments had been patterned with little stars and crosses, and even their cheeks and eyes had been painted. No attempt was made to re-colour them, but, as I wrote at the time, 'they had their faces washed and their garments cleaned'. Still more recent cleaning, of the stonework round the Angels has thrown them out in relief and enables them to be better seen from the ground. They are, indeed, as the late Professor Tristram called them, 'superb examples of the medieval stone-carvers' art'. At the time of the 1953 Coronation it was possible to examine the corresponding angels under the north Rose Window. They, too, are noble figures, but possibly because they may be by another carver, they seem somehow just to lack the grace and charm of those on the south.

The Censing Angels, at least, have always been there for those with eyes to see them, but the discovery or rather the re-discovery in 1936 of two great thirteenth-century mural paintings, dating from about 1280, on the south wall of the south transept was totally unexpected. They could not be seen, nor was there any record of their existence either in manuscript or in print. They came to light when it became necessary to remove two eighteenth-century monuments in order to clean the stonework at ground level. These monuments stood in front of two arched bays or recesses to the east of the door leading into St Faith's Chapel. At the time when these monuments were originally erected the face of the wall behind them had been covered with thin dark marble to act as a kind of background, and we noticed that round the edge of the marble in one of these recesses there were faint traces of colour. When this marble background was removed and the mortar or putty bedding on which it had rested had been very carefully and patiently cleaned off, to our astonishment there emerged from beneath it a great figure of St Christopher (9 feet high) painted in a warm lake colour against a green background.

I remember standing in front of this painting with the late Professor Tristram and saying to him 'do you think there is any chance of there being another figure in the next bay' and his replying that he thought there probably was, although there was no trace of colour to be seen. But when we started to clean this second bay, first a raised arm and then a head appeared until at length an even finer mural representing the Incredulity of St Thomas appeared. It was fascinating to see it gradually emerging while we speculated what the subject would prove to be. The whole thing seemed miraculous, for both these great figures were so well preserved that they required little or no 'touching-up' even after the lapse of nearly six centuries. Professor Tristram has described them as ranking 'amongst the most important of survivals of wall-paintings, not only in the Abbey, but in the whole of England.'

A rather different kind of discovery was made by chance in the autumn of 1930 in the Nave of the Abbey, which led to not unimportant results. One day I was asked to go and look at some apparently ancient stone foundations, running east and west, which had been encountered by the Abbey workmen a few inches beneath the surface when cutting a trench across the nave for a new heating pipe. As soon as I saw them I felt certain that they were part of the foundations of the nave of the Church of Edward the Confessor which was pulled down when the existing nave was begun in the fourteenth century. With the leave of the Dean and Chapter and under the direction of the Abbey Surveyor we opened up the ground and traced the foundations westwards until just within the existing west wall of the Abbey Church we found what had obviously been the western limit of the Confessor's Church. Many years before, some other foundations and pillar bases had been discovered showing the eastern limit, and from these and from this new discovery we were able to make a plan and to show that the ground plan of the Confessor's Church very nearly coincided with the ground plan of the present Church, except that the Confessor's transepts were much smaller and that the eastern apse would have cut across the site of the present Shrine of the Confessor. This had the interesting corollary that, as it was William I who set the precedent for coronations taking place at Westminster, he and subsequent sovereigns must have been crowned in the earlier church on almost the exact spot on which Queen Elizabeth II was crowned in 1953. The surprise of these discoveries was, first the size of the Confessor's Church, which was thus proved to have been larger than anyone had supposed, and, secondly, that no one had previously discovered these foundations, or at any rate had recognized them for what they were, although they were only just below the floor of the nave. We also opened the ground on the north side of the nave in the hope of finding foundations corresponding to those on the south, but without success. It was evident that any foundations which had been there must have been on the same line as the existing pillars, and must have been destroyed when the nave was re-built. It was very interesting, however, to see the massive circular foundations of the existing pillars merely resting upon the sand upon which the Abbey Church is built.[1]

But I think that the thing which perhaps gave me most pleasure in these years was the discovery in 1936 of the site of the anchorite's cell, with its rather delightful sequel. We had long been puzzled by a small blocked doorway in St Benedict's Chapel, which seemed to have served no obvious purpose as the sovereign's door in Poet's Corner was quite close to it. However, in the course of cleaning this Chapel, the stone *prie-dieu*, which formed part of the monument of Dean Goodman (d. 1601) and adjoined this blocked door, was removed. Behind it we found a small square Purbeck window-frame grooved for a shutter. I then remembered from the Account Rolls that the Abbey anchorite, who was usually a senior monk who had a cell of his own, was in the habit of making offerings at St Benedict's altar, although we had never known exactly where his cell was situated.

It seemed likely, therefore, that the door had led into his external cell, tucked away in the angle between the chapel and the transept, and from the interior of which he could have seen through the window the altar of St Benedict's Chapel. If so, it must have been through this door that Richard II passed to consult the anchorite before he went out to meet Wat Tyler, and, later again, it must have been through this door that the youthful Henry V passed on the evening of the day on which his father died when he spent the night with our anchorite and, according to tradition, vowed that he would lead a new life.

Sir Charles Peers, who had succeeded Sir Walter Tapper as the Abbey Surveyor, had the ground opened outside on the presumed site of the cell, but it had been much disturbed and we found no trace of foundations. So the matter remained in doubt.

[1] For a full account of these discoveries see a Paper by Sir A. Clapham and L. E. Tanner, 'Recent Discoveries in the Nave of Westminster Abbey', *Archaeologia*, Vol. LXXXIII (1933).

Now for the sequel. Some months later, when looking up a reference to something quite different in the *Autobiography of Thomas Raymond,*[1] I came across by chance the following story. It is in itself so delightful that, quite apart from the sentence which I have italicized, it is worth quoting. Raymond, it would seem, was living about the year 1629–30 with his uncle, William (afterwards Sir William) Boswell in what he described as 'a little straight howse built in a corner on the lefte hand as soon as you are out of the East door of Westminster Abbey (i.e. very much on the site of our cell) bellonging to one of the vergers of the Church, and is since demolished'. His uncle, he tells us, 'being wondered at and sometymes laughed at for the place of his lodgings, had this storey with other arguments to defende it, which I have heard him often relate for a real truth.'

In the latter tymes of Henry the 7th a prebendary[2] of this Church (haveing lived most of his life in his cloyster commeing little in the world) was perswaded by some friends to goe toe a maske at Courte where he hardly ever had beene, but never saw such a sight, the masks very glorious and the King and Courte in mighty gallantrie. The maske ended not till well towards morneing, and the prebendary returned home hugely satisfied and admyring the glories he had seene, and rose not that morneing till towards ten of the clock. And being very still these things much possessed his thoughts, and haveing received many civillities at this mask from several greate courtiers, he resolved to goe to Courte to returne them his thancks and again to feede his eyes with the glories there. And comeing to the Courte, the great gates were both open and no porters attending, and passing farther the yards were strewed with straw and horse dunge; not a creature to be seene. Goeing up stayres in the like case to the gard chamber, there he found only bare walls, dust and rubbish, and the tables and trustles throwne aboute. Then to the presence chamber where he had seene the cloth of state, rich hangings, yet nothing but dust and bare walls, and one corner a poore old man with a piece of candle in his hand – the Courte being that day removed – lookeing for pynns. This soe sudden and strange a change from what he had with admiration seene the night before strucke such a serious consideration into him of the mutability of the glories of this world that, returneing to his monastery, he within a while after bound himselfe an anchorite. *And in this very place where our lodging nowe is was his cell, haveing a little hole through the Churche wall, by which he could see the high altar and heare masse.* Where he in greate devotion lived and dyed.

---

[1] Camden Society, 3rd Series, Vol. XXVII, pp. 26–27.
[2] He means, of course, a monk.

Here then, not much more than an hundred years later was a living tradition that the house embodied part of the anchorite's cell, and, apparently, a mention of the very window which we had found behind Dean Goodman's monument. This unexpected corroboration seemed to make certain our identification of the site.

CHAPTER VIII

The War Approaches

Dean Labilliere – Sir Edward Knapp Fisher – The Latin Play, 1937 – The Search for Spenser's Grave – Medieval Floor Tiles – Photographic Exhibition – Evacuation of Muniments and Abbey Treasures – War Damage

DEAN FOXLEY NORRIS died in September 1937. Our new Dean was the Bishop of Knaresborough (Dr Paul Fulcrand Delacour de Labilliere, Plate 21). Hitherto his career had been mostly in the north of England, where he had been greatly liked, but to most of us at Westminster he was something of an unknown quantity. We soon found, however, that we had in him a Dean of great charm and modesty with a gentleness of manner and consideration for others which were singularly attractive. These qualities were combined with a strength of character and an unfailing courage which were to be cruelly put to the test in the war years which were to follow. For the first time, too, since Dean Armitage Robinson, we had a Dean who was deeply interested in the history and architecture of the Abbey. He read everything he could on the subject and liked to wander about the Abbey by day or, armed with a torch, by night, in order to verify some small point which he had come across in his reading.

Within a few months of his appointment as Dean two senior members of the Collegiate Body ceased to reside within the Close, the one by reason of promotion, the other by resignation. Dr Harold Costley-White, who had been Head Master of Westminster from 1919 to 1937, and a Canon of Westminster since 1936, was appointed Dean of Gloucester, and Sir Edward Knapp-Fisher resigned the office of Chapter Clerk which he had held since 1917.

As Chapter Clerk Sir Edward was a well known and conspicuous figure on all ceremonial occasions at the Abbey, to which he added a touch of dignity by always appearing in court dress with wig and gown. It had been a great delight to him to return to the Precincts

27 H.M. Queen Elizabeth II leaving the Abbey after the Maundy Service 1956.

28 Distribution of the Royal Maundy by H.M. Queen Elizabeth II at Rochester Cathedral 1961.

29 The author showing Nelson's cocked hat (with its green eye shade) to the late Mr Richard Dimbleby.

where he had been a boy at the School some forty years before, and he and Lady Knapp-Fisher made their house in Dean's Yard a centre of hospitality. The kindest and most friendly of men he retained a youthful gaiety of spirit to the end of his life and was equally at ease with all sorts and conditions of men. He came and stayed with me once on a fishing holiday in Dorset. Characteristically he made friends with the local station master, who played the organ at the village church, and finding that he was shortly coming to London invited him to come to the Abbey, where he allowed him (to his enormous delight) to play for a few minutes on the Abbey organ. When the following year I told him that his Westminster friend had been made a knight it drew from him the tribute 'If they made him an earl or a duke he would never be anything but the same kind and perfect gentleman!' This ability to establish friendly relations with all with whom he came in contact was of immense value to him in his work as Chapter Clerk. It happens that funeral or other services often have to be arranged at very short notice. On such occasions, it was truly said of him that 'conflicting claims were smoothed out, harassed officials were comforted, and all who came into contact with him went away happily convinced that he had been in complete agreement with all that they had put before him.' He had a way of saying 'I *quite* agree' which was immensely re-assuring. Before he retired his health had begun to fail, and it was perhaps fortunate that he was spared the responsibilities and anxieties which came to us all at the Abbey with the outbreak of the War.

Dean Labilliere made, I think, his first public appearance at Westminster after his appointment as Dean on the memorable evening (20th December 1937) when King George VI and Queen Elizabeth attended the Latin Play at the School. No sovereign had attended the Play since King William IV came to the *Eunuchus* in 1834, although the Prince Consort had come on three occasions and on one of these he was accompanied by the young Prince of Wales. As was customary when Royalty attended the Play the King and Queen were escorted across Little Dean's Yard by King's Scholars carrying torches, which were subsequently extinguished in the old iron torch extinguishers outside the door of No. 17 Dean's Yard. As the King and Queen entered the College Dormitory they were greeted by the 'Vivats' of the King's Scholars, thus repeating the 'Vivats' which had greeted their Majesties as they entered the Abbey Church at their Coronation a few months before.

When Queen Elizabeth I re-founded the School in 1561 it was laid down in the statutes that a Latin Play should be acted annually and 'because of the advantages which the boys would derive from a habit of correct action and pronunciation'. The Queen herself was present on more than one occasion, and I was amused to find by a bill of expenses preserved among the Muniments that the Dean and Chapter kindly provided 'butter beer and dredge (sweetmeats) for the children being horse' after their labours. The plays by Terence and Plautus, were acted annually up to the outbreak of the Civil War in 1642, and then after a break were revived and continued up to 1938. After the Second World War they were again revived but acted out of doors on summer evenings in Little Dean's Yard and with the actors in modern dress – thus rather curiously reverting to contemporary dress which had been the custom until classical costumes were introduced in 1839.

The Play as I knew it between 1900 and 1938 had altered little in essentials since the eighteenth century. It consisted of a serious Latin Prologue which drew attention to events in the world at large and at Westminster in particular, spoken before the Curtain by the Captain of College in evening dress, gown, bands, knee breeches and silk stockings. This was followed by the Play itself, and the evening closed with the Epilogue, a witty and scholarly satire in Latin on contemporary events, usually written by an Old Westminster, and full of topical allusions and puns, in which all the actors in the Play took part and appeared in modern dress.

It is difficult to recapture the atmosphere of the Play of those days, and the hold which it had on Westminsters of all generations. Some of the factors which contributed to it were, perhaps, the immense sense of tradition behind it; the setting in the College Dormitory with its walls covered with the names of former Westminsters; the layout of the auditorium, which preserved several eighteenth-century features – e.g. the division into various 'pits' (Seniors, Ladies, Masters, etc.); the organised 'claque' of the boys seated in the Gods induced at traditional places in the Play by the waving of the canes of the Gods' Monitors; and the exceptionally distinguished audiences which gathered year by year. I remember one night for instance when the audience included the Prime Minister, the Speaker, a Cabinet Minister, two ex-Lord Chancellors and two or three Judges. This no doubt was exceptional, but the records of those who have attended in the past are studded with the names of those famous in Church or State.

Dean Labilliere's interest in Abbey history led him to attempt to solve a mystery which has always intrigued those who have written on the Abbey. Edmund Spenser, the poet, died on 16th January

1598-9 and was buried in the Abbey. The Abbey Burial Registers only begin in 1607 so there is no actual record of his burial, but we know from the original inscription on his monument that the place for his grave was deliberately chosen so as to be 'near to that of Chaucer' at the south end of the east aisle of the south transept. Camden, who was living in the Precincts at the time and was probably present, tells us that the funeral was 'attended by poets, and mournful elegies and poems, with the pens that wrote them, were thrown into his tomb'. As Dean Stanley commented: 'What a funeral was that at which Beaumont, Fletcher, Jonson, and, in all probability, Shakespeare attended! – what a grave in which the pen of Shakespeare may be mouldering away.'

It was with this in mind that in the autumn of 1938 Dean Labilliere consented, at the request of the Bacon Society, to have the ground opened on the traditional site of the grave. Some notes which I made at the time take up the tale:

Nov 1st 1938
Tonight we began the preliminary work in connexion with the opening of Spenser's tomb. The work began at 6.30. as soon as the Abbey was closed to the public, and at eight o'clock I went along and found the Dean and his son and his daughter and son-in-law, together with Bishop [the Clerk of the Works], and the Abbey workmen. We got down to a depth of about 2 feet. Preliminary soundings and a little work had been done a few weeks before when the top of a coffin had been found, but when the Munich crisis threatened war the hole had been filled in again. We now got down again to within 6 inches or so of this coffin, and found that the grave (whoever it may have been made for – and there is no certainty that it *is* Spenser) had been cut out of solid stone foundations. These appear to be Norman, and may have been those of the Norman Chapter House. The grave is some 10 feet in front of the Spenser monument, a little to the east of the centre line of the aisle (or perhaps its head is on the centre line) and very slightly to the north of Drayton's monument. The grave was filled in with sand and stones, and at the east end we found some bones so went no deeper tonight.

Nov 2nd
At 4.30 a.m. the Daily - - - - - rang me up to know if I had any comments to make on a circumstantial 'story' which was appearing in the Daily - - - - this morning stating that 'the grey lead casket' had been brought to the surface, etc., etc., and that the only question left to the Dean, the 'clerk to the Bishop' (!), and others was whether or not to unseal it. My comments were brief. By 10 o'clock three more papers had rung up, and this and reporters continued all day.

Later in the morning Peers and I examined the work as far as it had got last night, and satisfied ourselves that the foundations exposed were probably Norman. We decided to open a little more to the east, and practically up to the stone seat, so that the whole length of the coffin would eventually be exposed.

Early that afternoon the Dean, Sir C. Peers, myself, Professor Plenderleith of the British Museum, the Duke of Rutland, some members of the Chapter, and three representatives of the Bacon Society, with one or two others assembled at the grave. My notes continue:

At first it was merely a question of uncovering the coffin, but as we began to see the outline emerge Professor Plenderleith himself removed the sand, etc., carefully, the supposition being that if any poems or odes were thrown into the grave they must be either on the coffin or by its side. We found that an interment or possibly two had taken place at some date above the lead coffin, and if the body had ever been coffined it must have been only a light wood shell to which perhaps some slight wooden fragments belonged. The skull and other bones were lying loosely in the earth, and these were, of course, carefully and reverently handed up to myself and the Duke of Rutland and put on one side. The skull and jaws, complete with teeth, appeared to be those of a young man. It then became apparent as we got lower that the lid of the lead coffin had collapsed into the coffin, slightly distorting it. We cleared away all the earth until the entire lid was disclosed and Plenderleith was able to feel that bones were underneath it. There was apparently nothing in the nature of a coffin plate nor means of identification, and beyond some rusty nails, a lead fitting (?) of some kind in the shape of a rough fleur-de-lis, and a scrap of pottery, nothing was found of interest in the filling of the grave, As it was now about 3.15 we decided to cease work until tomorrow norning. . . . From our investigation it would appear extremely unlikely that anything in the nature of M.SS. will be found.

Nov 3rd
On resuming our investigations today at $\frac{1}{4}$ to 11 we found that the earth on one side of the coffin had been taken out, but nothing had been found beyond two iron coffin handles, nails, etc. The other side was then excavated and the earth, etc., as before passed through a riddle, but nothing was found beyond the other coffin handles, bones, and a certain amount of the wood casing studded with nails. By lunch time the whole of the earth had been cleared and the coffin was photographed lying at the bottom of the grave. After lunch we raised the coffin to the surface and found a good deal of wooden casing underneath.

The position was now clear. There had been three interments in the grave. When the lead coffin had been placed in the grave, the first interment had been disturbed and the bones distributed round the coffin. Then later a third interment had taken place, and on finding the grave so shallow the lid of the lead coffin had been deliberately crushed in on to the skeleton at an angle, and the new burial had taken place on the top.

We lifted the lid of the lead coffin, and found that the greater part of the skeleton with the skull remained. It was not disturbed by us in any way. There was nothing to identify it, but it appeared to be of the 18th century, and I have little doubt that we looked on all that remained of Matthew Prior. It is possible that one of the other interments was that of Michael Drayton.

After Peers had examined the foundations in the grave – which he now thinks are not Norman but 13th century – we placed a stone in the bottom of the grave on which was cut a record that we had examined the grave, and then we re-lowered the coffin.

Later in the evening the Dean and myself drew up a statement for the Press and the B.B.C.

It was clear, therefore, that our investigation had been fruitless, and that not only had we failed to solve the mystery attaching to Spenser's grave, but that the grave itself was not in the place to which tradition had always pointed.

The presence of the Duke of Rutland (d. 1940) was due to the fact that he had somehow heard of the proposed search for Spenser and had invoked my aid to get the Dean to allow him to be present. I had come across him shortly before this. Knowing that he was much interested in his family archives at Belvoir, I wrote and asked him about a manuscript there which appeared to have Westminster interest. He at once most kindly brought it up himself for me to see. He was charmed with the Library and Muniment Room, and especially with its late fourteenth century tiled floor. At that time the Duke was generally recognized as one of the leading authorities on medieval slip tiles, but, although he knew of the Muniment Room floor, he had never before been able to see it. As it happened I had recently uncovered a portion of the floor which, previously, had been covered by a small wooden platform, and in consequence the tiles which had been beneath it still retained much of their original glaze. The Duke was so interested in these and the rest of the floor that a few days later he came again with the Duchess and together they spent some hours crawling about the whole floor making notes and sketching the heraldic and other designs on the tiles.

Curiously enough about the same time I was visited at the Library by Lord Ponsonby of Shulbrede who was also an authority on medieval tiles. He had written an extremely valuable Paper for the Sussex Archaeological Society on 'Monastic Paving Tiles' with special reference to the tiles which he had uncovered at his beautiful home, Shulbrede Priory on the border of Surrey and Sussex. He, too, was greatly interested in the Muniment Room floor and in the tiles which were on show in one of the cases in the Norman Under-croft Museum in the Cloisters. I remember that while we were in the Museum the attendant, wrongly assuming that I had my key with me, went off locking the door behind him. It was an agitating moment for Lord Ponsonby, who was then leader of the Labour Opposition, was on his way to the House of Lords where he had an important question on the Order Paper. It was only with difficulty and after some minutes that I managed through the grated window to attract the attention of a passing stranger and induce him to go in search of some one to release us just in time for Lord Ponsonby to hurry over to the House. Later that summer Sir Charles Strachey, who was then a voluntary member of my staff, took me down one day to luncheon at Shulbrede, and Lord Ponsonby showed us the remains of the Priory and the delightful mural painting in the Prior's room which represents birds and animals announcing the birth of Christ. 'Christus natus est', crows the cock. 'Quando? Quando?' quacks the duck. 'In hac nocte', answers the raven. 'Ubi? Ubi?' lows the cow, and the lamb bleats in reply, 'Bethlehem, Bethlehem.'

In the summer of 1939 I was able to arrange for an exhibition to be held in the Library and the Gallery of the Muniment Room of photographs of the Abbey and its sculpture taken by Mr R. P. Howgrave-Graham, F.S.A. Although it was not widely advertised it proved to be very successful and was visited by over a thousand people. I shall not easily forget the impact which these wonderful photographs made upon me some months before when he first showed them to me at his home and projected some of them on to a screen. Howgrave-Graham was an enthusiast, with an intense appreciation of the beautiful especially in gothic sculpture. The Abbey was an endless source of delight to him. He would take infinite trouble, often not without peril to himself and his camera, to photograph some rather inaccessible detail of sculpture or a corbel head, neither of which had probably been photographed before, so that there should be a record of them. An electrical engineer and teacher by profession, when he retired after the War it was a real pleasure to be able to add him to my staff at the Library so that he could devote much more of his time to his photography. His photographs illustrating a little book I wrote called *Unknown Westminster Abbey* (a King Penguin) came, I think, as something of a revelation to many architectural students and others.

Almost from the beginning of Dean Labilliere's tenure of the Deanery the war clouds had been gathering. At the time of the Munich crisis I had motored to Oxford with the most valuable of the Abbey Muniments and had deposited some of them in the cellars under the Radcliffe Camera and others at Chiselhampton House, the home of Sir C. Peers, a few miles from Oxford. When the tension eased I had brought them back, but the succeeding months were much occupied in making plans for the evacuation, if it became necessary, not only of the whole vast collection of muniments, but of such of the Abbey treasures as could be removed to the country.

When war became inevitable these plans worked out smoothly and easily. The Coronation Chair was sent at once to Gloucester where it remained in the care of the Dean (Dr Costley-White) and the Chapter throughout the War. Except for having been taken across to Westminster Hall for the installation of Oliver Cromwell as Lord Protector, this was the only time that the Chair had left the Abbey since it was made in 1300. The Coronation Stone, however, was buried in a secret place beneath the Abbey which was known to only a few of us, but a plan showing its exact whereabouts was sent as a record to the Prime Minister of Canada, and this plan is now preserved amongst the state archives of Canada.

The bronze effigies from the royal tombs, the contemporary portrait of Richard II, the stone statues of saints in Henry VII's Chapel together with the wooden stalls, the bronze gates and the grille round Henry VII's tomb, etc., were sent to Boughton House, Kettering, but were later moved to Mentmore, Buckinghamshire where they joined other national treasures. The most important of the Abbey Muniments and books from the Library also went to Boughton. I was not too happy about them for apart from possible bombing, the danger of fire was always in my mind. I was glad, therefore, to have the opportunity in 1941 of transferring them to Aberystwyth, where the National Library of Wales had made an air-conditioned cave some years before the war. There they remained, with manuscripts from the British Museum, etc., perfectly safely until peace was declared. The rest of the Muniments remained for some months in the Muniment Room at the Abbey which seemed to be reasonably safe, but as opportunity offered the whole collection was eventually evacuated to various country houses in Hampshire or to Chiselhampton House in Oxfordshire.

Much, of course, of the sculpture within the Abbey could not be moved, but was protected as far as it was possible to do so. The roofs, etc., were patrolled by a devoted band of fire watchers.

In September 1940 a bomb exploded in Old Palace Yard. The blast shattered such fragments of the original glass (mainly armorial shields and badges) in the east windows of Henry VII's Chapel as had survived from the destruction wrought in Cromwellian times. It also made a small hole in the wall of the easternmost chapel. When this chapel, after the War, was dedicated to the memory of the men of the Royal Air Force who were killed in the Battle of Britain, this hole was glazed and now remains as part of the memorial.

A far more serious raid took place on the night of 12th May 1941, when incendiary bombs were showered on the Houses of Parliament and on buildings in their neighbourhood. This was the night when the Commons Chamber was destroyed and Big Ben was damaged. Mercifully the fabric of the Abbey survived intact, largely owing to the efficiency of the fire watchers, although the roof of the Lantern, the low square tower at the centre of the building, was set on fire and destroyed. But the Precincts and the School suffered grievously. A large part of the Deanery was destroyed and four houses in the Little Cloister were completely burnt out. At the School the great Hall ('School') with its fine roof, the seventeenth-century Busby Library, and the College Dormitory were gutted, only the walls remaining.

A letter which I wrote a few days later gives my first reactions to that terrible night:

. . . All that really matters is that no one was injured and that at present the Abbey is safe and very little damaged. I was up there last week. It is distressing to look up at a great square of sky over the Lantern, but it was the *only* place where the roof could fall in without doing much harm. The whole burning mass fell in a heap in the central space between the Choir and the Altar steps and burnt itself out. The Choir stalls a bit singed and the 17th century pulpit a little damaged, but as far as I could see nothing else—hardly a chip. Laus Deo. The Library is also safe. An incendiary through the roof, and touch and go, but they got it out. A gaping hole, but the really valuable hammer-beam roof undamaged, and so too the 17th century bookcases. The books in 2 'bays' a sodden mass when you come to examine them, and the floor covered with charred debris. But again the one place where it could do least harm. At the Deanery, Jerusalem, Jericho, and the Tudor rooms over them, and College Hall are safe.

But all the most beautiful parts of the School (except Ashburnham House) have vanished in a night, and only bare walls remain. 'School' with its glorious roof is gutted. It is simply heart-breaking, and tho' I have seen it all it is still difficult to realise.

The Deanery and the lovely houses round the Little Cloister are just heaps of bricks. I could not have believed such utter desolation. The curious thing is that the monastic buildings have been laid bare. The medieval stone walls stand out everywhere in the ruins and all the Tudor and later work grafted on to them have disappeared. Charles Peers and I walked round, and in a stunned and rueful way noted that the whole place was alive with antiquarian discoveries – what an irony!

Every one is very brave and just humbly thankful for what has survived. There is no doubt that the thing was a concentrated attack on the Houses of Parliament (dear Big Ben with the dirtiest face you ever saw!) and we unluckily were near enough to catch it too. Mercifully it was only incendiaries and no explosives.

I just dare not think of the School, for we depended much on the charm of our buildings—still nothing can destroy the spirit of the place, and in time a new and even greater School will arise. It is a cruel blow.

My confidence was justified, and new buildings have taken the place of the old so that no trace of the devastation now remains. But for some of us the wounds inflicted on that terrible night, when so much that I had known and loved all my life was destroyed, have never completely healed.

CHAPTER IX

The Abbey Muniments and the Library

MY appointment, early in 1926, as Keeper of the Muniments of
Westminster Abbey had put me in charge of a collection which had
fascinated me ever since I was a boy at the School some twenty years
before.

In those days there might have been seen emerging from the east
cloister door at exactly two o'clock on any weekday afternoon a tall,
handsome, dignified, bearded figure clad in a tightly buttoned grey
frock-coat and top-hat, and with a large bunch of keys in his hand.
Sometimes, on a half-holiday, there was also to be seen in the same
cloister a Westminster boy. The frock-coated old gentleman was Dr
Edward J. L. Scott, sometime Keeper of the Manuscripts and Egerton
Librarian at the British Museum; the Westminster boy was myself,
hoping – and I was never disappointed – that Dr Scott would invite
me to come up the turret staircase and spend the afternoon in the
Abbey Muniment Room. And a queer couple we must have looked;
both of us in skull caps (for Dr Scott always insisted that I must wear
one, 'for dust is always falling here', and that I must keep my feet on
a bit of carpet 'to prevent the cold from the tiled floor getting into
your bones'), both of us with a box of manuscripts in front of us,
both of us completely happy and absorbed; except when Dr Scott
would come across to see how I was getting on or would lure me over
to his table so that I should get, all unsuspecting, a whiff of the disgusting stuff which he was using on a document in order to bring up
a word which was otherwise too faint for him to read.

Such had been my introduction to the great collection of documents, known as the Abbey Muniments, of which one day in the

distant future I was to become the Keeper and to hold that office for over forty years. I owe more than I can say to Dr Scott. He had the gift, so rare and so encouraging, of being able to appear to treat a boy as an equal, while all the time he was quietly allowing him to draw unreservedly on his own great knowledge and experience. He was the kindest, the most patient, and the most unselfish of men. For a quarter of a century (1893–1918) he devoted himself to the Muniments, which he found in an appalling state of neglect and decay. At first he had to combine the work with his post at the Museum and could only come in his spare time, but after his retirement in 1904 he spent his whole time in the Muniment Room. Day after day week after week, he arrived at exactly the same moment in the morning and departed equally punctually in the evening. It was, perhaps, not unfitting that at long last in 1918 death should have come to him quite suddenly in the Muniment Room while attending, according to his invariable custom, the Sunday morning service.

Gradually he had brought order out of chaos. With his own hands he sorted, cleaned, stamped, calendared and indexed over 50,000 separate documents besides calendaring two of the great Chartularies containing many hundred pages. His work was extraordinarily accurate and trustworthy, and he never missed anything. Again and again when I have imagined myself to have made some small discovery, I have found on the blue calendar slips an asterisk and a note in his fine legible handwriting (of which, by the way, he was extremely proud) showing that he had already noticed it. I sometimes used to comfort myself during the last war by thinking that if disaster overtook any portion of the collection, then evacuated in many places, Dr Scott's calendar gave so full a description of the contents of each separate document that the loss of the original document would not have been wholly irretrievable.

Not the least interesting feature of the Abbey Muniments is the place where they are kept. The Muniment Room at Westminster is a large room or gallery open on two sides to the Church and halfway between the floor of the south transept and the triforium. It is, in fact, above the vaulting of the east cloister, and by a clever piece of building it was incorporated into the Church by the thirteenth-century Master Mason who wanted to have aisles to his transepts. The other aisles are on the ground floor level, but here, owing to the position of the Cloister, he was forced to put his aisle, as it were, on the first floor. But by putting a large window at the south end he got the effect he wanted.

The original use of this gallery remains a matter of doubt. It seems likely that it was used as an office by the Monk Bailiff of Westminster a somewhat shadowy official of the Monastery whose work seems to have been mainly legal and connected with the records of the various abbey properties. It is probable that in the reign of Richard II (1377–99) it was turned into a Muniment Room and so it has remained ever since. At the same time the gallery was divided into two unequal portions by a partition, on which was painted a full size representation of the couched and chained white hart (Plate 23), the badge of Richard II, and this painting continues to dominate the northern portion of the gallery. The whole gallery is paved with slip tiles of the same date and many of these retain their original glaze. To about the same date, too, belongs the delightful cupboard or 'armarium' which stands against the partition under the painting of the white hart. A few years ago I was interested to find in the Treasurer's Accounts for 1380–81 a detailed account for the making of a cupboard at a cost of £3 14s. 9d. to be used as a receptacle for 'various memoranda' about the Abbey Manors. As in later accounts it is definitely stated that the 'armarium' was meant for 'munimenta' it may well be that these entries refer to this particular cupboard. There are also in the Muniment Room various chests of the twelfth, thirteenth, and fourteenth centuries which continue to be used for plans and documents although most of the muniments are now, owing to Dr Scott, beautifully kept in numbered boxes (over a thousand of them) in various more modern cupboards. It is a continual surprise to those who come and work – and they are many – on the Westminster muniments that provided a document contains a reference to a definite name or place it can, with the help of Dr Scott's calendar and index, be produced within a few minutes.

When I first knew the Muniment Room the only access to it was by means of the turret staircase from the east cloister, and it may be that the reason that Westminster has a collection of medieval and later documents unrivalled by any other cathedral in England is partly owing to this inaccessibility and partly to the fact that there was no serious break in the continuity of Westminster history between the earlier monastery and the later collegiate establishment. For a few years after the dissolution of the monastery in 1540 there was inevitable confusion and during those troublous times some of the Muniments were lost or destroyed, but the greater part of the collection remained and remains intact. It was owing to Dean Bradley (1881–1902) that the services of his old friend, Dr Scott, were enlisted with the fortunate results which have been already mentioned. But when in consequence of his labours and of those of his successor, the

Revd H. Francis Westlake, it was possible to make the Muniments accessible to students, the problem of space and accommodation for them became a pressing one. In 1932 Dean Foxley Norris had the happy idea of approaching the Pilgrim Trust, then recently founded by the late Mr E. S. Harkness an American citizen. The result was a most generous grant from the Trustees which enabled the late Sir Walter Tapper, R.A., who was then the Abbey Architect and Surveyor, to devise a scheme whereby the Library in the east cloister was connected with the Muniment Room. This he did by means of a very charming wooden spiral staircase in the Library leading up to a long gallery which he contrived over the leads above the cloister, with a door into the Muniment Room.

The Library (Plate 22) itself was formerly part of the monastic Dorter and retains its late fifteenth-century hammer-beam roof. It was turned into a Library between 1623 and 1626 by John Williams, Dean of Westminster and afterwards Archbishop of York, whose full length contemporary portrait has always hung over the fireplace. For a time it was one of the most important libraries in London, but as other libraries grew up it gradually fell into desuetude and except for bibliophiles was little known or used even by those residing within the Cloisters. When Washington Irving visited the Library in 1818 he tells us, in the charming little paper on it which he included in his *Sketchbook*, that the door was 'opened with some difficulty, as if seldom used'. It was a great delight to bring into use again this charming room with its original seventeenth-century bookcases and fittings so reminiscent of many of the College Libraries at Oxford or Cambridge.

While the scheme for remodelling the Library and Muniment Room was under consideration two of the Pilgrim Trustees, Lord MacMillan and Mr Stanley Baldwin, took the deepest interest in furthering it, and were charmed with the beauty and interest of these rooms and their contents. Mr Baldwin both then and afterwards visited the Library several times, assuring me that I had the most delightful job in the world and offering to exchange it for his own! I was struck by his real knowledge of the history of the Abbey and by his quoting with intense delight Lethaby's charming sentence: 'I want to think of it (the Abbey) here as it was when it stood in its first fairness, when Henry III, in 1262, ordered pear trees to be planted in "the herbary between the King's Chamber and the Church" evidently so that he might see it over a bank of blossom.' It had obviously appealed to Mr Baldwin as a Worcestershire man – the county of blossom.

I am tempted to recall a not unamusing incident in connection with his first visit to the Muniment Room when I was particularly anxious to enlist his support for the scheme then before the Trustees. It so happens that we have a very large collection of medieval Worcestershire documents owing to the fact that the Monastery held a number of manors in that county. As I knew Mr Baldwin's love for his native county it occurred to me to look through some of the Worcestershire boxes until I found a very perfect medieval document to which was attached a fine impression of the Great Seal of Edward III. This document I am afraid I put, rather deceitfully, on the top of the other charters in that particular box. Sure enough, says Mr Baldwin the next day 'I suppose that by no chance you have any Worcestershire documents here?' 'Oh yes,' say I, 'we have several boxes of them.' Then taking him to the cupboard I casually ran my finger down and picked out a box at random(!), and there, curiously enough, on the top was a fine charter, which I read to him, with the seal of Edward III attached to it! He was greatly impressed with the importance of our Muniments.

I remember, too, how thrilled he was when I told him how Francis Westlake and myself had found the scratch on the pavement in the Chapel of Edward the Confessor which Henry VI had caused to be made to mark the place where he had wished to be buried. The story is a curious and interesting one. Henry VI had a great desire to be buried among his forbears at Westminster, and on more than one occasion, somewhere about 1460, he came over by night from the Palace nearby to choose a suitable place. But it all came to nothing for Henry VI was ultimately murdered, and was buried first at Chertsey and then later at Windsor. But when it was proposed to move the body from Chertsey to Windsor the monks of Westminster made a determined but unsuccessful attempt to have him re-interred at Westminster, and they produced evidence of his own desire to be buried in the Abbey. Among the Muniments is a contemporary copy of the original depositions of those who remembered his visits to the Abbey many years before in order to choose a place for his burial. It is an extraordinarily interesting and detailed document. Not only does it give a very vivid account of these visits, but it also gives the actual words used by the King and others. Thus when the Abbot suggested that the then newly erected tomb of King Henry V might be moved to one side to provide space for a future tomb, the King replied 'Nay, let hym alone, he lieth lyke a nobyll prince I wolle not troble hym'. Eventually we are told that the King turned towards the tomb of King Henry III and 'nyghe the place wher the Reliques then stoode' he measured out with his own feet the length of seven feet pointing with his staff and saying 'Forsoth and forsoth here is a good place for us'. He then commanded that a mason should be called and ordered him to mark out the place which he had indicated with a pickaxe, 'whiche done the seide Kyng and lordys departed'. Some years ago it occurred to Francis Westlake and myself that a scratch made by a pickaxe on the thirteenth-century mosaic pavement must still exist. The difficulty was that the whole floor was then covered, as it is today, with thick linoleum. However, very shortly afterwards there was to be an Installation of Knights of the Bath, during the course of which the Knights were to go in procession from the Choir to Henry VII's Chapel by way of the Confessor's Chapel. So Westlake who was then Custodian, and myself went to the Dean and innocently suggested that it would look better if the ugly linoleum was taken up for the occasion and strips of red carpet laid in its place! The Dean entirely agreed – and so we were able to find the long wavering scratch, faintly but unmistakably marked on the pavement, which probably no one had identified since John Thirske marked it out with his pickaxe in the presence of the King some four hundred and sixty years before.

Such stories may perhaps show something of the extraordinary fascination which is to be found when one is engaged in what some people called 'grubbing about among your dusty old documents'. I was sometimes asked 'what is a muniment' and what do you mean when you call yourself the 'Keeper of the Muniments?' I was quite accustomed to be called the 'Keeper of the Monuments' or the 'Keeper of the Munitions', and I had even received a letter addressed to the 'Keeper of the Muses'! Oddly enough 'munitions' is not far out, for the word does in fact derive from the Latin word for a fortification ('munimentum'), and a muniment is properly a title deed or a charter of privileges which acts as a fortification against any who attempt to invade – in this instance – the Abbey's rights and privileges. From this restricted use the word has gradually become extended to cover any document or collection of documents.

As is generally known the Abbey is a 'Royal Peculiar', that is to say that the Dean is answerable to the Sovereign alone, and neither the Archbishop of Canterbury nor the Bishop of London can exercise any jurisdiction over or even come to take part in a service in the Abbey except by command of the Sovereign or by the invitation of the Dean and Chapter. It used to be the custom that the first time that a newly consecrated Archbishop of Canterbury or Bishop of London came to the Abbey he had to sign a document in the Jerusalem Chamber acknowledging the Abbey's 'peculiar' position, before he was admitted into the Church. There are in the Muniment Room many such documents going back to medieval times attested by the seals or signatures of successive holders of these offices. Even to this day a consecration of a bishop within the Abbey cannot take place except under a grant by the Dean and Chapter which begins 'whereas by ancient privilege belonging to the Collegiate Church of St. Peter, Westminster, it is not lawful for any Archbishop or Bishop to exercise any ecclesiastical jurisdiction or perform any part of the episcopal function within the limits of the same without leave first obtained from the Dean and Chapter . . .' etc., and ending, 'Protesting first that the said Grant nor anything therein contained shall not extend or be made use of in time coming to the infringement of the privileges of the said Church aforesaid'. There is a pleasant story of Dean Bradley, after a dinner-party at the Deanery, courteously escorting Dr Creighton, then Bishop of London, to the entrance of Dean's Yard and remarking as he left him, 'Now I return you to your Diocese'. Dr Creighton, himself an historian would certainly have appreciated the real sense of history behind the remark. In the same way Dean Ryle once told me with some amusement that as Prolocutor of the Lower House of Convocation he had just signed a letter addressed to himself as Dean of Westminster to ask permission for the Lower House to meet in the Church House within the Precincts of Westminster, and that he proposed as Dean of Westminster to write to himself as Prolocutor giving the necessary permission.

It was in connection with the Church House that I had the probably unique experience of firing off a thirteenth-century muniment with devastating effect. To explain how this happened it is necessary to say that the exemption of Westminster from episcopal control was not accepted in early days without demur. In 1222 the then Bishop of London, Eustace de Fauconberg, raised the issue directly and claimed episcopal jurisdiction over the Monastery. The monks, however, were able to produce (which seems exactly the right word) a remarkable charter of St Dunstan, Bishop of London (A.D. 959–60) which gave away every right which any bishop of London had ever claimed or was ever likely to claim over Westminster. This charter, with its even more remarkable seal, is still carefully preserved in the Muniment Room. Whatever may have been the real or imaginary basis upon which this exemption was founded, the so-called Charter of Dunstan has not been able to stand up against modern criticism. At the time, however, as Dean Robinson once remarked it did excellent work for Westminster. The matter was referred to arbitration and Stephen Langton Archbishop of Canterbury, with other bishops, was entirely

30   William III returns to the Abbey after the 1939–45 war. (*Left to right*) the author, Miss M. Usher, William III, the author's wife, F. Lane.

31　William III when re-invested with his robes.

convinced of its authenticity. The Abbey was declared to be wholly exempt from the jurisdiction of the Bishop of London for ever and subject only to the Pope. A further document embodying these conclusions and with the attesting bishops' seals in their original seal-bags is among the most important of the Abbey Muniments. As a consolation for any disappointment he may have felt the Bishop of London was given the Abbey manor of Sunbury, but the question of jurisdiction over Westminster was never again disputed and the 1222 award was subsequently many times confirmed and ratified.

When in the 1930s the charming terrace at the south end of Dean's Yard was pulled down and the site cleared for building the new Church House, the bed of the old mill ditch, which bounded the Monastery was disclosed. It was known that the mill stream had formerly flowed along the line of the present Great College Street, and about 1902 I saw the foundations of a bridge across it which were found under the street near the junction of Tufton Street and Dean's Yard. But the exact course of the stream from that point until it turned and flowed along what is now Great Smith Street had not been previously known. In due course the new Church House was built, with a chapel extending over the archway into Dean's Yard and beyond. It became clear, however, when the course of the stream was plotted on a plan, that the altar end of the new chapel was within the Abbey Precinct. It was then publicly announced that on a certain date the chapel would be consecrated by the Bishop of London. Now one of the specific prohibitions in the 1222 award was that the Bishop of London under no circumstances was ever to consecrate a church or chapel within the Abbey Precinct.

When I mildly pointed this out to the Dean (Bishop Labilliere) he took the line that it was an infringement of the privileges of the Abbey which he had sworn at his installation to uphold, and that the matter must be resisted. The upshot was the appointment of a Committee consisting of Lord Roche, sometime a Lord of Appeal in Ordinary, Mr Justice Vaisey and Professor A. Hamilton Thompson before whom the matter was argued by counsel representing the Corporation of the Church House on the one hand and the Dean and Chapter on the other. I gave evidence and produced both the 1222 award and the foundation Charter of Queen Elizabeth I.[1]

[1] The Charter is somewhat rubbed and not too easy to read. On quite another occasion when I had had to produce it in a Police Court the learned Magistrate had asked to have it passed up to him. After studying it *upside down* for a minute or two he returned it to me with the remark that it was very interesting! However no such contretemps occurred on the present occasion.

I contended that as the Elizabethan Foundation Charter of 1560 granted us 'all ancient privileges' the 1222 award was still operative. Furthermore, that the limits of the Close as laid down in detail by an Act of Parliament of Edward VI, which clearly mentioned the mill stream as the southern boundary, had never been superceded; all subsequent documents and Acts of Parliament (a curious fact) being content, as far as could be ascertained, merely to mention the 'Precinct' without further definition. After an interesting and learned discussion the Committee accepted my contention, but the matter, as so often, ended in a compromise. It was agreed that when the day came both the Bishop of London and the Dean should take part in the consecration without prejudice to the rights and privileges of the Abbey. However, I had fired off with effect my 1222 'muniment', which was not the less interesting from the fact that it was attested by the seals of some of those who had forced Magna Carta on King John.

It is difficult to give any idea of the extent and variety of the documents preserved in the Abbey Muniment Room. They range roughly from the Norman Conquest to the present day. There are, indeed, eighteen Saxon or pre-Conquest documents in the collection. But recent research has shown that most of these, although, perhaps, not all, are suspect and probably of later date. The kindest thing that can be said of them is that they may be very early copies of a lost original. The best known of these is a charter dated 785 by which King Offa grants land at Aldenham in Hertfordshire to the Abbey of Westminster which is described as being in the terrible or aweful place ('in loco terribili') called Thorney 'at Westminster'. This charter has always been most carefully preserved among our muniments and appears to be a genuine charter of the period.

Apart from Westminster and Middlesex the Abbey of Westminster held manors all over England, and most of the documents connected with these manors have been preserved. I have sometimes said, with no very great exaggeration, that some reference can be found among our muniments to anyone who was prominent in Church or State from the Norman Conquest onwards. Probably no other 'private' collection, for instance, has so fine and complete a series of charters with the Great Seal of England attached to them, and there is an equally fine series of documents from the fifteenth century either initialled or signed by the Sovereigns themselves.

Not less remarkable is the unrivalled collection of Account Rolls dealing with the internal affairs of the Monastery. From these the late Dr E. H. Pearce was able to compile a register of Westminster monks and to trace their careers from the day when they entered the Monastery to the day when either as sick or *stagiarii* ('old stagers' as Dr Pearce happily translated the word) they entered the Abbey Infirmary. The simple remedies which Brother Infirmarer could provide for them – ginger, poppy, liquorice, camomile, etc. – are duly set out in the Infirmarers' Account Rolls. If the illness was beyond his skill he called in a *medicus* – Dr Leech and Dr Pill were two early doctors whose names I have noted in the Account Rolls and on one occasion he even called in the aid of a lady doctor! But if all was in vain the Infirmarer made the last sad entry against their names that he had paid 6s. 8d. to the poor for their souls.

The Muniments are, of course, primarily a business and legal collection, and from the sixteenth century onwards they consist mainly of the kind of documents which would naturally pass through a Chapter Clerk's Office. There is very little personal correspondence and unfortunately successive Deans seem to have treated the letters they received on Abbey matters as their private property and consequently they have not been preserved among the Muniments. When in the nineteenth century the Ecclesiastical Commissioners took over the administration of the properties belonging to the Abbey, one of the main sources for additions to the Muniments came to an end. Curiously enough almost simultaneously a new chapter opened in the history of the Abbey. Under Dean Stanley the Abbey became a 'national' church in a fuller sense than ever before. It was unfortunate that at first very little attempt was made to preserve the general correspondence which that new development entailed. When I became Keeper it seemed to me that although official printed papers (e.g. Orders of Service, Procedure, etc.) were usually kept there was a good deal of correspondence at the highest level concerning special services and other matters which ought to be preserved as it showed how they gradually took shape. With the willing co-operation of successive Deans, who handed over to me their files as they were completed, it has been possible in the last few years to add some four thousand letters and documents to the collection dealing with a great variety of subjects (coronations, ceremonies and special services, funerals and memorials, gifts, etc.) mainly, but not entirely, of the last fifty years or so. They include holograph or autograph letters from prime ministers and statesmen, archbishops and bishops, lord chancellors, field marshals, admirals and air marshals, and, indeed, most of the prominent people of the time. These documents, although not immediately available for students, will eventually add very much to the value and interest of the Muniments.

Dr Scott, as has been said, had done a wonderful work in calendaring and indexing the greater part of the earlier Muniments. For the first time by means of his index, containing many thousands of typed slips, all the references to any particular person or place were brought together so that the documents in which they occurred could be easily found. The result has never failed to excite the admiration of all who have worked in the Muniment Room. But, even so, it remained true to say that in one sense the contents of the collection was still largely unexplored. Inevitably, faced with a collection of this magnitude, Dr Scott could only deal with and describe each document as it came to hand, but he had had neither the time nor the leisure to classify or analyse the results of his labours. Shortly after I became Keeper, therefore, I spent many months working through, with the aid of Dr Scott's calendar slips, the entire collection box by box and document by document. In the course of this 'stocktaking' I noted, classified and indexed anything which seemed to me to be of special interest (e.g. particularly fine medieval seals, royal and other signatures of distinguished persons, documents of special interest of all kinds, and documents suitable for exhibition in show cases, etc.). These notebooks have proved to be exceedingly useful. Having thus got a general idea of the scope of the collection I read a Paper to the Royal Historical Society, of which I was a Fellow, on 'The Nature and Use of the Westminster Abbey Muniments' which was subsequently published in its *Transactions*.[1]

In all this work I was greatly helped and was fortunate to have as my principal assistant Miss Dorothy Powell, a trained archivist and palaeographer, and also Mr Anthony Wood who eventually left me to become the County Archivist for Warwickshire. I also had as unofficial members of my staff, for greater or less periods, Sir Charles Strachey, Mr Kenneth Elphinstone, Mr A. G. Rawlings, Mr A. B. Tonnochy and others, who all did most valuable work. Sir Charles Strachey had had a long and distinguished career in the Foreign and Colonial Offices. After his retirement in 1927 and until the outbreak of the War in 1939 he spent many hours in the Muniment Room. He quickly made himself a competent palaeographer, and his fine classical scholarship and unique fund of out of the way knowledge were of constant value. He was the most persistent of men, no word however illegible was ever allowed to 'beat' him nor would he pass on until he had succeeded in reading it; no allusion was too obscure

[1] *Transactions of the Royal Historical Society*, 4th Series, Vol. XIX, (1936).

for him to fail to produce the solution within a day or two, usually triumphantly scribbled in his spidery handwriting on the back of an old envelope. It was a constant delight to work with him; he would produce the most brilliant emendations as apt as they were unexpected and one never knew what queer fancy or quaint flash of humour might be in store. It might be a simple jest, as when an enthusiastic young architectural student appeared one day in the Muniment Room with a camera and announced that he had come 'to photograph the boss' and was gravely told that he was 'sorry that he was not there that afternoon'; or, again, as when in reply to some query of mine which I have forgotten I received the characteristic postcard: 'I have no Hymns A & M to refer to, but I guess it is the casting down of the golden Crowns upon the glassy sea. Had the crowns strings attached, so that they could be recovered? Did they bounce, or skid away on the surface like stones on a frozen pond? Were there little cherubs to retrieve them? C.S.' His death in 1942 was a great loss to all of us.

A notable development which only became possible with an enlarged staff and greater facilities for dealing with them has been the increasingly large number of societies and visitors of all kinds who have come to see the Library and Muniment Room in recent years. It has been a great pleasure to welcome them and to arrange for them small exhibitions of some of our treasures.

In 1938 Queen Mary, in the course of what came to be known as her 'educational tours' for the young Princesses, visited the Library with Princess Elizabeth (now Queen Elizabeth II), Princess Margaret, and the Archbishop of Canterbury (Dr Lang). Characteristically Queen Mary at once 'spotted' and walked over to examine the best thing in the Library, which she greatly admired. This was the beautiful early sixteenth-century carved stone head of an Abbot (Islip) which I had rescued from undeserved neglect a few years before. She also showed great interest in the fourteenth-century Litlyngton Missal, the Liber Regalis (i.e. the manuscript of the coronation service believed to have been used by our medieval sovereigns at their coronations. 'A manuscript', as the Archbishop remarked with reference to the then recent Coronation of King George VI, 'which I have deeply studied, but never before actually seen'), and the original lease given to the poet, Geoffrey Chaucer, in 1400, of a house in the Precincts, which were among the things which I had put out in the show cases.

It happened that some months before, I had casually asked one of the clergy at St George's Chapel, Windsor, to let me know if he was ever offered a second-hand copy of Sir William Hope's great book on *Windsor Castle*, which I wanted for the Library. I had thought no more about it, but a few days before Queen Mary's visit I had been astonished and gratified by receiving a copy of the book (in three superbly bound volumes) autographed by King George VI. These had been sent to the Dean with a letter saying that it had been brought to the King's notice that a copy of this book would be of use to the Library. I showed these volumes to Queen Mary, and in reply to her question whether I had asked for them I said, 'Not exactly, Ma'am', and told her, somewhat to her amusement, the whole story. Whereupon she at once said, 'Perhaps you would like the Buckingham Palace Book to go with them?' The next day there arrived a copy of the late Mr Clifford Smith's *Buckingham Palace* with the inscription in the Queen's own hand, 'Presented to the Library in Westminster Abbey in remembrance of her visit by Mary. R. March 7th 1938'.

These were not the only royal gifts which the Library received during my time as Keeper. In 1926 a copy of Ackermann's *History of Westminster Abbey* (1812), specially printed on vellum with the original water-colour illustrations and magnificently bound in red velvet with brass embellishments, turned up at a London book-sellers. From internal evidence it could be proved that it had origin-ally been bound for, and had belonged to, H.R.H. The Duke of Sussex. It was offered to the Dean and Chapter, but at a price far beyond their means. The matter, however, evidently came to the notice of King George V and Queen Mary, for, on ascertaining that the Abbey coveted it, they and other members of the Royal Family bought it and presented it to the Dean and Chapter. King George himself recorded the gift on the fly-leaf of the book, and his signature was followed by that of Queen Mary and by all those who had subscribed towards its purchase. When King George handed the book to the Dean he chaffingly remarked, 'Now don't go and put this in the Library where no one will ever look at it', and for this reason it is displayed in a special case in the Nave of the Abbey.

These were notable accessions to the Library, and so, too, was the acquisition of the Langley Collection of prints, original drawings and engraved portraits connected with the Abbey which had been collected by the late Mr Percy Langley. After Mr Langley's death it had passed into the possession of his brother, and he had kindly given me many opportunities of studying this very extensive, interesting, and, indeed, in many ways unique collection. I had hoped for many years that it might eventually find a home at the Abbey, but it was not until after the War, during which it very narrowly escaped destruction by bombing, that the Dean and Chapter were able to purchase it for the Library in 1947.

CHAPTER X

The Royal Maundy

IN 1921 I was appointed Secretary of the Royal Almonry, and thus began an association with the annual Maundy Service which was to be an unfailing source of interest and pleasure to me for over forty years.

The service is of great antiquity. It derives its name from the opening words of the service which are taken from St John's Gospel: 'A new Commandment (*Mandatum*) have I given unto you that ye love one another.' From very early days Our Lord's humility in washing the feet of his Disciples was imitated in the Church, and the ceremonial washing of the feet of selected poor persons by a Bishop or Abbot, together with a distribution of alms and food, took place annually on Maundy Thursday.

The example of the Church was followed by Kings and other great personages. In England the annual distribution of the Royal Maundy by the sovereign can be traced back with certainty to the twelfth century, and it may well be that it goes back at least to the time of Edward the Confessor. At first the number of recipients of the Maundy seems to have been usually restricted to thirteen (i.e. the number of the Apostles and one extra to represent Our Lord). King Henry IV (1399–1413) seems to have been the first sovereign who decreed that the recipients should number as many old men and as many old women as he was years of age. This has always been the custom since then, with the addition, from an early date, of one more recipient of each sex to represent the uncompleted year of the sovereign's age.

The recipients can be chosen from anywhere in the United

32   Charles II before cleaning.

33   Charles II as he arrived for cleaning at the Victoria and Albert Museum.

34   Charles II rehabilitated.

35 Frances, Duchess of Richmond (d. 1702), when re-robed after the War.
The author's wife holds the stuffed parrot which belonged to the Duchess.

Kingdom, although for convenience they tend to be chosen from the district in which the service takes place. They have to be over a certain age and are usually recommended by their local clergymen to whom they are personally known as specially deserving cases. Each of them receives at the service, in the specially minted Maundy money (silver pennies, twopences, threepences and fourpences), as many pence as the sovereign is years of age. In addition they receive actual money payments amounting to between £4 and £5 in lieu of the clothing and provisions which were formerly distributed at the same time. They also receive further payments at Christmas, but these are not distributed ceremonially.

At the annual service on Maundy Thursday, which is usually held in Westminster Abbey, the recipients are seated on each side of the choir and at the east end of the nave. The Queen's Bodyguard of the Yeomen of the Guard are on duty in the choir and in the nave. The Maundy money and the alms given in lieu of provisions, in the traditional red and white purses, are placed on the silver gilt Maundy Dish, which is brought from the Tower of London for the service. This Dish with the strings of the purses hanging over the edge, is carried, by a very ancient and picturesque custom, on the head of one of the Yeomen in the Almonry Procession at the beginning of the service. He is preceded by another Yeoman who carries another Dish containing the rest of the alms which are contained in green and white purses. The Almsdishes are then placed on a table at the foot of the altar steps.

The High Almoner, or as he is usually called the Lord High Almoner, the Sub Almoner, and the Almonry Officials are girded with towels in remembrance of the feet-washing which was once part of the service. They, and others taking part, carry nosegays of sweet herbs.

During the course of the service there are two Distributions, when the sovereign or, in the sovereign's absence, the High Almoner, walks the length of the choir and into the nave and back again distributing the gifts first to the women on one side and then to the men on the other. During the Distributions traditional anthems are sung by the choir. The service ends with the Blessing and the National Anthem.

Curiously enough although I had always lived in the Precincts it was only the year before I was appointed Secretary that I saw the ceremony for the first time. To tell the truth I remember that although I had been interested I had not been particularly impressed. At that time before the advent of broadcasting the service attracted little public attention. It is curious to remember now, when the Abbey is filled to capacity, that in those days the Abbey was never more than half full, and the nave, for instance, was entirely empty. The service itself, with the presence of the Yeomen of the Guard and the Chapel Royal boys in their gold and scarlet uniforms, could never be anything but colourful, but the impression left on my mind was that there was nothing specially significant about it, and that it seemed to be in danger of becoming nothing but a picturesque and, perhaps, rather meaningless survival from the past.

It should be remembered that there was no record of any sovereign attending the service or making the distributions in person since James II did so in 1685, and there was no suggestion that the practice would ever be revived. In spite of the absence of the sovereign, however, the service survived and continued to be held annually, the distributions being made by the High Almoner or in his absence by the Sub Almoner. But the ceremonial washing of the feet of the recipients was discontinued in the eighteenth century and, as the years went on, the distributions of clothes and provisions during the service, which had led to disorderly scenes, were commuted for money payments. Beyond appointing a new High Almoner as vacancies occurred successive sovereigns took little or no interest either in the service or in the work of the Royal Almonry. On very rare occasions a member of the Royal Family attended the service, but by 1921 the royal connection was only kept alive by T.H. Princess Helena Victoria and Princess Marie Louise ('the hardy annuals' as they once described themselves!), one or other of whom, and usually both, made a point of attending the service almost every year until their deaths.

When I was appointed Secretary in 1921 the Very Revd Dr Armitage Robinson, Dean of Wells, was High Almoner. He had been appointed in 1906 when Dean of Westminster. Dr Armitage Robinson, with his strong historic sense, was intensely proud of his office and very tenacious of what he considered to be its rights and privileges. He liked to remember that two of his predecessors as Deans of Westminster had been High Almoners and to point out that he was one of the select few, like the Lord Chancellor, who was entitled to the word 'High' in the official designation of his office. In all matters connected with the Almonry he was a complete autocrat. He alone, like his predecessors, appointed the recipients to the various charities, instructed the Mint to coin the Maundy Money required for the service, and himself audited and signed the accounts at the end of the year. There was no personal contact with Buckingham

Palace. Correspondence with the Keeper of the Privy Purse, who was responsible for the annual grant for the charities, was confined to formal letters, and any suggestion that he should see the accounts or have any say in the distribution of the money was firmly discouraged.

The position, therefore, was not easy. Although my personal relations with the Dean were of the happiest description, any suggestions which I ventured to make about the service or the Almonry unless I could make it seem as if they came from himself were usually met by the remark that it had not been done in the past and that nothing must be changed. But none the less I felt that some changes were inevitable. The more I thought about it and the more I studied the history of the Maundy the more convinced I became that the service was, or could be shown to be, something much more than a picturesque survival. Here was something unique, perhaps the only Holy Week service which had come down to us unchanged in essentials from the remote past; something, like the coronation service, which was full of beauty and symbolic meaning, something in which magnificence and absolute simplicity and humility could be combined, and something which far from being meaningless could be shown to stress symbolically the importance of personal service and sympathetic understanding of the needs of the poor and the elderly even in an age when their care was passing more and more under the control of the State.

With these aims in view it seemed to me that as a first step it was essential to strengthen the royal connection with the service. Here I was greatly helped by the whole-hearted co-operation of the Revd Lancelot Percival, who had been appointed Sub Almoner on the death of the Revd Dr Edgar Sheppard in 1921. As Sub Dean of the Chapels Royal he was in close touch with the Court and through him it was possible not only to ensure that other members of the Royal Family should be invited to attend the service, particularly if the two Princesses were unable to be present, but to re-establish friendly relations with the Privy Purse and Lord Chamberlain's Department and by personal interviews smooth out the kind of misunderstandings which were inevitable when the only means of communication was by formal and rather frigid letters. It was not, however, until after the death of Dr Armitage Robinson in 1933 that it became possible to agree that the Royal Almonry, while remaining a separate establishment, should be given an office in Buckingham Palace, and that while henceforth the financial side should be under the supervision and control of the Privy Purse, the ceremonial side and all connected with the annual service should be left to myself as Secretary.

Here again I was fortunate inasmuch as the service had been held for so many years at the Abbey with its great traditions of perfectly ordered services. Owing to my lifelong connection with the Abbey I was able to work in close co-operation with those responsible fo the ordering of Abbey services, although from time to time I had to insist that the Maundy was not a Westminster charity and that the service was not an 'Abbey Service' but a service held at Westminster Abbey by command of the sovereign who, even if not present in person, was represented by the High Almoner.

But although in these early years I was able to make some small suggestions which added, so I hoped, to the dignity of the service, they did not amount to very much. And then something happened which was to alter the whole conception of the service for the future and was to give it a reality which had previously been lacking. It was as we came out after the 1931 service that Princess Marie Louise made the suggestion to me that the sovereign ought once again to make the distributions in person and added that she felt sure that King George would come if he was asked to do so. The result was that King George V and Queen Mary not only attended the service the following year but that the King consented to make the second distribution in person. It was an historic occasion, the whole service went without a hitch of any kind and it was a great success. The Abbey was flooded with sunshine, and the colour, pageantry, and beauty of the service made a great impression on the very large congregation.

King George, too, brought something to it which, perhaps, none of his predecessors could have done. For them it could hardly have been otherwise than 'a state occasion'. But King George with his complete naturalness, his ready sympathy, and his inherent friendliness – qualities so clearly shown later in that same year in the first of his Christmas broadcasts – brought a touch of intimacy into the service which it has never lost under his successors. On this occasion instead of handing the purses at the distribution to the Sub Almoner I walked immediately in front of the King indicating to him the recipients. My note at the time was: 'The King did the Distribution quite charmingly with a grave little bow and smile for each recipient. He was taken aback and quite flushed with pleasure when the old people quite spontaneously and one after another said "God bless Your Majesty", or "Long live Your Majesty", etc., as they received the purses.' As *The Times* put it in a leading article 'the presence of the King as his own Almoner showed that the Royal Maundy still expresses the will of the sovereign to be the friend and servant of the poor among his people; and at the heart of his Empire, in the noblest and most Royal of its churches, a stately ceremony holds out, for all to see, the example of charity and of service.'

For one reason or another King George V, although he expressed himself as greatly pleased and interested, was unable to attend the service again. But the precedent had been set, and his example was followed in 1936 by King Edward VIII. Since then it has become the custom once again for the sovereign to attend the service, unless unavoidably prevented from doing so, and to make both the distributions in person.

On the death of Dr Armitage Robinson in 1933 the Archbishop of Canterbury (Dr Cosmo Lang) had been appointed High Almoner in his place. This was a break with tradition for although nine Archbishops of York, including Cardinal Wolsey, had been High Almoners, on no previous occasion had the office been held by an Archbishop of Canterbury. It proved to be a very happy selection. It was a great pleasure to work with him and he was always helpful and charming to me in every way (Plate 26).

It was, of course, physically impossible for him ever to 'put a foot wrong' in matters of ceremonial. A highly symbolic service like the Maundy becomes increasingly impressive in proportion to the perfection and dignity with which the ceremonial part is carried out by the principal people concerned. There was never any anxiety with Archbishop Lang. He would give the most careful consideration to details and was always open to suggestions for any slight improvements which might occur to me. Nothing was ever left to chance. I remember, for instance, one occasion when if anyone had chanced to come unexpectedly into the Archbishop's study at Lambeth they would have been astonished to find the Archbishop, the Sub Almoner, and myself apparently engaged in some strange and intricate dance, rather like the Mock Turtle and the Walrus in *Alice in Wonderland.* We were, in fact working out exactly how the purses at the service could be passed to the King without awkwardness – slightly complicated by the fact that the Archbishop was unable to make up his mind, as we weaved in and out, whether at any given moment he was representing the King or himself as High Almoner!

Since the Abbey is a Royal Peculiar, whatever the occasion the sovereign is received at the west door by the Dean and Chapter. The Archbishop used to complain half humourously ('Of course I know that you *are* very peculiar') that neither as Archbishop of Canterbury nor as High Almoner could he accompany the Dean, and furthermore that at the end of the service the Royalties had departed before the Almonry Procession could reach the west door. To obviate this difficulty it was arranged that we should all go back to the Deanery after the service so that they should have an opportunity of meeting those who had taken part. These informal gatherings seem now to have become a regular feature. I remember on one occasion when we were all talking in the Deanery drawing-room the Archbishop telling the King, George VI, rather to his amusement, that I was 'the man who writes to the Mint and tells them to coin as much money as he wants'! It was true at the time, but the request for the coining of the Maundy money now goes direct from the Privy Purse.

Curiously enough, although for twenty years or more I used to write the formal letter to the Mint and they acted on my instructions, my annual request for the loan from the Tower of the Maundy Dish used in the service had to go through the Lord Chamberlain. The reason was that, in theory at any rate, my letter had to be authorized by the Sovereign before the Keeper of the Jewel House allowed any of the Regalia out of his keeping. The Dish itself is a perfectly plain silver gilt one dating from 1660 although it has the Arms and Cypher of William and Mary engraved in its centre. At the service it is filled with the red and white purses containing the Maundy money and the strings with which they are fastened hang over the edge of the dish.

Until 1936 at the first distribution I used to carry a brocaded silk bag which contained small 'wage-packet' envelopes with the money given to the old people in lieu of clothing. These envelopes I handed out as required to the Sub Almoner who passed them to the High Almoner to give to the recipients. I never liked it; it seemed to me that however one did it there was inevitably something furtive about handing a small and scarcely seen envelope, and that it was quite unworthy of the dignity and beauty of the service. After some thought, therefore, and being careful that nothing should detract from the second and principal distribution, I got approval for two new sets of purses to be made; the first white with green thongs for the men and the second a vivid Tudor green with white thongs for the women. These purses were similar to the red and white purses, but without long thongs and merely tied with a bow round their necks. They are now placed on a smaller Almsdish and carried by a second Yeoman but not on his head. They act as a most effective foil to the red and white purses, they can be seen by everybody and they are now, no doubt, thought to be traditional.

I was indirectly responsible for another successful innovation in this age-old service. It must always be remembered that the Abbey was originally designed in the thirteenth century for the practical needs of about fifty monks. But, except when the central space under the lantern is cleared for coronations, it was never meant for great ceremonies with very large congregations. The result was, and is, that for a service like the Maundy only those in the choir and under the lantern can see the actual distributions. This fact troubled King George VI and he asked me if some means could not be devised by which more people could see what was taking place. It occurred to me that instead of confining the distributions to the choir there might well be a few recipients placed in the nave. This idea was duly approved, and the sudden emergence twice during the service from under the organ loft of the Distribution Procession consisting of the Head Verger, the Secretary, the Sovereign, the High and Sub Almoners, the Asst. Secretary, the Yeoman carrying the dish with the purses, the Officer in command of the Yeomen in his cocked hat,[1] and the Sergt Major of the Yeomen, has proved to be not only very effective but has enabled many more of the congregation to see part at least of the Distributions.

King George VI was very much interested in the service and used to make suggestions about it to the late Bishop of Lichfield (Dr E. S. Woods) who had succeeded Archbishop Lang as High Almoner in 1945. He and the Queen made a point of attending the service, even during the War years (Plates 24, 25), unless they were prevented from doing so. It was a source of satisfaction that throughout those years there was no break with continuity and that the service continued to be held annually. I had some anxious moments with the sovereign present and the Abbey crowded to the doors, but by great good fortune we were disturbed neither by raids nor by flying bombs.

Since her accession Queen Elizabeth II has attended every service except those in 1954, 1960 and 1964, when she was unavoidably prevented from doing so (Plate 27). On these occasions the distributions were made on her behalf by the High Almoner (the Bishop of St Albans), by Queen Elizabeth, the Queen Mother, and by the Princess Royal (Countess of Harewood) respectively.

In 1955 the Queen commanded that the service should be held at Southwark Cathedral to mark the Golden Jubilee Year of the Diocese of Southwark. This, in a way, was a reversion to older custom. In medieval times and later the service was held wherever

[1] The Officers and Yeomen, being on duty, wear their hats during the service.

the sovereign was in residence at Easter. In the seventeenth century, however, it became customary to hold it in the old Chapel Royal (now the Banqueting Hall) in Whitehall. It continued to be held there until that Chapel ceased to be used for services in 1890, when Queen Victoria commanded that the Maundy Service should henceforth be held in Westminster Abbey. Until 1955 therefore, it was always held there unless the Abbey was not available, as for instance when it was being prepared for a coronation. On these occasions, the service is transferred to St Paul's Cathedral.

The service at Southwark proved to be so successful that the Queen decided that from time to time it should be held at other cathedrals, with the result that it has been held at St Albans Abbey (1957), in compliment to the Bishop of St Albans (Dr E. M. Gresford Jones) who had been appointed High Almoner on the death of the Bishop of Lichfield in 1953; at St George's Chapel, Windsor (1959); at Rochester Cathedral (1961 (Plate 28)); at Chelmsford Cathedral (1963); and since my retirement at Canterbury Cathedral (1965); at Durham Cathedral (1967) and at Selby Abbey (1969).

From a ceremonial point of view each of these cathedrals posed its own problems. At Westminster I made very full notes after every Maundy Service, and these were invaluable for the next year's service. They often reminded me of quite small points which I had noticed at the time as capable of improvement but which otherwise I might have forgotten. As a result I was able to add over the years a touch here and a touch there which helped, so one hoped, to make the ceremonial part of the service proceed with the smoothness and dignity of apparently effortless inevitability which was the ideal to which one endeavoured to attain.

But when the service was held at some other cathedral the procedure at Westminster could only be used as a foundation upon which to build. On these occasions the old people were chosen from the Diocese, and although one could leave much to the Diocesan authorities, there were civic and other processions which had to be timed to arrive at the cathedral without coming into collision either with each other or with the cathedral Clergy and Choir and the Almonry Procession who were probably forming up in the nave to await the arrival of the sovereign. Nor was the seating of the old people always easy where the space was confined and there was little room for the Distribution Processions to make their way round. At Chelmsford, for instance, where the Cathedral was originally the parish church, the aisles were very narrow, the floor very slippery, and the pews heavy, fixed, and immovable. The only

36   The Regalia Procession. Coronation of King Edward VII 1902. The Minor Canons carrying the Sceptres followed by Bishop Welldon (the Paten), Canon Henson (the Chalice), Canon Armitage Robinson (the Bible), Archdeacon Wilberforce (the Queen's Crown).

37   The Regalia Procession. Coronation of King George V 1911. Canon Barnett (the Orb), Canon Beeching (the Chalice and Paten), Canon Henson (the Bible), Archdeacon Wilberforce (the Queen's Crown), Canon Duckworth (the Imperial Crown).

38   The Regalia Procession. Coronation of King George VI 1937. The King's Scholars of Westminster School.

39   The Regalia Procession. Coronation of King George VI 1937. Canon Barry (the Bible), Archdeacon Donaldson (the Queen's Crown), Canon Storr (St Edward's Crown) followed by the Crossbearer and the Dean (Dr Foxley Norris).

way to seat the old people was to place one at the end of each pew practically all round the Cathedral, and the Distribution Processions, in consequence, had to take a long and complicated course. However all went well, and, at least, far more people than usual had a close view of the Queen and of the Distributions.

In all this, and indeed throughout my time as Secretary, I could have done little without the unfailing co-operation and help of successive High Almoners, of Deans and Chapters, and of all connected with the service, and especially that of Mr E. E. Ratcliffe, my Assistant for nearly forty years, and after his retirement of Mr Peter Wright, my eventual successor, upon both of whom so much of the detailed office work depended.

After the 1964 service I resigned the Secretaryship of the Royal Almonry which I had held since 1921, and after having been present and in attendance at forty-three consecutive Distributions of the Royal Maundy. It was a wrench to give it up after so many years, but it was a great privilege to have had the opportunity to help, in however small a way, to restore this unique and beautiful service, with its centuries of tradition, to something of its former position, and to re-establish once again the close personal connection between it and the reigning sovereign.

CHAPTER XI

The Wax Effigies

Origin of the Effigies – The 'Rehabilitation' of the Effigies – Charles II – The Duchess of Buckingham – The Duchess of Richmond – Eighteenth-Century Effigies – Lord Nelson – The Wooden Effigies

IT was in the Spring of 1932 that my friend, Mr J. L. Nevinson, then of the Textile Department of the Victoria and Albert Museum, came one day to look at some detail of the clothes of one of the wax effigies, which were then, and had been for many years past, kept in the upper part of Abbot Islip's Chantry Chapel. I had for a long time been distressed at their dilapidated and dirty condition, for the glass-fronted cases or presses in which they were kept had not been opened within living memory. While we were looking at them it suddenly occurred to me to ask him if he thought that anything could be done to clean them. On his replying in the affirmative I had a talk with the Dean (Dr Foxley Norris) about them, and on my assuring him that the clothes would not disintegrate if exposed to the air, he took the matter up with the authorities of the Victoria and Albert Museum, who agreed to clean each of the figures in turn.

Thus began a process which lasted until 1936 and aroused much public interest. As each figure was returned to the Abbey I wrote an article on its history for *The Times* and, as a result of my researches, I was able to establish the fact that these effigies were not only of great value to the student of textiles and costume, but that they had considerable importance as contemporary portraits in the round of historical personages.

These curious and unique figures are all that now survive at the Abbey of a custom dating back to very early times whereby a life-sized effigy of a sovereign or great person either carved in wood or later modelled in wax and dressed in the actual robes or clothes worn in life, was placed on the coffin in the funeral procession. On arrival at the Abbey the effigy was placed on a catafalque in the central space under the lantern where it remained for a week or more. It was then placed in a glass case near the grave, where it either remained or was removed and destroyed on the erection of a more permanent monument. The last survival of the custom, I suppose, are the emblems of kingship placed to this day on the coffin of a sovereign or the hat and sword which lie on the coffin at a service funeral. In 1839 those figures which still remained about the Church were collected together and placed in their cases in the Islip Chantry Chapel. A few people from time to time recognized their interest, but the general opinion was expressed by Charles Kingsley, then a Canon of Westminster, who writing in 1874 described them as 'old trumpery stuff not worth . . . looking at'. Certainly the eleven seventeenth- and early eighteenth-century figures, which were all that were on view, were a dilapidated collection, and I remember as a child being fascinated and rather frightened by the sinister appearance of Charles II which was not lessened by the fact that the feathers in his hat would shake in a mournful manner if anyone inadvertently touched the case (Plate 32).

This particular effigy proved to be one of the most interesting when we came to clean it. The face was probably taken from a cast made during life and it is unquestionably a portrait. It is curiously and uncannily lifelike and has the dark swarthiness and 'fierce countenance' which Evelyn noted as characteristic of the King. It is not too much to say that it is probably one of the most interesting and authentic likenesses of the King which exists. A contemporary who saw it together with the other effigies in 1695, and had probably seen the King in life, noted that 'the figures are curious, but yt of Charles ye 2nd exceeds all ye rest: 'tis to ye life, and truly to admiration'. I remember showing it to the late Arthur Bourchier, the actor, who was producing a play about Nell Gwyn, and how he insisted that Arthur Wontner, who was playing the King, should come and see it so that when he was made up he would resemble the effigy as closely as possible. The result was quite startlingly convincing.

When the time came for the figure of Charles II to make his pilgrimage to the Victoria and Albert Museum for cleaning an amusing incident occurred. The Islip Chapel is very cramped in space and we had some difficulty in getting the King down the steep flight of stairs. However, we placed him on a board and covered him with a rug, from beneath which his white kid shoes protruded. I followed behind carrying his black velvet high crowned Garter hat with its plume of ostrich feathers surmounted by an aigrette of black and white heron's feathers. This odd little procession, not unnaturally, caused some slight surprise as we passed through the Abbey. When we got outside into Dean's Yard a large red van from the Victoria and Albert Museum awaited us, and standing by the entrance to the Cloisters there happened to be a lady with a small boy. She gave one look at us and then hurriedly said to the boy 'take your hat off and don't stand there staring!'

The 'rehabilitation of Charles II', as *The Times* called it, was remarkable. Instead of the haunting, filthy, somewhat rakish figure which left us, there returned a figure of great dignity, 'every inch a king', with a curious suggestion of the charm which fascinated his contemporaries (Plates 33, 34).

No less remarkable, but from another point of view, is the effigy of Catherine, Duchess of Buckingham (d. 1743). This redoubtable lady, whose idiosyncrasies were a constant source of amusement to Horace Walpole and his contemporaries, prided herself on being a natural daughter of King James II by Catherine Sedley. It is recorded of her that she was once persuaded to go and hear one of the early Methodist preachers, and marvelled that their patroness, Lady Huntingdon, 'should relish any sentiments so much at variance with high rank and good breeding'. She added: 'their doctrines are most repulsive and strongly tinctured with impertinence and disrespect towards their superiors. It is monstrous to be told that you have a heart as sinful as the common wretches that crawl the earth.'

Her effigy was probably made at the time that her last surviving son (Edmund (Sheffield) Duke of Buckingham) died at the age of nineteen in 1735. His effigy, with its magnificent embroidered coat, and lying exactly as it was carried at his funeral, is in a case nearby, but the effigy of the elder son (d. 1715), a child of three, is in the same case as that of his mother. He is a pathetic little figure. He wears a handsome brocaded cap, while his body, as we found, is tightly laced with stays over which are elaborate embroidered satin and velvet clothes. At the back of his cerise-coloured velvet coat we found two slits which were evidently intended for the leading strings with which his mother guided his infant footsteps.

When we came to undress the effigy of the Mother we found to our astonishment that beneath her coronation robes she was complete, shall we say, from A to Z, with rose-satin and quilted linen petticoats, etc. Some of her paste jewellery had been sewn on to bits of old playing cards covered with black velvet. These I had framed and placed on the wall of her case. Although the effigy was made during her lifetime it was the last which was actually carried at a funeral.

The effigy of the other Duchess, 'La Belle Stuart' (Frances, Duchess of Richmond, d. 1702) is particularly attractive. It is a posthumous portrait, for the Duchess left in her will directions that her effigy should be 'as well done in wax as can be and set up . . . in a presse by itself . . . with cleare crowne glass before it and dressed in my Coronation Robes and Coronett'. It was modelled by Mrs Goldsmith at a cost of no less than £260 and was set up in the Abbey within a year of the funeral. The Duchess was the original model for the figure of Britannia on the coinage and the effigy preserves something of the charm which captivated Charles II. It is possible, too, to understand why Pepys spent a sleepless night thinking of 'the greatest beauty' he had ever seen in his life 'with her sweet eye, little Roman nose, and excellent taille'. This was after he had seen the Duchess and the other ladies of the Court 'talking and fiddling with their hats and feathers, and changing and trying one another's by one another's heads, and laughing', in July 1663. The robes on the effigy, which the Duchess wore at the Coronation of Queen Anne, must be the earliest peeress's robes which have survived.

It must have been about this time, for 'it had lived with her Grace for forty years', that she acquired the West African grey parrot which died within a few days of its mistress and was stuffed and placed in the case with the effigy. It was interesting to learn when I took it along to the Natural History Museum at South Kensington that it was by many years older than any stuffed bird that the authorities had ever seen and that it was probably the oldest stuffed bird in England. It shows no sign of its age! (Plate 35).

These effigies are all in what may be called the funeral tradition, but in the eighteenth century and until the invention of photography, full size wax figures or, on a smaller scale, little wax profiles mounted on plaques, were a regular method of representing famous personages, and a high degree of skill was attained in their modelling. Nowadays, except at Madame Tussaud's, it is almost a lost art. The custom, however, had a curious result at Westminster. As the 'funeral' tradition of these effigies died out at the Abbey the Minor Canons, Choirmen, and Vergers, whose inadequate salaries at that time were largely paid out of the money obtained from showing the tombs and effigies, found it profitable deliberately to buy new 'attractions' as opportunity served and to show them for a small extra fee. Such, for instance, was the origin of the effigies of Queen Elizabeth I, King William III and Queen Mary II, and Queen Anne.

The existing effigy of Queen Elizabeth was made in 1760 to replace an earlier effigy and in order to commemorate the bicentenary of the Elizabethan Foundation of the present Collegiate Church. Someone once indignantly wrote to me to say that surely the Dean and Chapter could provide a better effigy of Queen Elizabeth I, failing to realize that the figure is in fact an amusing example of a mid-eighteenth century 'Wardour Street' conception of what it was thought that Queen Elizabeth ought to look like. Unfortunately the original effigy which had been carried at the Queen's funeral was entirely destroyed in 1760. We had hoped that some portions of it might have been re-used, but such was not the case. The only interesting thing which we found when we came to examine the effigy was that underneath the Queen's petticoat was a genuine eighteenth-century pannier of red, blue, and white check stiffened with cane and with cushions on either side stuffed with hay. The effigies of King William and Queen Mary, and of Queen Anne, are rather stiff and 'waxworky', but there is contemporary evidence that they were greatly admired as good likenesses (Plates 30, 31). Queen Mary wears a pretty brocaded skirt which is probably French weaving of about 1700 and beneath it she has a curious brown leather petticoat painted with patterns and little Chinese figures in gold, but it seems improbable that the petticoat can ever have been worn as an actual garment. The effigy of Queen Anne was made after her death. It has a skirt of Louis XV yellow brocade, and she has a genuine contemporary Star of the Order of the Garter on her left breast. The wig was added in 1768, and by a mistake is made of black hair instead of dark brown as it should have been.

The effigies of William Pitt, Earl of Chatham, and of Nelson are much more effective, and, indeed, are of outstanding interest. It would be difficult to find a more masterly representation of the great statesman. The effigy was purchased in 1778, and it is believed that it was modelled in 1775 when Pitt is known to have given sittings to an American, Mrs Patience Wright. She had come to England in 1773 and had a considerable reputation in America for her life-size figures of Washington, Franklin, and others, none of which now survive. The attribution to her of our figure was confirmed by our finding the name 'Patience Wright' scrawled in ink on a bit of brown paper which had been used to mount part of the purple silk velvet coat on the effigy. There is no doubt of her skill as a modeller. The face, with its wide open blue eyes, is curiously and uncannily alive. The late Lord Stanhope very kindly allowed me to compare it with the portraits of Pitt and with the death-mask in his possession then at Chevening. The likeness was completely convincing, but there was more to it than that, for there was a tradition that Mrs Wright was in reality an American spy and that she had used her opportunities while Pitt was sitting for her to try to extract some information from him. Consciously or unconsciously she has given to the face of the effigy a faint suggestion of amusement about the mouth and a slightly quizzical expression in the eyes as if he was saying to himself, 'oh, no you don't. I see well enough what you are up to!'

When the effigy of Pitt was bought in 1778 and placed in one of the older cases or presses in the Islip Chantry Chapel, it was noticed that the roof of this press appeared at one time to have been painted. Not much notice was taken of this and as it interfered with the colour scheme devised to show off the effigy the remains of this painting were ruthlessly blacked out and defaced. Thereby a third of a great medieval work of art was irretrievably damaged. For when some sixty years later Edward Blore, the then Abbey architect, had the curiosity to remove the roof of this and the adjoining presses he found that the destroyed section formed part of what was probably the original thirteenth-century Retable, or back of the High Altar, and that the rest of it was still decorated with painting of exquisite craftsmanship. Although much of it is sadly damaged the Retable is now regarded as one of the major treasures of the Abbey.

The effigy of Nelson was quite deliberately bought in the Spring of 1806 because it was thought by the Choirmen and others that too many people were flocking to St Paul's to see the tomb and funeral car of the great hero. and it was felt that some sort of counter-attraction should be provided at the Abbey. There was a tradition that some of the clothes on the effigy had actually belonged to Nelson but perhaps because of the not very creditable circumstances surrounding its purchase very little was known about the origin of this figure, and, indeed, the same might be said about all these effigies until it was part of my work to investigate their history. I soon found however that it was of very great interest. Although, as I discovered, it was actually made by Miss Catherine Andras immediately after his death, I was able to prove that during his life he had sat for her and that, taking the pose and setting from the Hoppner portrait now at St James's Palace, she had succeeded in producing a remarkable likeness. Nothing could be more sensitive and attractive than the modelling of the face, and this is particularly noticeable when it is looked at in profile for the genius, the charm, and the slight suggestion of sensuousness about the mouth are all apparent.

At the time it was recognized at once as an outstanding success.

The Prince Regent – if by 'an illustrious personage' he is meant – considered it to be 'a strong and exact representation'. Lady Elizabeth Foster, shortly before she succeeded her friend Georgiana as Duchess of Devonshire, wrote to a friend that 'there is a wax figure of Lord Nelson put up in Westminster Abbey which is as if he was standing there'. My distant cousin, Miss Eyre-Matcham, told me that her grandfather, George Eyre-Matcham, who was a nephew of Nelson and as a boy knew him well, always said that the effigy was more like his uncle than many of the portraits. The likeness, too, was curiously demonstrated when some years ago I showed the effigy to the late Admiral Nelson-Ward and his brother who, of course, were directly descended from Nelson through Lady Hamilton. I made a note at the time that 'when the two brothers stood by the effigy the likeness was positively startling – one brother *was* the effigy from the forehead to the nose and the other from the nose to the chin – most curious and interesting!'

But we can go further than this. In a long forgotten book[1] I found an account of how the author had escorted Lady Hamilton herself to see the effigy. Much moved, she declared 'that the likeness would be perfect if a certain lock of hair was disposed in the way his lordship always wore it', and on disclosing her identity she was allowed to make the alteration. When I found this I immediately went into the Abbey and very carefully removed the cocked-hat which covered the head. Unfortunately the lock had been displaced at some later date and all I could do was to re-arrange it as it is shown in some of the portraits and as Lady Hamilton had wished. An examination of the hat, however, produced an interesting discovery. Inside the crown was a label of Messrs Lock, the well-known hatters in St James's Street, and there was also, which at first puzzled me, a crescent-shaped piece of green silk lining attached to the brim but turned up inside the hat. Messrs Lock courteously allowed me to examine their records, when I found not only that Nelson had been a customer, which they knew, but that on more than one occasion he had ordered a cocked-hat 'and green shade'. It was obvious, therefore, not only that the hat had actually belonged to Nelson but that what had puzzled me was in fact the green shade which when turned down protected from strong light his remaining eye. The Devis portrait of Nelson shows just such a shade in position (Plate 29). I gave Messrs Lock photographs of the hat and they now hang framed in their delightful shop.

This discovery led on to others. It became apparent that all the

[1] Benson E. Hill, *Recollections of an Artillery Officer* (1836), pp. 12–14.

clothes on the effigy had almost certainly belonged to Nelson. The stockings, for example, and the frilled linen shirt were found to be authenticated by the initial 'N' and coronet, and the full dress admiral's coat corresponded exactly in its measurements with the coat (now at Greenwich) which he was wearing at Trafalgar. Indeed the fact that the coat on the effigy was a full dress one while the cocked hat was an undress one would alone have pointed to their genuineness, for it is unlikely that such a mistake would have been made if they had been supplied for the effigy by a naval outfitter. A very curious incident occurred when the late Professor Callender, who had given me much help in my researches, and myself were examining the Trafalgar coat at Greenwich. As we lifted it out of its showcase a letter of which the existence was quite unknown, fell out of the pocket. It proved to be from Sarah, 1st Countess Nelson (the wife of Nelson's successor) to Lady Hamilton. It was dated 13 Feb. 1806, and referring to the Trafalgar coat the writer added (by an extraordinary coincidence) "tis thought a glass case hermetically sealed (the same as Miss Andras will do hers in Westminster Abbey) will be the best mode of preserving it from the injuries of the external air'. The only article on the effigy which remained in doubt was the sword, which is an ordinary naval dress sword and there was nothing to identify it as having belonged to Nelson. I may add that there was no sword-knot on the sword, and to supply this deficiency a sword-knot which was known to have belonged to one of the most famous of Nelson's admirals was presented anonymously a few years ago and added to the effigy.

When the last of the effigies had been cleaned, Mr Nevinson and myself read a Paper[1] on them before the Society of Antiquaries – one of the few occasions when I have seen that august body overcome with merriment as the slides with which it was illustrated disclosed the rehabilitation of King Charles II and the successive stages of the disrobing of an eighteenth-century Duchess!

During the 1939–45 War the effigies were again disrobed and placed in the disused London Tube which housed many other treasures from Museums while their clothes were separately stored elsewhere to preserve them from moth, etc. When the time came for their re-emergence the re-dressing of each figure proved to be a formidable and difficult task, in spite of the excellent series of photographs which had been taken during the 1933–36 cleaning. It was, however, most successfully undertaken by my wife and her friend, Miss Marjory Usher, and by their skill, after three weeks

[1] *Archaeologia*, Vol. LXXXV (1936), pp. 169–202.

intensive work, the clothes were replaced on the figures and with a few necessary repairs appeared to be little the worse for their war-time experiences. At the same time the opportunity was taken to place the effigies in the Norman Undercroft Museum in the cloisters where with plenty of space and with proper lighting in the cases they can now be seen to the best advantage.

Before the cases were finally closed we were honoured by a visit from H.M. Queen Mary, who spent the best part of an hour examining them and graciously helped me to display to advantage the Garter Robes of King Charles II. These robes are, with one exception, the earliest in existence in this country.

It remains to say a few words about the earlier wooden effigies sometimes known as 'the Ragged Regiment'. The earliest of these is of Edward III cut out of one piece of wood and hollowed out at the back. Unfortunately the best and most complete of these earlier effigies suffered severely during the 1939–45 War when they became saturated with water which had been used to extinguish a fire in the building underneath which they were thought to have been safely stored. They were in a desperate and apparently almost hopeless condition when my friend and colleague, the late Mr R. P. Howgrave-Graham, F.S.A., undertook to do what he could to salvage them. It was a most difficult and delicate job, for not only had they to be dried out but the plaster and paint on them had to be stabilized and prevented from peeling off before it was possible for them to be cleaned. With great skill and patience Mr Howgrave-Graham succeeded not only in saving them but in bringing out much of the original colouring in the most astonishing way. In the course of the work it was realized that these early effigies were much less crude than had been supposed, and that they have very considerable claims to be recognized, like the later ones, as portraits of those whom they represent. There seems to be very little doubt that the face of Edward III was the actual death mask mounted on a wooden core and it was noted that the left side of the face was slightly distorted suggesting the stroke from which it was known that he had died.

The face of Henry VII also proved to be a deathmask. It is most striking, full of character and with strong Welsh characteristics. So much so that we were amused and interested when a casual visitor to the library saw it there one day and immediately and innocently asked 'who is your Welsh miner?' Unfortunately the plaster body of the king was in such a state and so damaged that it had to be sacrificed, but not before we had extracted from the horrible mass of crumbled plaster and rotting hay with which it had been stuffed when it was first made no fewer than twelve separate plants which must have flowered in some Tudor field before the King's death in 1509.

Besides Edward III and Henry VII there is a full length wooden figure of Queen Katherine Valois (wife of Henry V), and heads of Queen Anne of Bohemia (wife of Richard II), Queen Elizabeth of York (wife of Henry VII), Queen Mary I (?), and Queen Anne of Denmark (wife of James I). All these heads or figures are now also on view in the Abbey Museum.

CHAPTER XII

Coronations

Edward VII – George V – George VI – Preparations – the
Regalia – Rehearsals – Elizabeth II

WHEN I retired from the Keepership of the Muniments in 1966
The Times somewhat rashly stated that I was the only living person
who had been privileged to be present at four coronations. This, as I
expected, at once provoked correspondence, and it transpired that
there were certainly five others then living who shared this distinction. They were H.R.H. Princess Alice, Countess of Athlone, the
Lady Patricia Ramsay, the Duke of Wellington (who was a Page
in 1902, a member of the Royal Household in 1911, a Gold Staff
Officer in 1937, and one of the four Knights of the Garter to carry
the canopy in 1953), the Earl of Macclesfield (who succeeded his
Grandfather as 7th Earl in 1896), and Mr Herbert Dawson who
had been a member of the Choir at all four coronations.

It is also worth noting that the Revd Dr Jocelyn Perkins (d. 1962),
who came as a Minor Canon to the Abbey in 1899, was present as
one of the Abbey Clergy at all four coronations, a record, I think,
without parallel in Abbey history.

The Coronation of King Edward VII in 1902 was in some respects
unique. There had been no Coronation in the Abbey for sixty-five
years. The records which remained of Queen Victoria's Coronation
were not encouraging. The service had been intolerably lengthy and
cumbrous, many mistakes had been made during its course, and the
whole had only been redeemed by the grace and charm of the young
Queen. As the then Archbishop (Howley) wrote in his copy of the
service, 'we ought to have had a rehearsal'. There were many, too,
in 1902 who felt, without knowing much about it, that the service
was something of an anachronism and without any great significance
except as a pageant. Fortunately a year or two earlier Dr Armitage

Robinson had been appointed a Canon of Westminster. He at once made himself a first-class authority on the whole subject, and his knowledge proved to be invaluable to all who were engaged in drawing up the service and the ceremonial. Finally he preached a sermon on the spiritual significance of the rite which was widely reported and made a profound impression. Then came the dramatic postponement of the ceremony owing to the sudden illness of the King. The announcement was made at the final rehearsal on the day before and, except to a very few persons, it came as a staggering shock. After a few minutes of complete silence the rehearsal was abandoned and, at the suggestion of the Bishop of Bath and Wells, an impromptu service of intercession took its place.

The postponed Coronation was fixed for 9th August, and much had to be done in the intervening two months by Dr Armitage Robinson and the Bishop of Winchester (Dr Randall Davidson) to shorten the service in order to save the King as much exertion as possible. Even so there was much anxiety. The King had barely recovered and it was feared that he might not be able to get through the service. The Archbishop, Dr Frederick Temple, was over eighty and was so blind that large scrolls with the words of the prayers printed in specially heavy type had to be held in front of him by the Bishop of Winchester during the Investing, etc. The Dean of Westminster, Dr Bradley, who was almost exactly the same age as the Archbishop, was equally tottery and had to delegate some, but not all, of his important duties to the Sub Dean, Dr Duckworth. When the great moment of the Crowning came and the Archbishop turned hopefully to take the Crown from the Dean, whose peculiar privilege it is to bring it from the High Altar, it was found that he had wandered away with it. Finally there was an agonizing moment when the Archbishop, having successfully retrieved the Crown, held it with trembling hands above the King's head before, to every one's relief, he managed to lower it into position. It was then seen that it had been placed with the back to the front. In endeavouring to rectify this the Archbishop made matters worse and one of the supporting Bishops and the Bishop of Winchester had to come to the rescue and get it straight, the King merely remarking in a low voice as though to excuse the Archbishop ' . . . it is very difficult to put it on rightly.'[1] The King's solicitude throughout for the Arch-

---

[1] Among the Abbey Muniments are notes on the ceremony made by the Bishop of Bath and Wells (Dr Kennion) who as one of the supporting bishops was standing on the King's left side and it is from these notes that the quotations are taken.

bishop was very touching. More than once he turned to one of his supporting Bishops and said, 'I am very anxious about the Arch-bishop', and suggested that the Bishop should go to his assistance, and more than once both the Archbishop and the Dean 'would certainly have fallen' if the Bishop had not been at hand to hold them up. In the end, however, the indomitable will of those taking the principal parts triumphed over their physical disabilities and the Coronation was brought to a successful conclusion. It was the first Coronation for at least two hundred years at which those who were present did not regard it as a mere pageant but were deeply impressed both by the solemnity of the service, and, let it be added, by the bearing and reverence of the King.

Of the actual ceremony I, as a small Westminster boy seated up in the Triforium, necessarily saw very little. But there lies in front of me a rather smudgy roneo'd family magazine, such as it was not unusual, at that time, for the younger members of many families to inflict on their long-suffering relatives and friends. It was edited by my brother and in it I find an article written by myself entitled, 'My Impressions of the Coronation by a Westminster Boy'. It gives a surprisingly good account of the splendour of the general scene and of the stateliness of the processions which passed up the Abbey beneath us. I can see quite clearly in my mind the King coming up the choir and I remember how struck we were with the way his robes and the cap-of-maintenance accentuated his remarkable resemblance to King Henry VIII. I can recall the thrilling effect of the traditional Westminster 'Vivats' then introduced for the first time into Parry's great opening anthem written for this Coronation, although we Westminsters were not too pleased at having our shouts of 'Vivat Rex Edwardus' set to music. However, we let ourselves go on the thrice repeated 'Vivat' which follows. Both at this and at the 1911 Coronation the arrangements for the comfort of the guests and for getting them away afterwards were curiously inadequate both within the Abbey and afterwards. When the service was over everyone living within the Precincts kept open house for those in need of refreshment, and my Father collected and took back to our house several resplendent but exhausted people whose carri-ages had hopelessly gone astray.

At this Coronation my name, to the no small satisfaction of a twelve-year-old boy, had duly appeared in the list of guests printed at the end of the late Mr J. C. Bodley's rather pompous official history of the Coronation. In the 1911 Coronation records a search for it among the guests will be made in vain. I was then in my second year at Cambridge, and although I was still a resident within the Close, for some reason there was no official invitation for me. The Head Master's sons were in the same position as myself and great was our disappointment. However, if the truth must be told, on the day we were quietly passed into the Abbey by the Head Master as part of the procession of masters and boys. The obliging Gold Staff Officer on the door presumed, I suppose, that we were all Westminsters and asked no questions, with the result that once again I found myself looking down on the scene from the Triforium.

This time I saw considerably more of the ceremony. It was possible to move about the Triforium, and eventually my Father and I worked our way along and managed to insert ourselves at the back of the press box at the north corner of the lantern. There by skilful balancing and manoeuvring it was possible to see a good deal of what was happening in the theatre far beneath us. There was at least one unforgettable moment. The Queen, who had just been out of my sight during her actual Coronation, rose immediately after she was crowned and turning towards the royal gallery or box began to circle the theatre on her way to her throne. At the moment the space in the theatre both in front of the altar and before the royal gallery was empty. Quite suddenly the Queen glided slowly into sight, moving as only Queen Mary knew how to move, her beautiful crown flashing on her head, a sceptre upright in each hand, and her splendid train held up by her Maids and extended at full length behind her. For a moment or two the Queen, her two Bishops, and her Maids were the only people within my view. Looking down on it from above it would be difficult to imagine anything more lovely – the very perfection of movement and grace. So she passed to make her low obeisance to the King which unfortunately I could not see, before she took her seat on her throne.

Almost equally graceful was the procession of foreign princes and princesses before the service began. Led with great dignity by the Crown Prince and Princess of Germany they came up the Abbey hand in hand and with arms almost fully extended and slightly raised. It was extraordinarily effective and could only have been done by those who had been taught to move gracefully from childhood. It was noticeable that at this Coronation, unlike that of 1902, the voice of the Archbishop (Dr Davidson) could be heard quite plainly – these were the days before amplifiers – and that the four great shouts at the Recognition together with later acclamations were led by the Westminster boys and taken up by the whole congregation with splendid effect. It was also the first Coronation at which photographs were allowed to be taken during the actual service. Old Sir Benjamin Stone, an amateur photographer of some note at the time, was given special permission by the King to do so. He was hidden away in a little box behind the tomb of Aymer de Valence in the Sanctuary and although his photographs were taken under great difficulties they provide a valuable and unique record of the service.

There was one little incident connected with the sermon which is of Abbey interest. When the Archbishop of York (Dr Lang) was first invited to preach the sermon he let it be known that he proposed to go to the pulpit preceded by his Primatial Cross. It was pointed out to him however that although he attended the service by command as Archbishop of York, the Rubric in the Coronation Service merely said that the sermon was to be preached by 'one of the bishops' present, and that it was in that capacity and not as Archbishop of York that he had been selected to preach it. Such being the case and to mark the distinction (not to mention the fact that the Abbey was a Royal Peculiar and that the Archbishop was not in his own Province of York) the invariable Abbey custom ought to be followed by which a preacher in the Abbey went to the pulpit preceded by the Abbey Cross. The Archbishop was unconvinced, but as nothing more was said it was assumed that he would conform to Abbey custom. However when the time came it was seen that he was making his way to the pulpit preceded by his own cross. Whereupon one of the Abbey clergy, seizing the Abbey Cross, quietly stepped out and led the little procession, doubtless to its greater dignity and certainly to the upholding of ancient custom and precedent.

At the Coronation of King George VI in 1937 there was no question of my gate-crashing. By then I was Keeper of the Muniments and was appointed a Gold Staff Officer. As no one then at the Abbey, except Dr Perkins, knew much about coronations even from the Abbey point of view, it seemed to me that I ought to try to make myself an authority on the whole subject. Actually, of course, with the precedents of 1902 and 1911 to go upon those in charge of the arrangements had little cause to delve into the remoter past, and I was always conscious both then and again in 1953, that mere antiquarian knowledge could be both unhelpful and tiresome and that all one should be able to do was to answer with authority any specific points which might be put to one. At the same time there were certain Abbey rights which it was important should be preserved and on which a watchful eye could be kept.

There was considerable doubt, for instance, who ought to be in

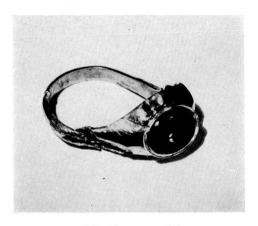

40   The Courtenay Ring.

41   The Essex Ring.

42   The Coronation Chair.

charge of the music at the Coronation, for although Sir Frederick Bridge, as Abbey Organist, had been in charge at the Coronations of King Edward VII and King George V, there were some who felt that Dr (now Sir) Ernest Bullock, the Abbey Organist, had not then sufficient experience and that Sir Walford Davies, as Master of the King's Musick, had a better claim. The Archbishop asked me to let him have a memorandum on the subject. In it I was able to show that although the Coronation Committee could recommend whom they pleased, subject to the sovereign's confirmation, the precedents showed that almost always the Abbey Organist was in charge. The result of my memorandum was that Dr Bullock was duly appointed with the proviso that he should take the Master of the King's Musick into consultation, and this seems to have settled the matter for the future.

I was also able to establish the right of the King's Scholars to take part in the Regalia Procession, and, for the first time, to have their right to acclaim Their Majesties 'in customary form' officially acknowledged in the Earl Marshal's printed 'Ceremonies to be Observed' at a Coronation.

Certain rights of the Dean and Chapter had inevitably (and rightly) shrunk in the process of time. It is a curious fact, however, that they still claim among other things the sovereign's robes together with the oblations and offerings, 'the Stage, Thrones, Royal Seats, Tapestry, Chairs, Cushions, Cloths and all the Ornaments with which the Stage and Church shall be embellished'; the blue cloth upon which the sovereign walks from the west door of the church to the stage; the poles which support the canopy with 'the four little bells that hang at each corner'; cloth for the robes of the Dean and Canons, and 'an hundred manchats, the third part of a Tun of Wine and Fish . . . for the said Dean and Chapter's Repast on the Coronation Day'. The Dean also claims to be 'the instructor of Our Sovereign' in the coronation ceremonies. These claims, which come down from remote times, are regularly sent[1] to the Court of Claims and are allowed by them with certain exceptions. They are now, however, largely commuted for a money payment to compensate for the losses which the Chapter funds sustain by having to close the Abbey during the preparations for the Coronation. But in the eighteenth century much of the furniture which had been used in the service was divided up into lots after a coronation and distributed among the Dean and Prebendaries. There is, too, a curious survival of these claims to this day in the actual coronation service. After the sovereign

[1] Until 1937 they were still sent both in English and in Norman French.

has offered the personal sword at the altar it has been the custom, certainly since the fourteenth century, for 'a great lord' to redeem it, or buy it back, for one hundred shillings in order to prevent it from becoming the property of the Abbey. These shillings are subsequently distributed among the Abbey personnel. In the eighteenth century, too, the nave and other parts of the Abbey were not required for official guests, and the gentlemen of the Choir and others were allowed by the Dean and Chapter, for a consideration, to erect stands and sell the seats to the highest bidders. Small wonder that Horace Walpole writing in 1761 should remark that 'the Prebends would like a Coronation every year'! Nowadays, of course, the whole of the Abbey is filled with invited guests, and merely a definite number of seats are allotted for the use of the Dean and Chapter and others officially connected with the Abbey.

In all such matters the Duke of Norfolk, as Earl Marshal, is the supreme arbiter, but he does not assume complete control of the Abbey until a day or so before the actual ceremony. Then, by one of the curiosities of English life, the leading Roman Catholic layman receives the keys of the Dean and of everyone else, and is supreme until the Coronation is over. Up to that time, as Dean Armitage Robinson was always very insistent, the Dean and Chapter remain the responsible and permanent guardians of the building and technically the Ministry of Works are only admitted to make the necessary arrangements. The distinction is, perhaps, a small one, for nowadays such care is taken of the fabric and the tombs that after the last Coronation, there was scarcely a scratch. But it was not so in the past and shocking damage, for instance, was done in the preparations for the Coronation of George IV in 1821.

The Dean is the principal assistant to the Archbishop during the actual service. In addition to other duties it is he who brings the various articles of the Regalia from the High Altar as they are required for the Investing, and it is from him that the Archbishop takes the Crown to place it upon the sovereign's head. To him, too, is delivered the Regalia on the day before the Coronation, and he is solely responsible for its care until, after being taken in procession on Coronation morning, it is handed over to the great Officers of State in the temporary annexe which is now erected for Coronations at the west door of the Abbey.

I remember being taken up on to the roof of the Deanery in 1902 to see the Regalia arrive in a state coach accompanied by an escort of household cavalry. Then, and again in 1911, the various objects were placed on the long table in Jerusalem, and the Dean having taken his seat at the head of it, those living within the Precincts were admitted and allowed to walk round the table. In 1937 the police, for some reason, were rather nervous about its progress from the Tower and in consequence the Regalia was brought down to the Abbey quietly and privately earlier in the day. The Dean, however, gave a small tea-party of about a dozen people to which he was kind enough to ask me. On this occasion we all sat round the walls of the Jerusalem Chamber, while the Yeomen Warders from the Tower stood behind our chairs – one to each side of the room except the fireplace side, with two more guarding the door and one standing by the table. A representative of Messrs Garrard's, the King's Silversmiths, then took each object out of its case and carried it round the room so that we were all able to see it really closely before he placed it on the table. It was intensely interesting to see the Regalia in this way and without any bars intervening. It was a very wonderful sight and I remember especially the flawless beauty of the Cullinan Diamond in the King's Sceptre and the Black Prince's Ruby in the Crown. I was amused, however, and somewhat disconcerted to notice that while this was going on the Warder immediately behind me was very imperfectly concealing a loaded revolver which he was holding beneath his tunic, and that all the others were similarly armed! Afterwards as we came out I chaffed the resident Governor of the Tower (Col. Faviell), who was a friend of mine, about this and pointed out to him that we were all supposed to be the Dean's personal friends. To which he very properly replied 'Yes, but it was the Regalia of England and I wasn't going to take any chances!' (Plates 36, 37).

There was in fact a curious incident connected with the Regalia at this Coronation which is referred to, but not quite accurately, in Archbishop Lang's *Life*. As it has been stated, the Dean is responsible for the safety of the Regalia while it is in his keeping and no one may remove any of it from Jerusalem without his express permission. On Coronation morning it is carried in procession by the Dean and the Abbey Clergy escorted by the King's Scholars of Westminster School, the Choir and the Children of the Chapel Royal, through the Cloisters to the High Altar and from there down to the Annexe. As the procession passed me in the Cloisters I had noticed with some surprise that the Sub Dean was carrying St Edward's Crown while the Dean was empty-handed. Afterwards he told me what had happened. As he was giving out the various objects to the clergy in Jerusalem he suddenly became aware to his consternation that the Imperial Crown was missing. All he could gather was that 'it had been sent for', but there was no time to make further inquiries for the Procession was due to start. As he said to me it was the worst ten minutes of his life for he had to go in procession without the slightest idea what had happened to the Crown for which he was responsible and it was less than two hours before the Coronation was due to begin! It was not until the procession reached St Edward's Chapel behind the High Altar that he found to his immense relief that the Crown had already been placed on the Altar. It appeared that some meddling official had blundered and had had it conveyed there without informing the Dean. It need not be said that steps were taken to prevent such a contretemps from ever happening again in the future, and the somewhat acrimonious subsequent correspondence relating to the incident was deposited among the Abbey Muniments (Plates 38, 39).

During the preparations for the Coronation I had had a 'pass' and this enabled me to go into the Abbey from time to time to see how things were progressing. I had also arranged for my friend the late Mr R. P. Howgrave-Graham, to be allowed to take photographs so that the Abbey should have a record of the progress of the work connected with the preparations. Quite early, indeed before the Ministry of Works came on the scene, it had been a great delight to see the two transepts completely empty of pews and chairs, and later, as the various stands were finished it was possible from them to have photographs taken of various details of the sculpture which are normally inaccessible. I was also in and out of the Muniment Room, for not all my documents had been evacuated, and sometimes found that rehearsals were going on below with various important persons trailing about in dust-sheets and suchlike to represent robes and using their bowler hats and umbrellas to represent coronets and swords. It was, however, at a Gold Staff Rehearsal in 1953 that the unforgettable sight was seen of the Duke of Norfolk standing on the steps of the throne in morning dress and wearing a coronet, with his Earl Marshal's Baton in one hand and a microphone in the other. Past and present could hardly have been more delightfully symbolized. All these weeks I was very busy writing articles, delivering nearly forty public lectures, and giving broadcasts on the religious significance of the ceremony, etc.

On the actual day I was in charge of the Library and part of the Muniment Room. For the first time use was made of the Library as one of the entrances to the Abbey and from an early hour my brother Gold Staffs and I were kept very busy passing people to their seats. As the door to the Cloisters could not be left unguarded

I worked out a scheme by which we all took quarter of an hour shifts on it. By this means those not on duty there were able to go up into the Muniment Room and see much of the ceremony provided that the next on duty punctually relieved the door-keeper whatever was happening during the service inside the Abbey. This worked out very well, although it was rather tragic to have to miss parts of the service. I had discovered a small vacant space in the gallery adjoining the Muniment Room and here I was able to place the stool which my Father had purchased after the 1911 Coronation. It was a perfect 'dress-circle' seat, for I was looking straight down on the theatre with the two thrones and the Coronation Chair in full view. Immediately below me in the same gallery was a solid mass of viscounts, while opposite and across the theatre were the peeresses both below and in the gallery above corresponding to that in which I was seated. It was a very curious sight for when they were all seated the crimson velvet of their robes could hardly be seen and they gave an impression of all being dressed alike in pearl grey and silver, a most lovely colour quite indescribable, while through them seemed to trickle streams of clearest water like little waterfalls due to the flashing of the diamonds, tiaras, and other jewels they were wearing. It had the most extraordinary effect and I noticed exactly the same thing in 1953.

I had made so close a study of the whole service, and knew, as one might say, every turn and twist of it and what had happened at previous coronations down the centuries, that it was completely absorbing to see the whole thing come to life before my eyes. It was, indeed, overwhelming, and this was partly due to the fact that both the King and Queen were so obviously under the stress of deep emotion that in some mysterious way it was communicated to the whole congregation. Archbishop Lang has noted the same thing and that 'the King (as many said afterwards) looked like a medieval knight awaiting his consecration with a wrapt expression in his eyes which turned neither to the right nor to left'. One of my outstanding memories is of him sitting thus completely motionless in the Coronation Chair before his anointing and while the Choir brought 'Zadok' to its triumphant close. So the service proceeded, no longer as Lytton Strachey wrote of Queen Victoria's Coronation 'like some machine of gigantic complexity which was a little out of order', but with every action falling inevitably into its place and charged with meaning and significance. Then came the great moment which no one who has been present at a Coronation can ever forget, when (to quote from my diary) 'the Archbishop, with the Dean on his left bearing the Crown, and the senior Bishops, were seen to be converging on the Coronation Chair amid a breathless silence. The Archbishop turned to the Dean and for a moment on taking the Crown he turned it in his hands first one way and then the other to make sure that he had it the right way. Then, after a superb' pause with the crown held steady as a rock above the King's head, he gently lowered it and 'reverently put it upon the King's head'. It was quite perfectly done.'

I just managed, as it happened, to see the crowning and then had to go down to the door. I quote again from my diary:

When I got back at 12.45 the Choir were singing the final Homage Anthem. When it was over the trumpets sounded a fanfare, the drums beat, and there came the three great shouts 'God Save King George' etc., real shouts this time with splendid effect. Thus ended the King's coronation. The scene at this moment was extraordinarily impressive and purely medieval. The King crowned and with his sceptres in his hands, sitting very still and upright on his Throne – every inch a king – surrounded by his Peers all wearing their coronets. The supporting Bishops on each side (I wished they had worn mitres), the king's sword and the three other swords to the King's right—a wonderful group. The Lord Chancellor (rather a figure of fun) with his coronet perched on the top of his wig and Mr Ramsay Macdonald were immediately behind the Throne. Lord Cork, with a good naval tilt to his coronet, bearing Curtana, and the Duke of Richmond completely squashed under the family ducal coronet which was of immense size. The Duke of Somerset just behind the Throne was a fine ducal figure . . . I had a look from the passage way under the clock where the effect of looking down on a solid mass of Peers all wearing their coronets was most extraordinary.

The Queen's coronation followed, where the outstanding memory, apart from the bearing of the Queen herself, was the supreme grace and dignity with which the Duchess of Northumberland, with the Percy lions embroidered on her long crimson train, moved about behind the Queen as her Mistress of the Robes. I missed the final Procession down the choir and nave as I was again on duty on the door.

We managed to get our people away fairly easily from the Muniment Room, but in other parts of the Abbey there was a long delay partly owing to the wet weather and partly owing to the carriage arrangements having broken down rather badly. A Peer told me an amusing story of something which happened during this delay. By some unforeseen combination of circumstances the clear voice of a Gold Staff Officer was suddenly heard coming over the loud-speakers with the remark 'The Earls have "hoofed" it, but the Barons are getting distinctly restive.'[1]

The Coronation of Queen Elizabeth II in 1953 by the marvels of modern science was able to be seen by so many millions of people either on television or on the films, that there is little to be said about it. Television was then comparatively new and it is curious now to remember that there were grave doubts whether or not permission should be given to televise the actual ceremony. So much so that in the early stages of the preparations a definite decision was given against it. It was not altogether surprising for it was not, I think, realized at first that it would be possible for it to be done within the Abbey without anyone knowing that it was taking place. We had had a not unamusing experience of television at the Abbey not long beforehand. It was desired to include a talk on Westminster Abbey in the ordinary evening programme, and the general idea was that the late Mr Richard Dimbleby should be conducted round the Abbey and shown the principal things in succession by the Dean, the Archdeacon (Dr Adam Fox) and myself. For this purpose on this particular evening, after the Abbey was closed, cameras, arc lamps, miles of cables, moving platforms for the cameras to follow us round, and much other paraphernalia made their appearance. Before the actual 'live' show we had a preliminary 'run through,' after which the producers came to the Dean and myself and said that they were very sorry but our bald heads were too like the monumental busts and that we should have to be made up! It was not therefore until we had been given pink cheeks and brown foreheads that we were allowed to appear.

Nothing, however, could have been more beautifully done or could have made a more profound or moving impression on all who saw it than the television of the actual Coronation ceremony.

At this Coronation I was again a Gold Staff Officer in charge of the Library, etc., and I watched the whole service from exactly the same spot and again seated on my 1911 Coronation Stool, as in 1937. In the earlier stages of the preparations I was able to give some small help on various points of the ritual and ceremony. The changes made by the Archbishop were not many, but they added greatly to the dignity and beauty of the service. For instance, the

---

[1] At the Coronation of Queen Elizabeth II in 1953, some hours after the Ceremony was over and most of those who had been present had returned to their homes and discarded their robes and uniforms, a solitary peer, in full robes and carrying his coronet, walked to St James's Park Station and took the underground to Sloane Square to the amusement of his fellow passengers!

presentation of the Orb was made a separate ceremony instead of being combined as formerly with the Investing with the Robe Royal. He also revived the ancient ceremony of the presentation of actual Bracelets. The Bracelets for some unknown reason, fell out of use in the coronation service in Stuart times, and Queen Elizabeth I is believed to have been the last sovereign who was invested with them. They are 'symbols and pledges of that bond which unites' the sovereign with her peoples. 'It was, therefore, peculiarly fitting that the new bracelets provided for the Coronation should have been presented by the Governments of the Commonwealth. Curiously enough the history and meaning of the Bracelets had got confused with the Armill or Stole and it was a great gain to disentangle their history and replace them in the service.

There were moments of extraordinary beauty in the actual service. No one who saw it could ever forget the mixture of grace, charm, dignity and humility with which the Queen bowed to the four corners of the theatre when she acknowledged the acclamations after she had been presented as 'Your undoubted Queen', or when she sat in the Coronation Chair, 'having been disrobed of her crimson robe', clothed in simple white, terribly alone, awaiting her anointing. Or later, again, when as the crowned Queen she received the homage of her husband and of the peers. One who was standing on the steps of the throne told me that he and those around him were so moved that they were almost in tears.

So much had happened in the world since the 1937 Coronation that it seemed to be more than ever necessary to insist on the religious significance and symbolism of the service and on its curious relevance in a rapidly changing world. With this in mind I wrote a book on the *History of the Coronation* which had a wide circulation, besides numerous articles for the more important daily and weekly papers on the service, the ceremonial, the regalia, the coronation church, etc. I also delivered about fifty lectures, besides home and overseas broadcasts, in which I tried to emphasize that the pageantry was merely the setting and was subordinate to the real significance of the service. It was all very strenuous and interesting and in the event, as one had hoped, it was exactly that aspect of the Coronation which made such a profound impression not only on the nation but on the world.

43 The North Front of Westminster Abbey. Painted (c. 1734–40) apparently to show the effect of a spire, etc., on the Abbey. This interesting topographical picture was found by the author at Toynbee Hall.

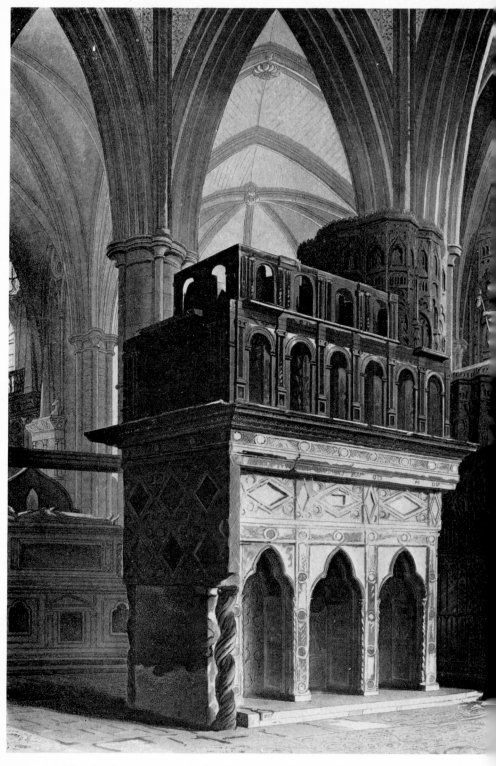

44 The Shrine of Edward the Confessor. From Ackermann's *History of Westminster Abbey* (1812).

45 The Urn in Henry VII's Chapel. Said to contain the bones of the Princes in the Tower.

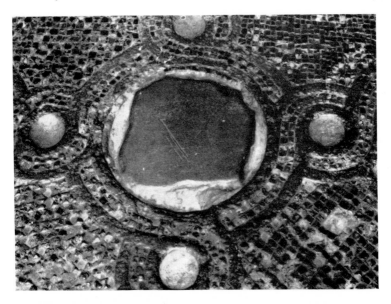

46 Relic Stone on Cosmati tomb in the South Ambulatory.

47   The interior of the Abbey after cleaning.

CHAPTER XIII

The Princes in the Tower

The Sarcophagus in Henry VII's Chapel–Opening of the
Urn–Historical Investigation–The Ages of the Princes–
Anatomical Investigation–Features of the Skulls–Historical
Evidence

In the north aisle of Henry VII's Chapel, near the tombs of two little
daughters of King James I and in a place aptly called by Dean
Stanley 'The Innocents' Corner', there is a white marble monument
supporting an urn or sarcophagus (Plate 45), designed by Sir Christopher Wren at the command of King Charles II. In the urn, which
measures about 29 inches long by 14½ inches high, there were alleged
to be deposited certain bones found in the Tower of London in 1674,
which the King was convinced 'by the most certain indications' (as
the epitaph states) were those of the Princes murdered in the Tower
(Edward V and his brother Richard, Duke of York). But the mystery
which has always surrounded their fate had also extended to the urn
in the Abbey. More than once it had been alleged either that the urn
was empty or that the bones therein were those of animals and were
not human bones at all. It was to settle those questions and also to
see, should they prove to be human bones, whether or not modern
medical science could deduce anything from them, that in July 1933 the
Dean of Westminster (Dr Foxley Norris) determined, although not
without considerable hesitation, to have the urn opened. He was
induced to do so by strong representations made by the late Lord
Moynihan, the well-known surgeon, and by other responsible
persons. As I am now the only person living who actually handled
the bones, it may, perhaps, be of interest to state what we found,
and the deductions which were drawn by us from our discoveries.

Some notes I made at the time tell the story of the actual opening:

July 6th 1933. Today at 9 a.m. the following assembled in the N. Aisle of
Henry VII's Chapel: The Dean, Sir Edward Knapp-Fisher (Chapter

Clerk), myself, Lord Moynihan, Professor William Wright (President of the Anatomical Society of Gt. Britain), Mr Aymer Valence F.S.A., the Dean's Verger (G. Drake), the Clerk of the Works (W. Bishop), Walter Wright (Asst. Clerk of the Works) Dr Jupe (photographer) and three of the Abbey Workmen.

The Urn containing the supposed bones of Edward V and his brother had been opened the evening before by the Clerk of the Works, and the top or lid was now supported by wooden blocks and the whole covered with a white sheet. A small temporary platform had been erected in front of it, and a table covered with a white tablecloth had been placed by Queen Elizabeth's tomb.

By Mr Dean's direction the sheet was removed and the Urn was seen to be full of bones. Professor Wright took these bones carefully out and placed them on a tray held by myself. The first removed was a skull which he handed to me and which I placed carefully and reverently on the table. The bones were transferred from the tray to the table until most of the table was covered by them.

It at once became apparent that these bones were those of two children of about the right age for the Princes. Parts of two skulls, two jawbones, two thigh bones were seen to be there and the thigh bones when placed side by side showed that one was slightly longer than the other. As the bones were placed on the table Lord Moynihan arranged them into groups.

A number of animal bones were found mixed up with the human bones and also one or two rusty nails. In view of these discoveries it was felt that the matter ought to be pursued further and a thorough examination made of the bones. It was decided therefore to close the Chapel for a few days so that Professor Wright could work there undisturbed, and the Dean asked me to exercise a general supervision over the proceedings.

Thus began an extraordinarily fascinating investigation which aroused considerable public interest.[1] There were in fact two sides to the investigation; the historical side, which was entrusted to myself; and the anatomical, which at Lord Moynihan's suggestion was entrusted to Professor William Wright, D.SC., F.R.C.S., F.S.A., of the London Hospital Medical College. Professor Wright, who was widely known as a distinguished anatomist, was at that time President of the Anatomical Society of Great Britain and Ireland. He was assisted throughout the investigation by Dr George Northcroft, O.B.E., a dental surgeon of wide experience especially in the dentition of

---

[1] For a full account, and the sources from which the quotations in this chapter are taken see, *Archaeologia*, Vol. XXXIV (1935), pp. 1–26, 'Recent investigations regarding the Fate of the Princes in the Tower' by L. E. Tanner and William Wright.

children, who was the immediate past President of the British Dental Association. Professor Wright and myself agreed that to some extent we would work independently and only compare our results when we had completed our investigations.

The first question I had to determine was the exact age of the Princes at the presumed date of the murder, August 1483. There was no doubt about the elder Prince, Edward V. It was known that he was born while his mother was in sanctuary at Westminster in 1470, but the precise day and month were unknown and unfortunately there is no reference to the event among the Abbey Muniments. An entry in the Patent Roll for 1472, however, recorded the retrospective grant to the Prince of the issues from the Duchy of Cornwall from Michaelmas 1470 to the 2nd November following 'on which day he was born'. In August 1483, therefore, he would have been twelve years and nine months old.

The age of the younger Prince was more difficult. The commonly accepted date of his birth, 17th August 1472, was impossible, for on investigation it was quite certain that his sister, Princess Margaret, was born on 10th April of that year. It was known, however, that in the following August (1473) both the King and Queen were at Shrewsbury. I was fortunate in having my attention drawn to an entry in a chronicle preserved at Shrewsbury which, although not contemporary, appeared to be based on local tradition. This chronicle definitely stated that 'this yeare (i.e. 1473) the ducke of Yorcke was borne in the blacke friars within the towne of Shrewsbury'. This seemed fairly conclusive and it was confirmed by a contemporary document, dated 3rd September 1473, then in the possession of Mr W. Westley Manning but since bequeathed by him to the Abbey. In this document Chester Herald acknowledged a gift from the Duke of Burgundy 'en ce present mois de septembre' when he had carried letters to the Duke from King Edward IV informing him of the birth of his second son. The younger Prince would have been, therefore, within a few days of his tenth birthday in August 1483.

When I told Professor Wright my results on these points he told me that from the evidence of the bones and particularly from the teeth he and Dr Northcroft had independently come to the conclusion that the age of the elder child was 'somewhere between the ages of twelve and thirteen' (Edward V was twelve years and nine months in August 1483), and the age of the younger child was 'about mid-way between nine and eleven' (the younger Prince was in fact within a few days of his tenth birthday). So far, then, we had reached the interesting and exciting conclusion that the bones in the

Abbey were those of two children of approximately the age of the Princes at the presumed date of the murder. It followed, therefore, that if, as some people think, the murder took place not in 1483 but some years later, then the Princes would have been too old for these bones to have belonged to them. In other words, if the murder took place in the reign of Richard III (1483–85) then our bones might have been those of the Princes, but they could not have been so if the murder took place in the reign of Henry VII (1485–1509).

But Professor Wright was able to tell me a good deal more than this. On the facial skeleton of the elder child there was an extensive red-brown stain. The wavy character of its margin seemed to show it was of fluid origin. Professor Wright had no doubt that it was a blood stain such as would have been caused by suffocation which 'is well known to be associated with intense congestion of the face'. The traditional account of the murder of the Princes states that they were suffocated under featherbed and pillows kept down by force 'hard unto their mouthes'. The elder child, then, had probably met with a violent death. Unfortunately the corresponding part of the facial skeleton of the younger child was missing so that it was not possible to know if there was a similar stain on it. Several other bones, especially of the younger child, were also missing. We know that after the bones were found in 1674 some at least were given away and others were scattered by the workmen who did not at first realize their importance. An eyewitness states that they 'cast the rubbish and them away together, wherefore they were caused to sift the rubbish, and by that means preserved all the bones'. Incidentally this may account for the animal bones which we found mixed up with the other bones in the urn although it is odd that these were not recognized as such at the time of the discovery.

Professor Wright's deductions on these points are so interesting that they may be quoted in full:

As to what happened after their death no one now can say, but I imagine that when placed in the elm chest in which they were found, Edward[1] lay at the bottom on his back with possibly a slight tilt to his left, that Richard lay above him face to face, and that when the chest was discovered in the

---

[1] It will be noted that Professor Wright for convenience assumed that the bones were those of 'Edward' and 'Richard'. This was, perhaps, unfortunate for it has led some people to suppose that we definitely identified the bones with those of the Princes. No such claim was made, and I was, in fact, particularly careful in the Paper which we read before the Society of Antiquaries to make no such identification, and to adopt a cautious and 'not proven' attitude throughout.

seventeenth century the workmen broke into it from above and near its middle. I am led to these conclusions from the fact that much more of Edward's skeleton is present than that of Richard's, since presumably lying deeper it was less disturbed, and from the fact that the extreme upper and lower portions (viz. the head and feet) of Edward's skeleton are so well preserved. The singular fact that of the atypical ribs no less than six should had been found, and that of these six, three were of the left side and belonged to Edward's skeleton, three of the right side and belonged to Richard's, and that similarly only the left clavicle of Edward and the right clavicle of Richard were present, strongly suggests that the left shoulder of Edward must have been in close contact with the right shoulder of Richard, as would have been the case had they lain face to face.

When we first opened the urn Lord Moynihan, who was putting the bones in order on the table, was immediately struck by something he saw in the formation of the skulls which suggested to him that the children were closely related. This point was subsequently taken up by Professor Wright and by Dr Northcroft, who on a further and more detailed examination noted certain peculiar features which were present in the skulls and jaws of both children and seemed 'of no small significance' as evidence of consanguinity between them. Dr Northcroft was able further to tell us that the elder child had quite definitely suffered from chronic toothache and that the disease was so extensive that it must seriously have affected his general health. Professor Wright also noted that the elder child's tear duct was abnormally enlarged.

So far, then, we had established that the bones in the urn were human bones, that they were the bones of children of approximately the ages of the Princes at the presumed date of the murder, that these children appeared to have been related to each other, and that one of them, as it would seem, had died a violent death. Furthermore there was no doubt that these bones had been found under a staircase at the Tower of London in 1674, and it is at least curious that the only account we have of the murder, whether we are prepared to accept it as based on truth or not, does in fact say that the murderers buried the Princes 'at the stayre foote, metely depe in the grounde under a great heape of stones'.

All this does not necessarily prove that the bones in the Abbey are those of the Princes, but it is at least legitimate to suggest that the evidence given above should not be disregarded but should be carefully weighed by those who attempt to solve this fascinating mystery. It is unfortunate that many of those who write so confidently about a subject which all serious historians admit is an extremely difficult and obscure one should too often have inadequate historical knowledge of the period and should impart into their writings a heat – one might almost say a virulence – which does nothing to elucidate the problem. No one now accepts the widespread partisan view which was taken of Richard III in Tudor times and was popularized by Shakespeare. It is generally recognized that his character was an extraordinarily complex one in which both good and bad were curiously mixed. Horace Walpole in his *Historic Doubts*, and on a more serious level the late Sir Clements Markham in his biography of Richard III, did well to clear Richard of many of the accusations which had been made against him. But Walpole never claimed to be more than a dilettante, and Sir Clements, although he took immense trouble over his book, was not a trained historian. Anyone who knew Sir Clements, and I knew him well and was much attached to him, would agree with the verdict of the *Dictionary of National Biography* which says of him that 'although assiduous in consulting authorities, he often accepted their data uncritically, for he was in all things an enthusiast rather than a scholar'. In view of this and of modern research it is exceedingly dangerous to accept his book, interesting as it is, as a first-class authority.

This fact is well known to historians, but in spite of this many who have plunged into the fray have based their arguments upon it, including the late Miss Josephine Tey who wrote a widely read and exceedingly plausible novel, *The Daughter of Time* (1951) on the mystery. By an ingenious device she imagined a modern detective lying in hospital and relieving his boredom by turning his mind to unravelling the mystery of the Princes. Step by step and with much parade of historical research Richard III is exonerated and the crime is inexorably brought home to Henry VII – which, incidentally, had been Markham's theory. The book is written with considerable ability, but unfortunately many of the 'discoveries' which seemed so convincing to Miss Tey's detective were known and had been taken into account by serious historians. The evidence of the bones in the Abbey, which one might have supposed would have appealed to a modern detective, if only to disprove its value, is not even mentioned.

Our investigations as to what could be deduced from the Abbey bones themselves had led us to certain definite conclusions, but it seemed necessary to probe a little deeper into the historical side of the question in order to see how far these conclusions were in agreement with the available evidence of the manner in which the murder was carried out and the date when it was commonly alleged to have taken place. Here it is inevitable that we should enter on controversial ground.

The crux of the matter is, of course, the amount of credit which should be attached to Sir Thomas More's *History of King Richard the Third*, which was written some thirty years after the death of Richard III and contains what purports to be a detailed account of the murder of the Princes. The *History* of which there are both Latin and English versions, was left unfinished. Neither version is a translation of the other, but it is now generally agreed that both were written by Sir Thomas More, and that he was at work on them between 1514 and 1518. The English version alone contains the account of the murder.

More was born either in 1477 or 1478. As a boy he was brought up in the household of Cardinal Morton (d. 1500), who was struck by his intellectual alertness and prophesied that he would prove 'a marvellous man'. The supposition is that More derived much of the information embodied in his *History* from the Cardinal, who had been deeply implicated in the plots which led to Richard III's defeat and death on Bosworth Field in 1485. More himself was only a boy when Richard died, and therefore, as the late Professor Pollard wrote,[1] his book as history 'stands or falls by the value of its oral information'. There are many who would dismiss this information as mere biassed hearsay but, while no doubt More relied largely on what Morton had told him, it is often forgotten, as Pollard has shown, that when he wrote there were many still alive and well known to More who had played a prominent part in the events of the reign of Richard III, and who would have been able to give what, to More, would have been a first-hand account of scenes in which they had taken part.

At the same time it cannot be denied that judged by modern standards the *History* leaves much to be desired. More never names the authorities for his statements, he does not scruple, after the pattern of classical historians, to put speeches into the mouths of his characters, and he gives the false impression that he was writing as if he was contemporary with the events which he records. Above all the *History* is obviously biassed in the sense that he was reflecting the intensely hostile view of Richard III as it had been held by Morton, and was still held by many of his friends. But More had considerable independence of mind, as a judge he was accustomed

---

[1] *Historical Essays in Honour of James Tait* (Manchester, 1933), pp. 223–38.

to weigh evidence, and by 1514 when he wrote the *History* he was not likely slavishly to follow the current Court opinion of Richard III unless he had convinced himself that it had at least some foundation in fact.

It is not, however, the *History* as a whole which concerns us here, but the extraordinarily vivid and apparently circumstantial account which he gives of the actual murder of the Princes. How far, if at all, can this be trusted? On this the older generation of historians are agreed. Sir James Ramsay, for instance, called it 'an uncritical narrative' but 'believed it to rest on substantial fact'; Dr Gairdner thought that it 'must bear some resemblance to the truth', and these views have the support of Sir Charles Oman, Professor Pollard, Mr C. L. Kingsford, Dr Busch and others.

Mr P. M. Kendall, however, in his authoritative *Richard the Third* (1956) will have none of this. In an Appendix on 'Who murdered the little Princes?' (pp. 392–418) he submits More's narrative to a devastating criticism and he considers that it 'is manifestly discredited by the circumstances of its origin, by its inaccuracies and incongruities' etc. But Mr Kendall was writing before the publication of the Yale Edition of the *Complete Works of St Thomas More* (1963). In this edition the Editor, Professor R. S. Sylvester, re-examines the *History of King Richard III* with great thoroughness and scholarship, and in his valuable Introduction and Commentary[1] goes some way to re-habilitate More as an historian. Of the murder he writes, 'Any consideration of the essential truth or falsity of More's account must deal with the immense amount of specific detail (names, places, etc.) that he introduces into it. In this he is far removed from most other contemporary narrators, who for the most part merely adduce rumours.'

More, himself, was well aware of these conflicting rumours. He prefaces his account by saying 'I shall rehearse you the dolorous end of those babes, not after euery way that I haue heard, but after that way yt I haue so heard by suche men & by such meanes, as me thinketh it wer hard but it should be true' and he ends by saying, 'thus . . . I haue learned of them that much knew and litle cause had to lye . . .'. These two statements coming from a man of the character and integrity of Sir Thomas More cannot, I think, be lightly disregarded. No one, probably, will ever know what exactly happened within the walls of the Tower, but they seem to show that More himself, whatever source or sources he was drawing upon, believed

---

[1] I am much indebted to this Introduction for what is said about More in the preceding paragraphs above.

THE PRINCES IN THE TOWER

that his account, although as was his wont he cast it into narrative form, was nearer the truth, and certainly more detailed, than any other which he had heard.

But whether More's account is to be accepted or not is of less importance, from the point of view of our investigation of the bones, than when the murder actually took place. It became necessary, therefore, to re-investigate the evidence for the usually accepted date, which is somewhere in the summer of 1483.

Sir James Ramsay, in his *Lancaster and York*,[1] went into this question fully. From four practically contemporary sources he was led to place the date of the murder between the end of July and the end of September 1483 – the most probable dates being between 7th August and 15th August when Richard III was at Warwick, from which place More states that Sir James Tyrell was despatched to the Tower to carry out the murder. These dates would fit in with other evidence. Lord Hastings, a staunch adherent of the late King, Edward IV, had made no secret of his fears for the safety of the young Edward V. On 13th June of that year at a council meeting at the Tower Richard accused him of treason and he was immediately led out and executed.[2] Three days later the little Duke of York was sent to join his brother in the Tower. *The Great Chronicle of London*[3] states that not long after the execution of Hastings the Princes who had been seen 'shooting and playing in the garden of the Tower' were 'holden more straight'. Mancini,[4] who was a foreigner in England at the time, writing in December 1483, also reports that 'after Hastings was removed, all the attendants who had waited upon Edward V were debarred access to him. He and his brother were withdrawn into the inner apartments of the Tower proper, and day by day began to be seen more rarely behind the bars and windows, till at length they ceased to appear altogether'. He adds, 'I have seen many men burst forth into tears and lamentations when mention was made of him (i.e. Edward V) after his removal from men's sight; and already there was a suspicion that he had been done away with'. Neither the reference in the *Chronicle* nor the statement in Mancini were known to Ramsay, for they had not been published at the time he wrote, and the quotation from Mancini has the additional

[1] Vol. II, Appendix pp. 510–14.

[2] Markham and Miss Tey state that he was executed a week later, after a regular trial, but the *Inquisitio Post Mortem* made by Richard's officials, states definitely that he was executed on 13th June.

[3] Edited by A. H. Thomas and I. D. Thornley (London 1938).

[4] Dominic Mancini, *The Usurpation of Richard III*, ed. by C. A. J. Armstrong (Oxford 1936), pp. 113–15.

interest that it is the last known contemporary reference to the Princes before they disappeared.

At the end of July 1483, too, the Duke of Buckingham, who up to that time had been high in the trust of Richard III and was on progress with him through the kingdom, suddenly and for unexplained reasons left the King at Gloucester and set out for his castle at Brecknock where he had Cardinal Morton in his custody. He and his prisoner became very friendly and during August and September they began to plot that Richard should be deposed and that Richmond (the future Henry VII), who was then in exile, should marry a sister of the Princes. It is known that this project had the secret approval of the two mothers, the Lady Margaret (then Lady Stanley) and the Queen Dowager. They were in touch with the conspirators through the agency of Reynold Bray, 'the most faithful servant' of the Lady Margaret and her husband Lord Stanley, and Bray is known to have visited Brecknock at Morton's invitation early in September. Suddenly at the end of the month a message was sent to Richmond by the conspirators suggesting that he should land in Wales, join in a rising with Buckingham, depose Richard, and claim the crown. Now whatever Buckingham and Morton, both marooned at Brecknock, may have suspected they could hardly have made this suggestion if the rightful King, Edward V, was still alive, and the supposition is that before sending this message they must have had definite information from someone they trusted that the Princes were dead.

As a matter of fact the rising led by Buckingham when it came in October was a failure and was completely crushed by Richard. Buckingham was caught and executed. Richmond, who had set out with the intention of raising his standard in the western counties, as soon as he learnt that Richard had already reached Exeter without opposition, sailed back to Brittany without having set foot in England. But if the rising had failed it had, at least disclosed widespread disaffection.

There is not the slightest doubt that from this time onwards ugly rumours began to circulate both at home and abroad. Richard must have known of them. He had been personally popular, and he never entirely lost his popularity especially in the provinces, but he could hardly fail to notice, as Mancini tells us – and coming from a foreigner who was in London at the time it is very significant – that 'when he exhibited himself through the streets of the city he was scarcely watched by anybody'. He could have scotched the rumours at once by producing the Princes, just as Henry VII in 1487 produced the real Earl of Warwick from the Tower and paraded him through the streets to confute Lambert Simnel's claim to be that nobleman. He did not do so. As Professor Pollard pointed out, 'Richard III neither denied nor attempted to disprove the fact of their death; he put the blame on no one else and he made no pretence that they had escaped'.

In the Act of Attainder against Richard III passed in the first year of the reign of Henry VII reference is made among the charges to the 'unnatural mischievous and great perjuries, treasons, homicides and murders, in shedding of Infants blood . . . committed and done by Richard'. This, at least, is suggestive, for to what can the 'shedding of Infants blood' refer unless it is to the Princes?

On 18th January 1486 Henry married Elizabeth, the sister of Edward V, with the avowed object of uniting the Houses of Lancaster and York. To liquidate her two brothers a few months after the marriage (between 16th June and 6th July 1486 as Markham argued) so that his wife should be the unquestioned representative of the House of York, would not seem to be the happiest foundation even for a dynastic marriage and, if he did so, it is difficult to see how Henry was able to suppress any rumours of such a crime having taken place. There are, however, no hints of any such rumours and, although Henry had many enemies, none of his contemporaries seem ever to have suggested it. Ten years later, in 1496, Giovanni de Bebulcho was probably expressing the common view when in writing to the Duke of Milan he reported that the Florentine, Aldo Brandini, had told him privately that Henry VII was feared and disliked by the people and 'if fortune allowed some Lord of the blood royal to rise and he (Henry VII) had to take the field, he would fare badly owing to his avarice; his people would abandon him. They would treat him as they did King Richard, whom they abandoned taking the other side because he put to death his nephews to whom the kingdom belonged'.

The mystery of the Princes in the Tower remains and, perhaps, will always remain, unsolved. One of the few certain facts is that the bones now in the urn in Henry VII's Chapel, whether they be the bones of the Princes or not, were found within the walls of the Tower, and it would be a strange coincidence if two other children of the approximate ages of the Princes were also buried there. At the time of the examination of the bones, after reviewing with great care all the available evidence, I came to the conclusion that there was 'at least a reasonable probability that the traditional story of the murder, as told by More, was in its main outlines true', and that it took place in August 1483. Professor Wright, from an examination of the bones, stated at the same time that from a medical point of view there was nothing to prevent these bones from being those of the Princes and that the evidence in favour of it was 'definitely more conclusive than could, considering everything, have reasonably been expected'. Further than that neither of us would go.

*   *   *   *   *   *

Since the publication of our Paper in *Archaeologia* in 1935 three important contributions to this fascinating problem which have been made by responsible historians should be mentioned.

(1) As has been mentioned above Mr P. M. Kendall in his *Richard III* totally discards the traditional story as told by More, but he seems to have little doubt that the Princes were murdered during the reign of Richard III. As he puts it: 'The most powerful indictment of Richard is the plain and massive fact that the Princes disappeared from view after he assumed the throne and were never again reported to have been seen alive' (p. 410). With regard to the bones Mr Kendall thought it 'very probable that these are indeed the skeletons of the Princes', but before coming to this conclusion he submitted the anatomical and dental evidence set forth in our Paper to Dr W. M. Krogman, Professor of Physical Anthropology in the Graduate School of Medicine of the University of Pennsylvania, Dr Arthur Lewis, Orthodontist, of Dayton, Ohio, Professor Bertram S. Kraus of the Department of Anthropology, the University of Arizona, and to an English doctor, Dr Richard Lyne-Pirkis of Godalming, Surrey.

They were of the opinion (a) that it was not possible to determine the sex of either child (b) that the stain on the jawbone was 'not a bloodstain resulting from the suffusion of suffocation', and (c) that the precise ages of the children, as estimated by Professor Wright and Dr Northcroft, were open to doubt although they agreed that in spite of this, if the bones were really those of the Princes, both children were still young enough to have met their death as historically stated i.e. in August 1483 (pp. 497–8).

The opinions of these experts cannot, of course, be disregarded, but it should not be forgotten that Professor Wright, Dr Northcroft, and Lord Moynihan had had the advantage of examining the actual bones, and that they were eminently qualified to give their opinion on them.

(2) In 1954 Professor A. R. Myers wrote an exceedingly interesting

article on 'The Character of Richard III' (*History Today*, August 1954). This, in Mr Kendall's opinion, offers 'the best concise discussion of the sources available for an estimate of Richard's career and the essential qualities of his character (p. 433 n.). In this article Professor Myers refers to the bones and states that he asked Professor R. G. Harrison, Derby Professor or Anatomy in the University of Liverpool, to evaluate the medical evidence as given in our Paper. As a result of this Professor Myers says: 'In spite of some difficulties in the evidence which he (Professor Wright) did not discuss, he appears to be correct in his conclusion that the bones were consistent with the sizes and ages of the two princes in 1483.'

(3) Finally, the late Mr Geoffrey H. White, O.B.E., F.S.A., the learned editor of the *Complete Peerage*, in a most important Appendix (J) to Vol. XII, Pt II 'The Princes in the Tower' (pp. 32–9), sums up the reasons for attributing the murder of the Princes (a) to Richard III or (b) to Henry VII and remarks that 'a strong case can be made out for either view if the arguments on the other side were ignored'. He also discusses very fully, impartially and fairly the evidence regarding the bones in the Abbey, and concludes, as indeed was the conclusion of Professor Wright and myself, that 'it seems necessary to record a verdict of "not proven".'

CHAPTER XIV

Problems and Discoveries

The Essex Ring – Caxton's First Printing Press – Death Masks at Islip – An Eighteenth-Century Picture – Lost 'Treasures' – The Cross of Edward the Confessor

In the course of a long life at the Abbey I have been continually surprised at the scope and variety of the problems, large and small, which I have been called upon either to solve or to elucidate. Some of these have involved considerable research, others have been straightforward and have presented little difficulty. Apart from queries concerning the muniments a large part of my correspondence concerned the monuments and interments within the Abbey Church and Cloisters and the heraldry and genealogy connected with them. Some of these were not without humour; for instance, an American lady called Dux wrote to me recently to say that she had seen a large monument in Henry VII's Chapel and that as the inscription on it contained her rather unusual surname she wondered if it was connected with her family. After some thought, and by a process of elimination, I came to the conclusion that what she must have seen were the words 'Antonius Phillippus, Dux de Montpensier' on the monument to the Duc de Montpensier who died while an exile in England in 1807. He was the brother of Louis Philippe, afterwards King of France.

The problems connected with the wax effigies, the urn alleged to contain the bones of the Princes in the Tower, and the position of the anchorite's cell have been already described, but one or two others come to mind which all presented points of interest.

In July 1927 the late Mr Ernest Makower presented to the Abbey the so-called 'Essex Ring' which he had bought at Christie's a few days previously, and I was present at a little ceremony by the tomb of Queen Elizabeth I when the ring was formally given into the keeping of the Dean and Chapter. The ring is a gold one set with a sardonyx cameo portrait of Queen Elizabeth (Plate 41). The inside is rather prettily enamelled with blue flowers (perhaps forget-me-nots) on a gold ground. It appears to have been made for a female finger and to have been subsequently enlarged. In view of the tragically romantic story attached to the ring it seemed to me to be necessary to investigate its history afresh and to try to see what truth, if any, lay behind it.

The traditional story is, briefly, that a ring was given by Queen Elizabeth I to her favourite, Robert Devereux, Earl of Essex, and that she told him to return it to her if he was ever in serious trouble and she would pardon him. When he was under sentence of death as a traitor it is said that he endeavoured to do so, and threw it out of a window to a boy begging him to take it to his friend and cousin, Lady Scrope, one of the Queen's Ladies. By mistake the boy took it to her sister, Lady Nottingham, who was one of Essex's bitterest enemies. Her husband forbade her to take any action, and Essex went to his execution on 25th February 1601.

This story first appears at length in a tract published in 1650 entitled *History of the most renowned Queen Elizabeth and her great Favourite, the Earl of Essex. In Two Parts. A Romance.* It was often re-issued and was widely accepted as true. Unfortunately it is full of such obvious historical errors that the late Sir Sidney Lee, in his article on Essex in the *Dictionary of National Biography*, had no hesitation in dismissing it as 'quite worthless as an historical authority' and, further, that in the absence of any contemporary evidence the whole story 'is quite apocryphal'. Most historians have been content to accept his conclusions.

But none the less it seems clear that very shortly after the execution of Essex there was some kind of story in circulation which connected a ring with the Queen and Essex. John Manningham, whose gossiping Diary covers the period January 1602 to April 1603, had been told that the Queen 'wore a ring, which the Earl of Essex gave her, unto the day of her death'. In this connection I was interested to see some years ago at Gorhambury a portrait belonging to Lord Verulam which was then traditionally said to be of Queen Elizabeth in which she is depicted wearing a ring which is pinned to her dress just above her heart. This ring, however, appears to be set with a precious stone and not with a cameo portrait.

Then, again, Clarendon, writing 'in his younger days' but before the publication of the tract in 1650, had heard that shortly after the execution of Essex upon 'the delivery of a Ring or Jewel by some

Lady of the Court, the Queen expressed much reluctancy for his death'. He dismisses it, however, as 'a loose report' which he himself did not believe. It is, of course, possible that the author of the tract may also have heard some such 'loose report' and writing nearly fifty years after the execution recklessly mixed fact with fiction.

It is curious, too, that Louis Aubery, Sieur du Maurier, in his *History of Holland* (1680), when writing of Prince Maurice (the brother of Prince Rupert of the Rhine), thought it worth while to retell the ring story in detail. He definitely states that it was told to his father by Prince Maurice himself, who had himself been told it by Sir Dudley Carleton, the well-known diplomat in the reign of James I.

Furthermore Lady Elizabeth Spelman, whose great grandfather, Sir Robert Cary, had been much about the Court at the time of Queen Elizabeth's death, added some further details, presumably based upon family tradition, including the picturesque story that when Lady Nottingham, on her deathbed, confessed to the Queen that she had kept back the ring, the Queen exclaimed 'God may forgive you, but I never can!' It has been pointed out, however, that Sir Robert Cary himself makes no mention of this story in his Memoirs, but it must be remembered that Lady Nottingham was Cary's sister and if some such scene really took place it is conceivable that he was unwilling to give currency to a story which redounded little to the credit of one who had been one of the Queen's most intimate and trusted friends.

Such then is the historical evidence, or lack of evidence, for the traditional story and, it must be admitted, that it rests on a very insecure foundation. Something of the kind may have happened, but, if so, the details seem to have got hopelessly distorted. It remained to see whether or not anything could be gathered from the ring itself and what was known about its history. It is unquestionably a genuine sixteenth-century ring, and it has a long family tradition behind it connecting it with Essex. This tradition states that after Essex was executed the ring was returned to his widow and was given by her to her daughter, Lady Frances Devereux, who married the 2nd Duke of Somerset. From her it was said to have descended from mother to daughter until it came into the possession of Lady Louisa Carteret who married, in 1733, Thomas (Thynne), Viscount Weymouth, and was the mother of the 1st Marquess of Bath. There is no doubt at all about the mother to daughter descent which can be easily proved through six generations to Lady Weymouth, but although I remember looking up the Wills of some of those to whom it was said to have belonged I could find no mention of the ring in any of them. This, although disappointing, did not necessarily disprove the traditional story, for it might well have been that the ring was a gift by the mother in her lifetime to her daughter.

The ring remained with the Thynnes at Longleat until it passed into the possession of the Revd Lord John Thynne, Sub Dean of Westminster, a son of the 2nd Marquess. It was shown by Lord John at a meeting of the Society of Antiquaries in 1858, with the traditional story attached to it, and was exhibited again at the Tudor Exhibition in 1890. On the death of Lord John's eldest son in 1910 it was sold and bought by the 1st Lord Michelham. When he died in 1927 it again came up for sale at Christie's, and was bought, as has been said, by the late Mr Makower and presented by him to the Abbey.

The traditional connection of the ring with Essex is strengthened, in a way, by the remarkable fact that there is preserved at Ham House a lock of hair, enclosed in a ruby ear-ring, which is said to have been cut from the head of Essex on the day of his execution. This ear-ring, like the ring, is known to have belonged to Essex's daughter, Frances, Duchess of Somerset, and there is at Helmingham a portrait of the Duchess by Van Dyck which shows her actually wearing the ear-ring.[1] The interesting thing is that the tradition in the Tollemache family is that it passed from mother to daughter, in exactly the same way as the ring, until it came into the possession of Lady Grace Carteret (the sister of Lady Louisa Carteret who brought the ring to the Thynnes), who married in 1729, Lionel (Tollemache) 4th Earl of Dysart.

There is, therefore, the double tradition passed down from generation to generation[2] in well-known families concerning both the ring and the ear-ring with its lock of hair, and there can, I think, be little doubt that both are genuine relics of Essex. We may, perhaps, go one step further and suggest that the ring with its cameo portrait of Queen Elizabeth may well have been given by the Queen to Essex when he was high in her favour. But the romantic story which was subsequently attached to it can be neither proved nor disproved.

Another problem which comes to mind concerned the exact place where William Caxton set up the first printing-press in England.

[1] E. D. H. Tollemache, *The Tollemaches of Helmingham and Ham*, where the portrait is reproduced as an illustration.

[2] Lord Bath told me in 1927 that the family had never had any doubt about the tradition.

It was known to have been in Westminster, and it was assumed that Caxton's well-known advertisement, issued about 1482–3, in which he bids his customers 'to come to Westminster to the Almonry at the sign of the Red Pale', settled the question, for the monastic Almonry was situated at the west end of the Abbey more or less at the east ends of the modern Victoria Street and Tothill Street.

Many years ago, however, my predecessor, Dr Scott, drew attention to a series of entries in the Sacrist's Account Rolls preserved in the Muniment Room which showed that at an earlier date, probably as early as September 1476, Caxton was already established in a shop not in the Almonry at the west end of the Abbey, but somewhere near the east end of the Abbey and Old Palace Yard. These entries showed that Caxton continued to rent this shop even after he had moved to the Almonry in 1482–3. The only clues as to its position were that it was somewhere near a large house known as St Albans and that there were two shops, one of which was rented by Caxton, which were described in the Accounts as being near or next to the Glasshouse. St Albans was roughly on the site of the green by Henry VII's Chapel whereon now stands the statue of King George V, but the site of the Glasshouse was unknown.

Thus the matter remained until 1954 when the Dean and Chapter, on the successful conclusion of the million pounds appeal for the upkeep of the Abbey, had the happy inspiration of erecting a tablet not only to commemorate Caxton's connection with the Abbey but, as the inscription on it states, 'the great assistance rendered to the Abbey Appeal Fund by the English-speaking Press throughout the world'. When the erection of this tablet was first suggested I was consulted as to a suitable site. It then occurred to me that it might be worth while to re-examine the entries in the Account Rolls and, more especially, to trace the subsequent history of the shop after Caxton's death in 1491–2, which had not previously been done. The result was unexpectedly rewarding. Caxton was succeeded in his shop by his assistant, Wynkyn de Worde, and shortly after Wynkyn moved to Fleet Street in 1499–1500, James Bookbynder, who had been living next door, added the Caxton shop to his own. It was interesting to find that the two shops, or rather the one shop, continued to be rented by a succession of 'bookbynders' until 1531–2, when the Sacrist's Account Rolls come to an end.

It was the 1508–9 Roll, however, which gave me the clue for which I had been hoping. In that Roll the reference to the glasshouse disappeared and thenceforth what was obviously the same shop was described in successive Rolls either as being 'next to the Chapter

House' or as 'lying next' or 'nigh to' the south door of the Abbey Church. As I wrote in a Paper which I read before the Bibliographical Society[1] in February 1956: 'We can say, then, with certainty, that the first printing-press was set up in 1476 in a house adjoining or close to the Chapter House, on the left hand side of the path leading to the south or Poets' Corner door, and that the shop was more or less associated with the production of books from that date until 1531–2.'

The tablet, therefore, was placed on the wall just outside the Poets' Corner door, and within a few feet of the site of Caxton's shop. It was unveiled on 12th November 1954 by Col. The Honble J. J. Astor, Chairman of the Press Council, at a ceremony attended by representatives of the newspaper and printing industries.

It may seem curious that Caxton should have set up his press in what, at first sight, would seem to be rather an obscure place within the monastic precinct. The clue, I think, is to be found in other entries in the Account Rolls which show that Caxton and his neighbours were in the habit of paying a small extra rent for permission to set up a stall or booth in front of their shops 'in the time of the Parliament'. It must be remembered that at that time the Lords sat in the Palace of Westminster while the Commons met either in the Chapter House or in the Refectory of the Monastery. Members going to and fro between the Palace and the Monastery would necessarily pass these booths, and they would be the kind of people who would be likely to buy the books which Caxton would display.

When Caxton moved to the Almonry in 1482 it was to premises to which was attached 'a certain chamber lately built over the Almoner's gate there'. This was a definite clue, and by a fortunate chance the house with the room over the gateway became in the sixteenth and seventeenth centuries the house leased to successive Masters of the Choristers of the Abbey. As such it was possible by a careful study of later leases and plans to determine its exact position. It was nearer to the west end of the Abbey than had been previously thought. It stood, in modern terms, exactly at the junction of Great Smith Street and Victoria Street where there is now a vacant space on ground belonging to the new offices of the Board of Trade. It might well provide an admirable site for a statue to the Father of English Printing.

Discoveries and problems were not only confined to Westminster. The Abbey at one time owned manors all over England and, as

[1] 'William Caxton's Houses at Westminster' (Transactions in *The Library*, 5th Series, Vol. XII, No. 3 (September 1957), pp. 153–66.

part of my work and as a pleasant object for holiday tours, I made it my business to try to visit as many as I could of the Abbey Livings or places which had in any way been formerly connected with Westminster. Several Easters before the War were spent at Malvern (where the Priory was a daughter-house of Westminster) with my friend John Carleton, the present Head Master of Westminster, but then an Assistant Master, who even as a boy at the School had shared to the full my Westminster interests. Together we visited the large number of churches connected with Westminster in the lovely Worcestershire country side. It was very interesting to see for oneself places, 'familiar in my mouth as household words' from the documents connected with them in my keeping in the Muniment Room – Deerhurst, Pershore, Longdon, Eckington, and the rest. Always there was the half-hope that we might find something of particular Westminster interest such, for instance, as the memorials and relics at Ruthin of Gabriel Goodman, the Elizabethan Dean of Westminster, or the monument, with his spurs hanging above it, of John Williams, Dean of Westminster and later Archbishop of York (d. 1650) in the tiny church of Llandegai, near Bangor, both of which we saw on another of these expeditions.

But the most curious and intriguing 'discovery' was at Islip, an Abbey Living, a few miles north of Oxford where I found two death masks fixed in the wall of the vestry of the parish church. One of them was slightly damaged, but they appeared to date from the seventeenth or early eighteenth centuries. No one could tell me anything about them, and there was no tradition to suggest whom they might represent. Death masks as a rule were only taken of distinguished persons, and to find these things in a small country church was most unusual and unexpected. The fact, however, that Islip had been intimately connected with the Abbey since the time of Edward the Confessor, who was born there, at once suggested to me a possible Westminster origin for the masks.

The most distinguished Rector of Islip was probably Dr Robert South (Prebendary of Westminster and Rector of Islip from 1678 to his death in 1716). He rebuilt the chancel at Islip and built the (old) Rectory there where he spent much of his time. He was the former pupil and life-long friend of Dr Busby, the famous Head Master of Westminster, and one of the executors of his will. He is generally thought to have been the 'favourite pupil' who appears in the well-known posthumous portrait of Busby by John Riley which hangs in the Hall of Christ Church, Oxford.

But a glance at South's face, with its snub nose, as carved on his monument in the Abbey showed that the death masks could not possibly be of him.

On the other hand we know from Anthony Wood that 'Busby never permitted his picture to be drawn. The moment he was dead his friends had a cast in plaster taken from his face and thence a drawing in crayons, from which White engraved his print, and Bird carved his image' on his monument. He does not say what became of the death mask.

Busby left no near relations, and South was a bachelor. It is, at least, not improbable that South, as Busby's executor, removed the death masks to the Rectory at Islip, and that from there they ultimately found their way into the parish church.

A discovery of rather a different kind may also be recorded. Some years ago several clues led me to Toynbee Hall in search of a large and interesting picture of the north front of Westminster Abbey painted c. 1734–40 and showing the houses which then stood right up against the Abbey but were almost always omitted in prints and drawings (Plate 43). The Warden was interested, but was quite sure that they had no such picture. But the Warden was mistaken for on looking round it was found to be hanging over the side-board in the main dining-room! It was subsequently bought for the Dean and Chapter by the late Lord Wakefield of Hythe, and now hangs in the Chapter Library. The sequel was curious. About a year or so later I went to stay at an hotel where I had never stayed before. Coming down to breakfast on the next morning I was astonished to see hanging on the wall, exactly opposite to my table, a picture of the north front of the Abbey evidently painted at the same time and by the same artist as the Toynbee Hall picture but from a slightly different angle. I suppose that I showed too much interest, for the proprietors, although willing to sell, put an exorbitant price on it, and it slipped through my fingers although I did manage to have it photographed. On my next visit I found a new proprietor and the picture had gone no one knew where. No doubt sooner or later it will turn up again, and we will hope at a more reasonable price.

I have often wondered what happened to much that is known to have once belonged to the medieval Abbey of Westminster. The relics and the almost incredible wealth of plate, etc., of the Monastery disappeared almost without trace at the Dissolution in 1540, and only the contemporary Inventories tell us what once was there. The splendid cloth-of-gold cope, chasuble, and chalice veil at Stonyhurst, the no less splendid fifteenth-century chasubles at Wardour Castle and at Ushaw College, Durham, and a few fragments elsewhere are apparently all that remain of the pre-Reformation vestments once at Westminster. The Litlyngton Missal and the *Liber Regalis* are still treasured possessions at the Abbey, and there are a few books and manuscripts in some of the larger libraries which can be identified as having come from monastic Westminster. Occasionally a Westminster charter or manuscript turns up in the sale room or in a private collection, and one or two of these it has been possible to buy back for the Abbey.

But not always. Soon after I became Keeper the late Mr John Burns, the former Labour leader and Cabinet Minister, came one day to the Library. He was well known as an enthusiastic collector of books on London, of which he had an extensive collection and it was he who coined the phrase 'liquid history' for the River Thames. On this occasion he produced from a despatch case one of the manuscript Indenture volumes bound in its original blue velvet, connected with the foundation of Henry VII's Chapel, remarking as he did so that he didn't suppose that I had ever seen anything like it before. Very gently I had to tell him that I knew these volumes well, and that several of them (I forbore to say the rest of the set) were among the muniments. Somewhat taken aback he replaced it in the case, and I have never seen it since.

This leads me to remark that wonderful as the Westminster Muniments are there is no doubt that the collection was once very much larger. Many documents were lost or destroyed at the Dissolution in 1540. When, for example, John Feckenham, the Abbot of the restored Monastery at Westminster in the reign of Queen Mary Tudor, was pleading before the House of Commons in 1555 for the retention of the ancient right of sanctuary at Westminster, he could only bring two charters with him to support his case, explaining 'that if he had not other charters than those to show, they would not thereby take advantage, but impute it to the iniquity of the times wherein they were perished, declaring how, as by a miracle, those (i.e. the two charters) were preserved, being found by a servant of my Lord Cardinal's (Pole) in a child's hand playing with them in the street'. Such losses were, perhaps, inevitable owing 'to the iniquity of the times' as Feckenham put it, but less excusable seems to be the fact that some of my predecessors were unable to resist the importunity of noblemen and others who wished to add a desirable manuscript to their private collections.

It was not only manuscripts. Some things have been given away, more or less deliberately by former Deans and Chapters. The pulpit which stood in the choir of the Abbey from 1775 to 1824 is now at

Trottiscliffe in Kent. It found its way there in 1824 because the then Abbey Architect and Surveyor, Benjamin Wyatt, happened to have a friend who lived in that parish. With its elaborate canopy supported by a single pillar in the form of a palm tree it fits somewhat incongruously and with difficulty into that charming little Norman Church. The dull little pulpit which Wyatt designed to replace it in the Abbey, together with other woodwork and the attractively carved wooden case which contained part of the Shrider Organ presented by George II to the Abbey for his Coronation, can now be found at Shoreham a few miles from Trottiscliffe. Shoreham is an Abbey Living and they were transferred there between 1847–51 by the then Vicar (Canon E. Repton) who was also a Prebendary of Westminster, when the present choir stalls, etc., were erected in the Abbey. Still more strange was the fate of the great classical altarpiece which stood in the Abbey from 1708 to 1820. It was originally designed by Grinling Gibbons and Arnold Quellin for the private Chapel of Queen Mary of Modena at Whitehall. After the dismantling of that Chapel, the altar-piece was given by Queen Anne, at the suggestion of Sir Christopher Wren, to the Abbey. In 1820 during the preparations for the Coronation of King George IV it was decided to remove the altar-piece in order to provide extra seating by the erection of a large gallery behind the high altar. After the Coronation it was not replaced. Part of the marble of which it was composed was sold, but the sculptured portions were given to a former Prebendary of Westminster, Bishop Walker King of Rochester, who erected some of the carved panels in the parish church of Burnham-on-Sea, a living which he held in commendam with his bishopric, and there they remain to this day.

These losses are well known, but I have often thought that there must be other, smaller, things which are either 'said to have come from Westminster Abbey' or lie unidentified in local museums, private collections, or antique shops. Two such may be mentioned which almost certainly exist and would be of great interest to find, although so far they have eluded every effort to locate them. In 1807 a stone capital, elaborately carved with small figures, was found embedded in a wall near the Abbey. It was carefully drawn and engraved at the time, and the broken inscription on it showed that two of the figures represented William Rufus and Gilbert Crispin, Abbot of Westminster (1085–1117), and that it had almost certainly come from the Norman Cloister of the Abbey. It was bought shortly after it was found by Sir Gregory Page Turner, a well-known connoisseur of the time for the somewhat large sum of one hundred guineas. Unfortunately this important Romanesque work of art, although it can hardly have been destroyed, seems to have completely disappeared and cannot now be traced.

The other object which has disappeared was a much more precious relic. At the time of the Coronation of James II in 1685 one of the workmen engaged 'in removing the scaffolds' after the ceremony accidentally made a hole in the coffin of Edward the Confessor. One of the Choirmen, hearing of this, climbed up on to the Shrine to investigate, and putting his hand through the hole drew out a gold cross and chain. The Dean, on being shown it, insisted that it should be presented to the King. This was accordingly done, and there is evidence that it was highly valued by the King who often showed it to those about the Court.[1]

It has often been said that the cross was finally lost during the King's flight to France in 1688. But this was not so. I was able to show that either before or after the King's death in 1701 it passed into the possession of the Queen, and that on her death in 1718 among the things which were sent to her son, Prince James (the Old Pretender) was 'a box containing a Cross and a Chain found in the tomb of St Edward in 1685'. Eleven years later Prince James writing from Rome on 17th June 1729 mentioned that on that day 'my son Charles Edward (the Young Pretender) . . . gave the Pope St Edward's Cross and Chain'.

In view of the fact that the presentation to Pope Benedict XIII was not previously known I suggested to Dean Labilliere that inquiries might be made through the Apostolic Delegate whether or not anything was known at the Vatican about the Cross. The Vatican authorities were much interested and made a thorough search for the Cross, but had to report that it was not 'in the Vatican Museum, nor in St Peter's, nor in the Vatican Galleries, nor in St John Lateran, nor with the Dominicans (of whose order was Pope Benedict XIII)'. They could only suggest either that the Pope gave it to some religious community or that on his death it passed into private hands.

There the matter rests. It may, and probably does, still exist, and if it should ever come to light it would be perfectly possible to identify it from the very full and detailed description of it which was given in a pamphlet published very soon after its discovery in 1685.

[1] The full story is given in a Paper I wrote on 'The Quest for the Cross of St Edward the Confessor', *Journal of the British Archaeological Association*, 3rd Series, Vol. XVII (1954), pp. 1–11.

CHAPTER XV

More Problems and Discoveries

The Burial Place of James I – An Unrecorded Burial – The
Position and original appearance of the Confessor's Shrine

It is just over a hundred years since Dean Stanley noted that there
was some uncertainty as to the exact place of burial of King James I
in the Abbey. The Abbey Register gave one place, but such other
records as existed were, as he put it 'provokingly vague', although
they all pointed to a vault somewhere in Henry VII's Chapel. The
Abbey Register stated quite clearly that the King was buried 'in
King Henry VII's vault', but this was not enough for Stanley. He
loved exploring and he persuaded himself that he must first eliminate
all other possible places by opening up each of the other Royal
vaults in turn.

There was not then the public curiosity which today surrounds
anything which takes place at the Abbey, and so night after night
the Dean with a few of the Abbey staff was able to carry out his
self-imposed task undisturbed. On one occasion the historian Froude
was present. Speaking of it afterwards he said: 'it was the weirdest
scene – the flaming torches, the banners waving from the draught
of air, and the Dean's keen eager face seen in profile had the very
strangest effect. He asked me to return with him the next night,
but my nerves had had quite enough of it.'[1]

Vault after vault was opened, and much valuable information was
obtained and recorded by the Dean.[2] He tells us of the deep impression made upon his mind when he opened the vault of Queen
Elizabeth I in the north aisle of the Chapel and saw that it contained

[1] Sir M. E. Grant Duff, *Notes from a Diary*, Vol. I, p. 235.
[2] A. P. Stanley, *Memorials of Westminster Abbey*, 5th ed. (1882), Appendix
pp. 499–526.

only the coffin of the great Queen actually resting on that of her half-sister Queen Mary I – 'partners of the same throne and grave, sleeping in the hope of resurrection'.[1] He contrasted it with the appalling sight which met his eyes when the corresponding vault in the south aisle was opened, and 'a vast pile of leaden coffins' in hopeless confusion was disclosed. Among them were those of Mary, Queen of Scots, Henry, Prince of Wales, Elizabeth of Bohemia ('the Winter Queen'), her son Prince Rupert of the Rhine, and mixed with these the tragically numerous progeny of James II and Queen Anne, none of whom survived infancy or childhood. A vault, as Stanley put it, containing 'the wreck and ruin of the Stuart dynasty'.

In 1934 I took the Crown Prince Rupprecht of Bavaria round the Abbey. As we stood above this vault I remember thinking how curious it was to be standing there with the man who had fought for the Germans in the 1914–18 War but whom many still regarded as the senior representative and rightful heir of the House of Stuart, while he discoursed on his Stuart ancestry, in which he took a deep interest.

At length the search for the coffin of James I drew to a close, and Stanley was able to write 'every conceivable space in the Chapel had now been explored, except the actual vault of Henry VII himself'. There, to the Dean's genuine surprise, if not, perhaps, to that of others, the missing coffin was found, and thus, as he wrote, 'curiously confirmed the accuracy of the Abbey Register'!

In 1943 Dean Labilliere, who shared something of the curiosity of his Victorian predecessor, became interested, for some reason which I have forgotten, in the Hanoverian vault under Henry VII's Chapel. This was the one vault which Stanley had not opened for it had presumably been made in the middle of the eighteenth century. One day the Dean told Canon Fox, Canon Don, Mr John Carleton and myself that he had had the entrance to the vault opened up and suggested that we should go and see it. The following is the account I wrote at the time:

The entry to the vault is immediately under the Font, thence descending by a broad flight of steps we found ourselves in a crypt of 4 bays obviously constructed not at the time of the building of the Chapel but in the 18th century, and this was borne out by a pencil inscription on one of the walls stating that it was begun in 1737. The crypt was perfectly dry, quite inoffensive and without smell, with clean white walls, and the vaulted roof was several feet above our heads. It reminded me of the vaulted arch

---

[1] So reads the inscription of the monument to Queen Elizabeth I.

and passage under the clock tower of the Horse Guards which was built a few years later.

At the extreme east end [of the vault] was an immense and rather fine black marble sarcophagus with bronze handles (rather like a medieval cope chest) which contained the coffins of George II and Queen Caroline. On the top in white marble were crossed sceptres, crown etc, and name plates. These appeared to be separate and were lying on the black marble lid of the sarcophagus. On each side were large boxes covered in leather presumably containing entrails, etc, and leaning against the east wall the 2 side planks from the 2 coffins removed in accordance with the King's instructions so that his remains and those of his wife should be mingled together.

In each of the bays were very magnificent coffins of the other Hanoverians covered in leather and velvet and with silver fittings. There were scarcely any signs of decay.

The scene was impressive, and it was interesting to see the coffins of Frederick, Prince of Wales ('Poor Fred'), and of 'Butcher' Cumberland (alone in the bay nearest the entrance). The sight of the latter was too much for the Scotch blood of [Canon] Alan Don who broke into vituperation and vilification to our amusement and the Dean's gently murmured 'De mortuis' etc.

The surprise was the spaciousness of the vault, the central aisle leading up to George II's sarcophagus being entirely empty, and the other coffins placed, as it were, in the three little side chapels on each side.

These were the last royal burials within the Abbey; almost all subsequent burials have taken place at Windsor. The names of all those buried in the Hanoverian vault are inscribed on the pavement of the Chapel above, but occasionally an unmarked grave (usually medieval) comes to light and sets a problem in identification.

One day in October 1953 I was in the Abbey with the Surveyor (Mr S. Dykes Bower) when we were met by the Clerk of the Works who greeted us with the words 'we have made a discovery'. He then produced from his pocket a gold ring, set with an oval ruby (Plate 40), which had just been found by an Abbey workman. A few days before, a small hole had been noticed at the edge of a Purbeck marble slab in the floor of the Confessor's Chapel. On probing this hole, and by the light of a torch, it was seen that there was quite a considerable cavity beneath this slab. As there was some danger of a subsidence the Surveyor had given orders that the slab should be carefully lifted. It was then that the ring was found some little way beneath the surface lying in loose earth together with two human leg bones.

The ring itself was certainly medieval. It was a little twisted, but the ruby was undamaged. It was set in the lid of a small hinged recess probably meant to contain a tiny relic. It opened perfectly easily.

Further investigation revealed the outline of a skeleton lying in a grave lined with Reigate stone and apparently extending almost to the foot of the steps of the north turret of Henry V's Chantry Chapel.

The identity of this skeleton was a puzzle. There was no record of anyone having been buried in this place. The only two persons definitely recorded to have been buried beneath the floor of the Confessor's Chapel were John de Waltham, Bishop of Salisbury (d. 1395) and Thomas of Woodstock (d. 1397) the youngest son of Edward III, and the position of their graves was known. I found, however, that Dart in his *History of the Abbey* (1723) had noted, without giving his authority, that Richard Courtenay, Bishop of Norwich (d. 1415) was said to have been buried near the Shrine of the Confessor 'without monument or inscription'. This seemed to be a clue, and I suggested that if this was in fact the grave of the bishop we should probably find that he had been buried with a crozier on his right hand side. My suggestion proved to be correct. On scraping away more earth part of the staff and the foliated head of a wooden crozier were revealed.

Richard Courtenay was a son of Sir Philip Courtenay of Powderham, and had been Dean of Wells and Chancellor of Oxford University before becoming Bishop of Norwich. He was the trusted counsellor and close friend of King Henry V whom he accompanied to France in 1415. At the Siege of Harfleur, however, he fell ill and died in the King's presence. The King felt his loss deeply and commanded that his body should be taken to England and buried at Westminster.

A contemporary spoke of the Bishop as having been of lofty stature, and this agreed with the measurements which we took of the skeleton, which showed him to have been about six feet tall. Beyond uncovering the skeleton sufficiently to allow a careful measured drawing and photographs to be taken of it, it was not disturbed in any way. A photograph was also taken of the crozier in order that there might be a record of it preserved amongst the Muniments. After the crozier and the two leg bones had been replaced the grave was filled in and sealed. The ring was not replaced, but is now exhibited in the Museum.

There was one curious little point in connection with this discovery. It was quite evident that the grave had been disturbed at some early date. The leg bones had been deliberately broken off below the knee, and were found, as has been stated, lying in the earth *above* the remains of the coffin. Furthermore the whole body seemed to have been pushed westwards with the result that most of the bones were slightly out of their normal positions. The explanation appears to be this. A few days before Henry V left Southampton for France in September 1415 he made his Will. In it he left instructions that he was to be buried in the Abbey in the place where the relics were then kept and that above his tomb there was to be a Chantry Chapel approached by two turret staircases – exactly as it appears at the present day. No doubt when Bishop Courtenay died at Harfleur the King commanded not only that he should be buried at Westminster but that the grave should be made as close as possible to the place where he himself had determined to be buried. But when the Chantry Chapel was eventually built at the east end of the Confessor's Chapel in 1441 it must have been found that the only way to provide space for the foundations of the northern turret staircase was to shorten the bishop's grave and move the body slightly to the west.

The late Professor Lethaby thought that the building of the Chantry Chapel also involved the moving of the Confessor's Shrine 'a few feet farther west', but there does not seem to be any evidence to support this theory. Nevertheless the Shrine has always been something of a problem. In 1958 Mr J. G. O'Neilly, A.R.I.B.A., who was then working as an assistant to Mr S. Dykes Bower, spent a considerable time measuring and examining the structure of the Shrine as it exists today. The conclusions which he came to were of considerable interest and value and were embodied in a Paper which he read before the Society of Antiquaries.[1] To that Paper I contributed a short historical introduction.

As is well known the Shrine (Plate 44) was set up just seven hundred years ago in 1269. It was designed by Peter the Roman Citizen and decorated with the finest mosaic of the Cosmati school. When first erected it must have been, as Lethaby called it, 'the shining beacon of the whole church'. At the Dissolution of the Monastery in 1540 it shared the fate of similar shrines throughout the country. But at Westminster the destruction was marked by two facts which were unusual if not unique. In the first place, although the golden feretory in which was encased the body of the saint was plundered, the body itself was quietly and secretly buried. It may be, although we have no evidence of this, that a hint was dropped that Henry VIII did

[1] *Archaeologia* (1966), Vol. C, pp. 129-154.

not wish that the body of the royal saint who had also been one of his predecessors on the throne, should be desecrated. In the second place, although the Purbeck marble base of the Shrine was dismantled either in whole or in part, the stones which composed it, although stripped of their rich mosaic decoration, for some reason were carefully preserved.

It was possible, therefore, for Abbot Feckenham, during the brief revival of the Monastery (1556–59) under Queen Mary I, to set up the Shrine again more or less in its original form and to replace the body of the Confessor within it. The remarkable fact is that he was able to do it at all. It was eighteen years since it had been dismantled, he himself had had no previous connection with Westminster until he was appointed as its Abbot, no documentary evidence or contemporary drawings of the Shrine showing its exact form are known to exist, and even the memories of former monks cannot have been of much practical use. Even at the present day it was difficult enough, as we found, to re-assemble the grille round Henry VII's tomb when it was returned to us after the last war, although we had an excellent series of photographs to help us and each piece had been carefully labelled and numbered.

It was not surprising, therefore, that Feckenham in hurriedly putting the Shrine together again made various mistakes and misplaced many of the stones. It was these mistakes, some of which were already known, which Mr O'Neilly set himself to disentangle with a thoroughness which had never before been undertaken. The results of his investigations seemed to me to be an important and suggestive contribution to the history of the Shrine. They may be briefly summarized here.

(a) He had no doubt that the Shrine was totally dismantled in 1540, and not partially as some had thought, and that Feckenham had had to rebuild it from the ground. In no other way did it seem possible, for instance, to account for some of the stones composing the niches or recesses in the base being obviously out of place and wrongly matched.

(b) By exact measurements of each slab and by carefully following up such clues as the patterning of the matrices which formerly held the mosaic work, etc., it could be shown that practically all the component parts of the original Purbeck marble Shrine base, however wrongly placed, were in fact incorporated in the present structure. A few pieces were missing but their size and shape could be ascertained from, so to say, their corresponding opposite numbers. It followed, therefore, that it would be perfectly possible to re-assemble the Shrine correctly in what was presumably its original form. This had not been realized before.

(c) The present Shrine stands on a rectangular platform of which the edges, composed of long Purbeck stones, form a single surrounding step. At present there is a space of between one or two feet between this step and the original thirteenth century mosaic pavement of the Confessor's Chapel. Mr O'Neilly suggested that the Shrine originally stood on four steps instead of one. He was able convincingly to show by means of a scale model that if stones similar to those of the existing step were used the lowest of the four suggested steps would come exactly to the edge of the pavement. One of the stones forming the present step at the east end of the Shrine has two depressions in it which are traditionally said to have been made by the knees of those who knelt at the Shrine. To kneel on it in its present position is impossible, but if it was turned round and moved so that it formed one of four steps on the south side the knee holes would come directly in front of one of the recesses in which I had long noticed a number of small scratched crosses which presumably had been made by pilgrims.

Another of the steps has a small oblong stone (about the size of a small brick) let into it and apparently kept down and sealed by an iron staple. As there is no mention of this stone in any of the books I pointed it out one day to the Dean and the Surveyor and we decided to investigate. After removing the mortar round it the stone was lifted out and there was revealed, as I had suspected, a most carefully made little oblong recess. It had a ledge all round it just below the surface on to which must have fitted a lid hinged to the staple. Unfortunately the recess was empty but no doubt it had been made originally to hold a relic.

(d) It had always been supposed that the present wooden canopy or superstructure with its arcades inlaid with blue and gold glass mosaics was part of Feckenham's work. On close examination, however, both the Surveyor and Mr O'Neilly became convinced that the high standard of its craftsmanship suggested an earlier date for it than the hasty reconstruction of the Shrine in 1557, and that it might well have been a pre-Reformation addition dating from the late fifteenth or early sixteenth century. Feckenham did a good deal of restoration to the cornice of the Shrine upon which it now rests, but it was suggested that if this work was removed and if what appeared to be the form of the original cornice was restored then the canopy would exactly fit to its edge and was so constructed that it would have acted as a cover to the original, but lost, gold feretory enclosing the body of the Confessor.

(e) At the west end of the Shrine there was an altar[1] of which the original reredos slab above it still remains. It is supported on two twisted columns which have long been known to have been wrongly used by Feckenham for this purpose. Sir Gilbert Scott twice opened the ground round them in 1850 and again in 1868. He found that only half of each of these columns was above ground. On the second occasion he turned one of them upside down in order to show the mosaic work on it which was still intact below ground. From this column one can get some idea of how magnificent the Shrine must have been when the whole of it was covered with mosaic. It is probable that these two columns originally stood on each side of the Shrine, perhaps supporting statues or candles. There would seem to be no reason why they should not be replaced in these positions.

Mr O'Neilly found that behind the present altar there remained two small pilasters, and suggested that the reredos originally rested on them. He further suggested that it was possible that the small Cosmati tomb, now in the south Ambulatory, which contains the bones of children of Henry III and Edward I and is traditionally believed to have been moved from the Confessor's Chapel, was in fact the original altar. He found that its shape and measurements would exactly correspond to the space for the altar in his conjectural reconstruction of the Shrine. It may have been so, although it can only remain a suggestion. It is worth noting, however, that the top slab of this little altar tomb has four circles in it surrounded by mosaic work. One of these circles is filled with mosaic, two others, which had presumably lost their mosaic, were filled by Dean Stanley with marble brought back by his father-in-law, Lord Elgin, from Greece, but the fourth circle is filled by a roughly cut brown stone (Plate 46) (about 6 inches by 6 inches). Lethaby first noticed this stone and wondered if it had some special significance as it was certainly inserted at the time the tomb was made. Some years ago the Dean allowed me to submit some tiny shavings from it to the authorities at the Geological Museum. They told me that the stone was 'unquestionably of foreign provenance, probably from the Mediterranean area'.[2] We know that Edward I brought back various stones and relics from his Crusade. He may well have had one of them inserted into the top

---

[1] The present altar was erected in 1902.

[2] For further information about this tomb see Joan D. Tanner, 'Tombs of Royal Babies in Westminster Abbey', *Journal of the British Archaeological Association*, 3rd Series, Vol. XVI (1953).

slab of the tomb which contained his children, and he would have been the more likely to have done so if that tomb was also the altar at the west end of the Shrine. The exact significance, perhaps, of this particular stone will never now be known, but it is one of those problems and mysteries which add so greatly to the endless fascination of the Abbey and its contents.

CHAPTER XVI

War and Post-War

Evacuation of the Muniments – Life at Houghton – Marriage –
War Damage at the Abbey – Restoration Work – The Deanery
– The Coffin of Anne, Duchess of York – 900th Anniversary
Celebrations – Retirement

I HAD not intended to bring these recollections of Westminster
beyond the outbreak of War in 1939. The War made a definite break
with the past, and of the pre-War Collegiate Body only the Revd
C. Hildyard, Minor Canon and Sacrist, Mr John D. Carleton, then an
Assistant Master at the School and now Head Master, and myself still
remain at Westminster. Much, of course, has happened in the quarter
of a century since peace was declared, but it seems better to confine
myself to such events – some of these have already been mentioned –
as more particularly concerned myself and my work at Westminster.

During the war years I was in exile in the country. My house at
Westminster had been badly blasted in one of the early air raids, but
I was fortunate in finding a cottage at Houghton near Stockbridge.
It was a district I knew well from many happy days fishing the
Compton stretch of the River Test, and it had the further advantage
that I could easily get to London when necessary, and could also
ensure that the Abbey Muniments were not suffering any damage
from being exposed to damp or other unsuitable conditions in the
Hampshire houses and elsewhere to which they had been evacuated.

At Houghton I was drawn into various war activities (Red Cross,
War Savings, etc.), and joined the ranks of the local Home Guard.
Those were, from one point of view, the great days of the Home
Guard, when all alike were animated with a spirit of comradeship and
a single purpose[1] and, mercifully, no one doubted that we could deal

[1] A friend of mine was amused to find in his local H.Q. Battalion Orders:
'L/Corporal His Grace the Duke of X reverts to the rank of private at his
own request'!

with whatever might come our way. We were part of the 10th (Romsey) Battalion of the Hampshire Regiment, and our local officers, as was typical in those days, included the Rear Admiral of the United Kingdom (Admiral Sir Hubert Brand), the head gardener of a nearby country house, and the well-known sporting artist and horse-man, Lionel Edwards, who organized a mounted section which patrolled the downland in the direction of Salisbury.

As an historian it amused me to remember that no less a person than Edward Gibbon had served with the South Hampshire Militia in an invasion scare in 1756 and subsequent years. Rather un-expectedly he was able to reflect in later life that the military know-ledge which he had acquired while exercising his Company, over very much of the same countryside which we were guarding nearly two hundred years later, had given him 'a clearer notion of the phalanx and the legion' and that such knowledge 'had not been useless to the historian of the Roman Empire'! It was pleasant, too, while our Houghton roads and woods were crowded with troops and lorries on their way to embark at Southampton for D day, to recall a tradition that Henry V, too, on his way to Southampton in 1415 had camped with his army in a field by the River Test a few hundred yards from my cottage, and that the field was still locally known as 'Agincourt'.

As the fear of invasion receded I was able to remove many boxes of the Abbey Muniments and to store them in my cottage. It seemed to me that they were safer there than in large country houses standing in their own grounds which might well be a target for the bombs of a solitary daylight raider. It was a great relief to have them under my immediate care again, and to be able to distract my mind for an hour or two daily by retiring into the Middle Ages in order to work on a box of medieval documents.

These years in the country, apart from the war, were profoundly to affect my own personal life. I made many new friends, and in January 1945, to my great happiness, I became engaged to Joan, the eldest daughter of the Honble Assheton N. Curzon, the youngest brother of the Statesman and former Viceroy. She, too, was in exile from London in the neighbouring village of Broughton, and shared many of my antiquarian and genealogical interests. The war was then nearly over, and we were married at the Nave Altar in Westminster Abbey by Dean Labilliere on 9th June 1945, spending part of our honeymoon at Kedleston which had been kindly lent to us by Joan's cousin, Viscount Scarsdale.

Many of the Curzons had been at Westminster, including the 1st Lord Scarsdale who had built that great Derbyshire house. While he was at the School (c.1745) he and three of his schoolfellows carved their names on the Coronation Chair (Plate 42), an act of vandalism which caused an august Personage, on being shown the names a few years ago, to express the hope that they had been well flogged for it. But no one at that time seems to have treated the Chair with any special veneration, and visitors to the Abbey, like Addison's Sir Roger de Coverley, sat in it without hesitation. It was not until the middle of the nineteenth century, I think, that some care began to be taken of it, and a barrier was put round it to prevent any further mutilation.

Westminster was a somewhat desolate place when we returned to it after peace had been declared. Much of the Precincts was in ruins, and in those days it seemed impossible to foresee that within a few years so much would have been so skilfully re-built or repaired that it would be difficult to remember how great had been the destruction. The Library, as has been already said, miraculously escaped serious damage, but all the surrounding buildings suffered to a greater or less degree. In the Chapter House, which almost adjoins the Library, all the windows had been shattered. These large windows had been filled with stained glass depicting persons and events connected with the history of the Abbey and Palace of Westminster. They were part of the mid-Victorian restoration by Sir Gilbert Scott after the Chapter House had been rescued from 'the ruthless disfigurement and deterioration' caused by its use for nearly three hundred years as the storehouse for the national records. The glass, by Messrs Clayton and Bell, was good of its kind and for its date, but it had made the Chapter House somewhat dark.

When the question of restoring these windows after the War was under consideration, Miss Joan Howson, the stained glass artist, found that some of the scenes and figures in the Victorian glass were either intact or only slightly damaged, and that if they were re-set on to plain quarries there would be sufficient to fill three of the six large windows. I was then consulted about the filling of the remaining three windows. It happened that a few years before the War I had found in the Bodleian a rough sketch of the outside of the Chapter House. It was drawn about 1610 and showed three of its windows in which there were still what were obviously thirteenth-century shields with the coats of arms of Edward the Confessor, Henry III, Provence, etc. I strongly urged, therefore, that this precedent should be followed. My suggestion was adopted, and I was asked to draw up a list of suitable coats of arms. The result is a splendid spread of heraldry embodying forty-seven large shields with the arms of Sovereigns, Abbots, Deans, and others connected with the history of the Abbey. I also wrote the inscriptions for the panels at the base of each window describing what each window represented.

I was also concerned with some of the historical problems which arose in connection with the rebuilding of the greater part of the Deanery. Those who knew the Deanery before the War will remember it as a beautiful but rambling house of many dates and full of steps and staircases. Much of it went up in flames in the air raid of 12th May 1941. Dean Labilliere told me how he had watched, helplessly, the terrifying sight of the roof of the Lantern falling in flames on to the floor of the Abbey, and how he had seen that the Houses of Parliament, 'School', the houses in the Little Cloister, and two houses in Victoria Street were all on fire at the same time – 'and then I turned and saw that the Deanery with all I possessed had also burst into flames'.

Fortunately the Jerusalem Chamber, the Jericho Parlour with the early sixteenth-century panelled rooms above it, and the room adjoining Jericho, which of late years has come to be known as Samaria, escaped damage. But the greater part of the long gallery in the Deanery with the rooms opening out of it, the main staircase, and the 'Tudor rooms' extending over the west cloister were completely destroyed, while the drawing-room and the two fourteenth-century rooms above the entrance to the south cloister were gutted and only the walls remained. These two rooms were originally part of the Abbot's Lodgings and, curiously enough, the fire disclosed their original stone exterior north wall, which had been encased in the later Deanery and completely hidden by layers of decanal wall papers.

In the rebuilding it was decided to leave this wall exposed, so that once again as in the days of the monastery the Abbot's Lodgings stand out as an oblong stone building approached by a separate entrance and staircase from the Cloister below them, although they are still connected by an internal doorway with the rebuilt Deanery. Until the sixteenth century the Abbot's residence or lodgings were known as the Manor of Cheynegates and I was instrumental in getting the name revived for this little building, and the rooms themselves named Langham and Litlyngton after the Abbots by whom they were built. The name Cheynegates, which often appears in the monastic account rolls, was something of a puzzle, and it was thought to mean the house with the chained gates. But I think that there is no doubt that in reality it is derived from the French word *chêne*, meaning an oak, and it was interesting to find that the ancient family of Cheyndutt or Chenduyt bore as their punning coat of arms an oak tree within a border of acorns.

The Langham room, which overlooks Dean's Yard, was used by successive Deans as their Library. The fire destroyed its late seventeenth-century panelling, and also, unfortunately, the long narrow secret chamber reached by a ladder which was found quite unexpectedly behind the fireplace and panelling in 1864. It was supposed to have been the place where Dean Atterbury carried out his Jacobite plotting before he was tried and exiled in 1723. For the further, or Litlyngton, room the architects, (the late) Lord Mottistone and Mr Paul Paget, designed a new open timber roof with an oak cornice.

In connection with this Lord Mottistone wrote to me:

... This cornice was originally intended to be embellished in the normal way with a series of carved bosses of conventional foliage. It so happens however, that the foreman, Mr George Markham, on the job is an amateur sculptor in wood and has done one or two remarkably good portrait heads. In view of the fact that it is such a rare thing to find that a foreman on a job is an enthusiastic artist in woodwork, and bearing in mind that portrait heads of those connected with a building project were such a usual feature of medieval work, we feel that it might be a very good idea to substitute for the originally proposed bosses a series of carved heads representing some of those connected with the Abbey and with the work of restoration now proceeding at the Deanery. . . .

The result was a series of half-size heads, carved in oak, representing the Dean (Dr Don), the Chapter, the Surveyor, the Architects, and others including myself (a perfectly recognizable likeness!). It was pleasant thus to revive an ancient custom of which there are some notable medieval examples within the Abbey Church.

It was a great sadness that Dean Labilliere did not live to see the restoration of the Deanery and other buildings. He had felt it his duty to remain at Westminster throughout the War, and his steadfast courage and unruffled calm had been an inspiration to everyone. But there is no doubt that the terrible strain of those years, however little he showed it outwardly, undermined his health and led to his death on 28th April 1946. He was succeeded by Dr Alan Don, who had been appointed a Canon of Westminster and Rector of St Margaret's on the death of Canon Vernon Storr in 1941.

Apart from the erection and dedication of war memorials in the Abbey such as the Battle of Britain Chapel in 1947, the outstanding events in the first few years of Dr Don's tenure of the Deanery were the marriage (1947) and subsequent Coronation (1953) of Queen Elizabeth II. At the beginning of 1953 the Dean issued an appeal for 'a million pounds from a million people' for the maintenance of the fabric and for other objects connected with the Abbey. The target was reached in just over a year, and the sum subscribed provided the means for much urgent repair to the roof and exterior of the Abbey.

Above all it enabled the completion of the scheme for cleaning the whole of the interior of the Abbey, on which a beginning had been made at the east end and in the south transept in the years before the War. Unfortunately the bombing and collapse of the roof of the Lantern and the further dust and dirt inseparable from the erection and dismantling of the stands and galleries for the Coronation had covered this preliminary work with a fresh layer of grime. But, at least, this cleaning had shown that the dull, dark, uniform brown of the interior as it had appeared for generations was simply a thick coating of dirt on the original stone. Now, as the work again proceeded it was fascinating to watch, month by month, the transformation as the pure white stone gradually emerged. No chemicals, soap or detergents were used, the stonework was simply washed with water after the dirt had been softened and loosened by workmen using fibre brushes. By the end of 1965 the whole of the interior down to the west end of the nave had been cleaned. In the words of Mr Stephen Dykes Bower, the Abbey Architect and Surveyor, under whose care and supervision this great work was carried out, 'the view of the Abbey, on entering at the West Door, is no longer one of sombre gloom, but of lightness and radiance – a symphony of white stone, grey marble, gilding and colour' (Plate 47).

In these years I was concerned with an event at the Abbey which, at the time, aroused a good deal of public interest. One day in December 1964 I was rung up by the Director of the London Museum who told me that during excavations on the site of the former church of the Minoresses of St Clare, in Clare Street in the City, a small lead coffin had been found. On it was a Latin inscription which when translated read:

Here lies Anne, Duchess of York; daughter and heir of John, formerly Duke of Norfolk, Earl Marshal, Earl of Nottingham, Earl of Warenne, Marshal of England and Lord of Mowbray, Segrave and Gower; the late wife of Richard, Duke of York, the second most illustrious Prince of Edward the Fourth, King of England, France and Lord of Ireland; who died at Greenwich on the 19th day of November in the Year of Our Lord 1481 and in the 21st year of the reign of the said Lord King.

Anne Mowbray, as the inscription stated, was the (child) wife of Richard, Duke of York (the younger of the Princes in the Tower). She had died, during the lifetime of her husband, at the age of eight or nine, three years after her marriage. Here was a puzzle. There was not the slightest doubt that originally she had been buried in the old Lady Chapel of Westminster Abbey. When that Chapel was pulled down in 1502, to make way for Henry VII's Chapel, it was always believed and, indeed, definitely stated, that like others who had been buried in the Lady Chapel, she had been re-buried within the Abbey. Yet she was now found on the site of a City church, and the inscription on the coffin made her identification certain. It could only be assumed that the Abbey tradition was incorrect, and that either in 1502 or a few years later the body must have been transferred to the Church of the Minoresses, in which church, as subsequent research was to show, her mother, the Duchess of Norfolk, and other members of her mother's family were buried.

I saw the body a few days after the coffin had been opened, and a very distressing sight it was; and, again, after it had been cleaned and beautifully laid out as a skeleton in its lead coffin. She had masses of brown hair. After consultation with the authorities, the Dean (Dr. E. Abbott)[1] decided that she should be re-buried in the Abbey. I suggested that a grave should be made in one of the small chapels at the east end of Henry VII's Chapel very near to the probable site of her original burial place, and within a few feet of the tomb of her sister-in-law, Henry VII's Queen, Elizabeth of York.

There on a summer evening, after having laid in state covered by the Abbey Pall in the Jerusalem Chamber, the body of the child Royal Duchess was laid to rest. It was a deeply moving and impressive little service conducted by the Dean in the presence of a representative of H.M. The Queen, Lord and Lady Mowbray, Segrave, and Stourton (representing Anne Mowbray's family), the Home Secretary, the Director of the London Museum, and one or two others.

If, for a moment, we may assume that the bones in the north aisle of Henry VII's Chapel are really those of Anne's husband, Richard, Duke of York, it is a curious fact that I should have been present at the re-burial of both these children nearly five hundred years after their deaths.

One other event may properly be mentioned here. From December 1965 to December 1966 the Abbey celebrated the 900th anniversary of its Foundation by Edward the Confessor and of the Dedication, on 28th December 1065, of the great Abbey Church which he had

[1] Dr Abbott has been appointed Dean on the resignation of Dr Don in 1959.

caused to be built. Those celebrations were a time of great activity for all members of the Collegiate Body. Special services, exhibitions, musical performances, dinners, lectures, and functions of all kinds followed one another week by week throughout the entire year.

As regards myself, apart from giving broadcasts to listeners at home and abroad, I was specially concerned in helping to arrange and choose the exhibits for an Exhibition of Abbey Treasures in the Norman Undercroft, and in advising how they should best be displayed so as to give a kind of panoramic history of the development of the Abbey from the earliest times to the present day. The Exhibition was opened by H.R.H. Princess Margaret, and was subsequently visited by H.M. The Queen. On both these occasions I had the honour of showing and explaining the various exhibits to the Queen and the Princess. It was estimated that about 190,000 people visited the Exhibition during the year.

To commemorate the 900th Anniversary a new, comprehensive, and beautifully-produced history of the Abbey called *A House of Kings* was written by past and present members of the Collegiate Body together with two independent scholars. To this book I contributed a chapter on Coronations, and was able to give some help with choosing suitable illustrations.

A copy of the book was presented to H.M. The Queen when Her Majesty and Prince Philip attended a Collegiate Dinner in College Hall on 6th July 1966. It was an historic occasion, for, so far as is known, no sovereign had dined with the College since the sixteenth century. After the dinner the Queen and the Prince made a short conducted tour round the Abbey, partly in order to see the cleaned interior stonework and the newly installed lighting arrangements. Those who were present will not easily forget the beauty of the silent and empty Abbey as first the vaulting and then gradually, chandelier by chandelier the entire church became flooded with light.

The 900th Anniversary celebrations had begun with a great and splendid Inaugural Service which was attended by H.M. The Queen and most of the Royal Family. The final service was a more 'domestic' occasion and, although there was a very large congregation, it was primarily meant for all those who had taken an active part in the celebrations, and for representatives of the many societies for whom special services had been held throughout the year.

It seemed to me that with the close of this memorable year the time had come for me to relinquish the Keepership of the Muniments. It was a wrench to give it up, for like the Secretaryship of the Royal Almonry and the Clerkship of the Weavers' Company, I had held the post for forty years, but the blow was considerably softened for me by the desire of the Dean and Chapter that I should not entirely retire from the scene but that I should retain the Librarianship and so remain a member of the Collegiate Body.

APPENDIX

INSTRUCTIONS FOR THE MORNING PREACHER IN WESTMINSTER ABBEY

This poem was written by Canon H. C. Beeching about 1909 and circulated among his Westminster friends (see p. 48).

As soon as little Benjamin has struck the notes of ten,
The scarlet-cassocked boys march in, in stroll the white-robed men,
The tonsur'd priests they follow next; then verged along are seen—
You with the Residentiary and, last of all, the Dean.

The Preacher must arrive before 10 o'clock and walk with the Canon in Residence.

When you have reached the pulpit, say a collect; do not bawl;
And keep your face religiously towards the *decanal* stall;
Be short and pithy; and though 'up-to-date', to please the town,
Kindly supply a skeleton for H——k to take down.

Of the collect before the Sermon, and the manner of preaching.

Now when you preach at Westminster, the first thing you must say
Is that miracles and prophecy have vanished clean away,
With Balaam's ass and Satan, up the empyrean vault,
And that relics must be swallowed with a largish pinch of salt.

What the Preacher must say of the Bible.

If you're a scholar you may talk of J, and E, and P.;
And make Leviticus yield place to Deuteronomy;
Quote Schmiedel on S. Paul; and for the Psalms let Cheyne tell
They're a buried-word enigma on the name Jerahme-el.

If a Doctor or Bachelor of Divinity.

Then you must say about the Creeds that every honest man
Believes as many articles as honest persons can,
And that the clever hymn that goes by Athanasius' name
Is a very (something) picture in a very (something) frame.

Of the Creeds.

The Preacher supplies epithets at his discretion.

APPENDIX

What he must not tell.

But when you preach at Westminster be sure and never tell
The cultured congregation there of things like 'heaven' and
    'hell';
And if you have to mention God—to show that you're well-bred
Say 'th' unconditioned intellect' or 'absolute' instead.[1]

He must praise the architecture of the Abbey,

Last, should you be ambitious to be asked to preach again
Omit not to apostrophise 'the venerable fane',
'The long-drawn aisle and fretted vault', and other handsome
    things,
And make that fine quotation about 'ruin'd sides of Kings'.

and the music.

Returning through the Cloister home, the music you must
    praise—
It never was so wonderful in Blow's or Purcell's days—
From Sir Frederick's[2] 'echo' rendering of some new discovered
    'Op',
To the little husky solo with the *vox humana* stop.

The joy of preaching in the Abbey is increased by the sight of the Chapter.

O' tis a very pleasant thing at Westminster to preach,
To see the Dean[3] and the Sub Dean[4], the Archdeacon[5], all
    and each,
The angel-Bishop[6] up aloft, and Henson bold and bland,
And poor old Beeching fast asleep, his beard upon his band.

---

[1] i.e. favourite phrases of Archdeacon Wilberforce.
[2] Sir Frederick Bridge. [3] Armitage Robinson. [4] Duckworth.
[5] Wilberforce. [6] Welldon.

SELECT READING LIST

Further information about some of the subjects mentioned in the foregoing chapters can be found in the following papers and articles.

L. E. TANNER and A. W. CLAPHAM, 'Recent Discoveries in the Nave of Westminster Abbey', *Archaeologia*, vol. LXXXIII (1933), pp. 227–36.

L. E. TANNER and J. L. NEVINSON, 'On some later Funeral Effigies in Westminster Abbey', *Archaeologia*, vol. LXXXV (1936), pp. 169–202.

L. E. TANNER and WILLIAM WRIGHT, 'Recent Investigations regarding the fate of the Princes in the Tower', *Archaeologia*, vol. LXXXIV (1935), pp. 1–26.

L. E. TANNER, 'William Caxton's Houses at Westminster', *Bibliographical Society's Transactions* in *The Library*, 5th Series, vol. XII, No. 3 (1957), pp. 153–6.

L. E. TANNER, 'The Quest for the Cross of St Edward the Confessor', *Journal of the British Archaeological Association*, 3rd Series, vol. XVII (1954), pp. 1–11.

J. G. O'NEILLY and L. E. TANNER, 'The Shrine of St Edward the Confessor', *Archaeologia*, vol. C (1966), pp. 129–54.

R. P. HOWGRAVE-GRAHAM, 'The Earlier Royal Funeral Effigies', *Archaeologia*, vol. XCVIII (1961), pp. 159–69.

ACKNOWLEDGEMENTS

Many people have been kind enough to express interest on hearing that I was engaged in writing these recollections, and I owe much to their encouragement. More especially am I grateful to the Archdeacon of Westminster (The Ven. Dr Edward Carpenter) who very kindly read the typescript and made many helpful suggestions; to the Head Master of Westminster and Mrs Carleton; to my publisher, Mr John Baker; and to Mr James Campbell, the Editor of the Pembroke College Annual Gazette, who kindly gave me permission to incorporate some passages from an article in the Gazette which I wrote a few years ago on the College in my time. Above all I am indebted to my Wife whose help and encouragement have been constant and unfailing.

For the use of certain illustrations I am indebted to: Keystone Press Agency Ltd – Plates 24, 25; Fox Photos Ltd – Plates 27, 35; Kent Messenger – Plate 28; B.B.C. – Plate 29; International News Photos – 34 and The Sport and General Press Agency Ltd – Plate 47.

INDEX